Risk, Courage, and Women

risk, courage, and women

contemporary voices in prose and poetry

edited by

KAREN A. WALDRON

LAURA M. LABATT

JANICE H. BRAZIL

UNIVERSITY OF NORTH TEXAS PRESS | Denton, Texas

10 9 8 7 6 5 4 3 2 1

Permissions:
University of North Texas Press
P.O. Box 311336
Denton, tx 76203-1336

∞ The paper used in this book meets the
minimum requirements of the American
National Standard for Permanence of Paper for
Printed Library Materials, z39.48.1984. Binding
materials have been chosen for durability.

LIBRARY OF CONGRESS CATALOGING-IN-
PUBLICATION DATA

Risk, courage, and women : contemporary
voices in prose and poetry / edited by Karen A.
Waldron, Laura M. Labatt, Janice H. Brazil.
p. cm.
Includes bibliographical references.
ISBN 978-1-57441-233-8 (alk. paper)
ISBN 978-1-57441-234-5 (pbk. : alk. paper)
1. American literature–Women authors. 2.
Women–Literary collections. 3.
Courage–Literary collections. 4. Risk-taking
(Psychology)–Literary collections. 1. Waldron,
Karen A., 1945–
11. Labatt, Laura M., 1943– 111. Brazil, Janice
H., 1951–

PS508.W7R57 2007   810.8'09287-dc2
22007005473

contents

acknowledgments

A collaborative manuscript of thirty-seven authors and eighty-one pieces of prose and poetry requires not only the involvement of many talented and dedicated writers, but their cooperative effort toward a final goal. The book began with deep respect for the courage and risk-taking of so many women and concluded with a work that let them tell of their individual journeys. Working together through the book's evolution afforded opportunities both for theme-building and team-building.

With deep appreciation and admiration, we thank our authors, remarkable women who made choices to move ahead during circumstances that would have made the best of us falter. They shared both original and published work freely, dedicating all net proceeds from book sales to fund breast cancer treatment for uninsured women. They also offered significant suggestions and reflections as the direction of the book evolved. For many, our initial connections developed into email bonds as we came to know and sustain each other personally during difficult periods and also to share individual joys.

Of the many additional men and women who gave time, encouragement, and wonderful advice, the following were exceptionally supportive:

Dr. Maya Angelou, who shared not only her brilliant writing, but a personal conversation to introduce the book. Her remarkable life is emblematic of the courageous woman, and we are very grateful for her poignant insights;

Aaronetta Pierce and Dr. Amy Freeman Lee, close friends of Dr. Angelou, who collaborated in creating the framework for her participation and shared in developing the vision for this manuscript;

Barbara Ras, Trinity University Press, who guided us to a number of our superb authors and became our "ear" as we formulated initial themes and directions;

Benjamin Harris, Trinity University Reference Librarian, unfailingly positive and excited about the work, who spent countless hours assisting our exploration of literature in risk and courage for book and chapter introductions;

Michael J. Kutchins, whose ongoing computer expertise was incredibly valuable in melding together the extensive writings of so many into one final manuscript. His patience and problem-solving were essential to bringing this project to fruition;

Jack Ko, who guided us through the final stages of publication with wisdom and outstanding counsel. He made each problem seem imminently solvable;

Jean and Robert Flynn, who introduced us to the University of North Texas Press and provided on-going wisdom concerning book publication. Through her writing, Jean also shared her incredible story of terrible loss and rich fulfillment;

Paula Oates, University of North Texas Press, who first saw the potential of this book to impact many lives. With an excited, "I want to work with you on this manuscript," she took it forward;

Ronald Chrisman and Karen DeVinney, University of North Texas Press, who have believed enough in this work to bring it to fruition despite the extensive demands of such a complex and collaborative project;

The WINGS ("Women Involved in Nurturing, Giving, and Sharing") organization, which has sponsored tremendous care through treatment, surgery, and counseling for so many uninsured women with breast cancer. You honor us all.

strong women

Pat Mora

Some women hold me when I need to dream,
rock, rocked my first red anger through the night.
Strong women teach me courage to esteem,

to stand alone, like cactus, persevere
when cold frowns bite my bones and doubts incite.
Some women hold me when I need to dream.

They walk beside me on dark paths I fear,
guide with gold lanterns: stories they recite.
Strong women teach me courage to esteem.

They watch me stumble on new trails I clear.
In hope, feed me their faith, a warm delight.
Some women hold me when I need to dream.

In their safe arms, my visions reappear:
skyfire voices soar, blaze, night ignite.
Strong women teach me courage to esteem.

They sing brave women, sisters we revere
whose words seed bursts of light that us unite.
Some women hold me when I need to dream.
Strong women, teach me courage to esteem.

Reprinted from *Communion* (Arte Público Press, 1991).

women involved in nurturing, giving, and sharing (WINGS)

All net proceeds from this book will be donated to the WINGS foundation, to provide critical treatment services for women diagnosed with breast cancer. WINGS was formed to fill the vacuum that exists between detection and medical attention for uninsured women. It works to fund the treatment for those whose mammograms indicate anomalies. It provides diagnostic testing, surgery, chemotherapy expenses, as well as services not traditionally offered, but sorely needed, such as outpatient medication and psychological counseling.

WINGS creates a network of physicians, healthcare facilities, laboratories, and other professional services for breast cancer victims, including general and gynecological surgery, hematology/oncology, radiology, pathology, reconstructive surgery, and anesthesia. The more than 200 involved physicians and service providers agree to reduce their customary fees to ones that WINGS can afford to pay from donations. Uninsured women are referred to WINGS by physicians and radiologists. Once deemed eligible, they are provided all necessary treatment at no cost.

Aware that breast cancer is the leading cause of cancer death in women between the ages of 40 and 55, and approximately 180,000 new cases of breast cancer occur each year in the United States, Kathryn Safford, M.D. and Terri Jones co-founded WINGS in 1999. Breast cancer survivors themselves, they were moved to action after learning that thousands of women die each year due to lack of health insurance or enough funds to pay for breast cancer treatment. In 2000, they received a $50,000 Use Your Life award from Oprah's Angel Network. She said that they "found a way to give help and hope and life to women facing a death sentence." Her awards go to "those who make a difference." They also received start-up funds from the Susan G. Komen Breast Cancer Foundation. Currently, their ongoing operations are funded totally by donations and grants.

Risk, Courage, and Women

introduction

Karen A. Waldron

> When my dreams showed signs
> of becoming
> politically correct ...
> then I began to wonder.
>
> ADRIENNE RICH: "North American Time"

The genesis of this book came from years of observing women who grew beyond political correctness to take amazing risks as a matter of course or necessity, resulting in extraordinary outcomes. Through personal choice or life situations, they made courageous decisions to stand fast or to risk pushing ahead into the unknown. Some were quietly steadfast while others were directly confrontational. Age and experience did not appear to be their reasons for accepting and mastering life's challenges, but instead it was a determination to learn more about themselves through going beyond socially accepted boundaries. Many times, they risked the loss of freedom, love, and physical well-being by working toward a higher belief such as the good of others. As a result, they not only changed their own lives, but moved toward justice and equality for women, minorities, animals, the disabled or ill, and the impoverished.

We decided to create a literary work where brave women would simply tell their stories. Our goal was to explore *why* these women took risks and demonstrated extraordinary courage, with the outcome of inspiring other women to fulfill their own dreams. In the words of Edna St. Vincent Millay, we wanted to examine those inner qualities or needs that forced them to

> Soar, eat ether, see what has never been seen;
> depart, be lost,
> But climb."
>
> *"On Thought in Harness"*

We felt that if we came to understand writers' "real selves" (Benstock, 1988) through their own telling, we could gain insights that would encourage our readers to develop their own personal strengths.

In selecting our authors, we chose women from diverse backgrounds who were known to be outstanding writers. Importantly, they had a demonstrated history of risk-taking towards positive outcomes for themselves and others. As Bauhn (2003) suggests in her review of women and courage, each writer is one who is self-assertive and has freed herself from tradition and superstition in order to explore the world's possibilities while taking charge of her own destiny. Yet, we considered only those works where the author becomes "Everywoman," or as Viola reflected in Shakespeare's *The Twelfth Night*, "I am all the daughters of my father's house ...."

We selected authors and pieces that fulfilled the critical need of allowing readers to relate to each author even if individual life situations were different. As Heilbrun (1997) reflects,

> Biographies of women will offer unmet friends provided the subject of the biography has encountered struggles or dilemmas or crises of choice that the reader can learn from, as one would from a friend's. We like, I think, to read as women about women who have braved the terrors and the hopes we share, at least to some degree. Courage in women always catches me up, moves me to compassion and the desire to offer them succor, sustenance if possible...The secret of unmet friends is that they have called upon the same strengths to escape or endure the same kinds of situations. (153)

The book evolved much as a child grows, with unexpected turns, poignant moments, and divergence from original expectations. Initially, we asked *When have you taken a risk that has changed your life?* and for those who wanted to tell stories of mothers, grandmothers, and brave women, *When has someone you know or admire taken a risk that has changed her life?* It all seemed direct and easy.

Yet, early on, Janice Brazil commented, "I tell my stories in poetry. That's how I write." So the book expanded its genre, and Janice's poems, along with those of Pat Mora, Rosemary Catacalos, and Bárbara Renaud González became part of its very core. We agreed with Long's observation (1999) that "Telling women's lives often involves new or mixed genres . . . The fullness of women's accounts reproaches the leanness of generic autobiography, and contradicts its claim of universality"(55). As we expanded the genre, poetry, essays, and stories flowed organically together. Our themes expanded as Bonnie Lyons shared poems of powerful Biblical women, while Gaynell Gavin, Joan Loveridge-

Sanbonmatsu, and Mitsuye Yamada explored not only specific risks, but the power of moral necessity to support the oppressed, lending to uncommon demonstrations of courage.

While we have compiled this book primarily for an audience of students in literature and Women's Studies classes, we also see its significance for community literary study groups exploring the nature of women's risk and courage. Although it deals with women's reflections and observations, thematically it is also a book for male readers who wish to understand better the inner self of each of us. As Adrienne Rich noted in her Commencement Address at Smith College (1979), while it is critical to gain the most skill and knowledge possible from our professions, "most of your education must be self-education." We believe that this education begins in childhood, and for the privileged, gains focus through the university. Truly "At the end of the day...," it culminates later in life as each of us reflects upon the way that we have used these insights towards personally courageous acts.

We learned much along the journey of this anthology: that while our authors were themselves from diverse backgrounds, they did not focus their identity on race, ethnicity, age, or sexual orientation. Instead, they answered our thematic questions and wrote about uniquely shaping experiences. Yet, too often the world finds it hard to distinguish achievement from diversity, as Professor Demetrice Anntía Worley writes in "Dancing in the Dark":

> I present papers in white academia.
> I match their foreign movements.
>
> My jerky fox trot is invisible to them.
> They see a waltz of standard diction.
>
> "She speaks so well for a black woman ..."

Many of our writers went beyond diversity issues by passionately embracing communities originally outside their own. Paula Cooey immerses us in her mother's dedication to teaching Appalachian children to dance, while Ruth Kessler introduces a non-Jewish woman who risked her life to shelter Jews during the Holocaust. Connie Curry's award-winning work on supporting African Americans during the Civil Rights movement explores the lives of Mississippians Mae Bertha Carter and Winson Judson as they engaged in "civil disobedience."

A goal of this book has been to encourage readers to expand beyond a sense of "us versus them" through embracing all communities. In "Stock," Hilda Raz speaks brilliantly to a mother's poignant acceptance of her transgender son:

Sarah was born to Hilda who was born to Devorah, who was born to her mother, Hilda. Sarah was like me, someone who says in the silence over the newly lit candles, make with us celebrations of joy or of mourning, rites of passages for one another, the kneading of bread, the salving of wounds, flesh healing between stitches, the slow unlearning of silence, the slow recession of nausea, weakness, the intolerable flesh cut off by the friendly surgeon engaged with the help of the other. We will never leave you, never turn our eyes from each other, never shake off the fingers entwined with our own, never refuse presence at births or deaths, you are my child. I am your mother. Who is of my flesh. Aaron.

Such acceptance of life outside the typical is not without pain, as Doris Sage reveals in her description of time spent in prison for her protests of the School of the Americas' role in El Salvador. Yet, as Adrienne Rich notes about Madame Curie, "Her wounds came from the same source as her power." In our selection of authors, it was paramount that they be very courageous women.

From the onset, one of our most difficult tasks was to consider *Courage* itself in a manner that takes it beyond a "battlefield quality" (Bauhn, 2003). We found that reasons that women take risks and demonstrate courage may be quite different from those of men (Meccouri, 1999). We agreed with Walton's (1986) reflections that typically society looks to wartime experiences, the Presidency, or major business risks for examples of courage. But, as she notes, women are under- or not-represented in these areas, negating opportunities to be considered courageous if these are our only criteria. She writes,

The view of courageous action as a sudden outburst of will manifested in aggressive actions should immediately be countered by the fact that some of the most courageous acts are deliberated through a period of solitary reflection and are quiet acts of high principle. Far from being aggressive, such an act or refusal to act may be a deliberate forfeit of one's own interest for the sake of others. (9)

Indeed, in her essay, "Belfast: A Woman's Story," journalist Estelle Shanley castigates herself for not remaining in Northern Ireland to train the women there to work with the press. Years later, she continues to regret allowing her family to pull her home from her work there because of their concern for her safety. But in this "Catch-22" situation, we observe the relative nature of courage. Which of us would have even considered going to the Belfast war zone in 1980? Yet, she measures her courage not by her risks taken, but by forsaking her own needs for that of her family. Such are the pulls that women face.

Carol Gilligan (2002) asserts that it is important to acknowledge that women are conditioned to nurture others before meeting their own needs. Bauhn (2003) adds: "The often ignored fact is that courage is by no means incompatible with the 'softer' virtues of compassion and empathy; on the contrary, courage may be fuelled by one's perception of other people being in need of one's support" (8). Indeed, in his book *Emotional Intelligence*, Goleman (1995) underscores empathy as a critical variable in emotional well-being and in successful relationships.

In her exploration of "Feminisms and the Self" (1995), Griffiths elaborates that women's most significant definition of self is found in relationships with others, either as individuals or groups, rather than in those situations that are unaffected by relationships. However, she adds that "While all children— and adults—need to accommodate themselves to the wishes of others some of the time, a requirement to do so all the time leads to what are described as feelings of being inauthentic, or a loss of a real self" (87).

Muske (2000) agrees, describing how women are diverted from knowing and loving themselves because their lives are consumed by attaching to men and raising children. She observes how this "division of spirit" both enlivens and frustrates the need for common speech among women, and how having a literary voice provides opportunities to shatter women's frequent silence. Muske explores Adrienne Rich's powerful resolve,

"And I start to speak again."

She reflects how Rich's voice models for each of us how our desires for an historical, as well as truth telling or real self, can merge into a single dramatic voice.

Women might ask how far they have come from Emily Dickinson's plaintive, almost chat-room-like cry,

I'm nobody / Who are you?

For still today, we see that a major aspect of a woman's courage may be to stand alone and speak, despite fear and the possibility of loss. Clearly, through social actions and acquiring a literary voice, breaking out of silence can involve tremendous risk along with substantive fear. Bauhn (2003) observes that all of us have fears of injury and death, as well as that of failure and social ostracism. She adds that these primary fears may be restrictive enough that we become unwilling to take risks despite the greater social and personal importance of the outcomes.

Indeed, Aristotle's ethical theory supports that the courageous person fears what should be feared, such as disgrace, both personally and for one's family. While he observes that feelings of fear are natural, he states that they must be managed in order to fulfill the outcome of courage: the creation of good for self and society (*Nicomachean Ethics*).

How does this theory impact women, both as activists and writers? Clearly, as nurturers, women find great personal meaning in their relationships with others. Therefore, ostracism and disgrace become profound inhibitors of their desire to act. The fear of loss of others' respect and regard may warrant tremendous risk to a woman. The greater the risk, the greater the fear and the amount of courage necessary to act.

The themes of this book developed as we realized from many authors' pieces an even greater fear: that life may be spent without making a difference. Their organization emerged in two stages: the arrangement of topics based on the source of the woman's strength to take risk, and the subsequent thematic sequencing. As authors submitted poetry, stories, and essays, we found that their work clustered around their discussion of the source of their courage. Some elected profound risks from a personal inner strength that sustained them. Risk nourished and gave substance to their lives. For others, it was a faith that things would be better in the future despite current adversity. Sometimes religious, sometimes intuitive, their belief carried them. A third group of authors wrote about deliberating painfully, at times for years, before choosing to take a risk. This process of choosing freely and carefully gave them the strength to move forward. From these inner workings of sustenance, faith, and choice, we developed the initial chapters of the book.

But there were a number of authors who found their source of courage by reaching further *outside* themselves. The tapestry of their attachments enabled them. Some relationships were positive and familial, while others emanated from the pain of love and attempts to comprehend human complexity. Additional authors relied on the true, or "real" self, taking forth the power they drew from themselves, Nature, and limitations of their physical being. Having determined their needs at the very core of their being, they refused to be silenced by societal obstacles. The final group of themes described authors who crossed boundaries imposed by tradition, discrimination, and fear of mortality. Through their actions, some experienced a personal impact, while others changed the lives of thousands. In Maya Angelou's terms, they demonstrated "The Power of One."

As we organized these themes into the book's subsequent chapters, we began with the most inward-looking theme, *Sustenance for Living*, and moved gradually and sequentially away from the self into relationships with others.

We completed the sequence with those themes moving outward by challenging traditional barriers to women.

Our thematic organization begins and ends with the words of Dr. Maya Angelou. In an interview shared as a preface for this book, she reflects,

> Years ago, I deduced that it costs everything to win, and that it costs everything to lose. So, if I didn't take a risk, if I didn't take a dare, then I would lose everything .... I wish women could see themselves Free. Just see and imagine what they could do if they were free of the national and international history of diminishment .... See yourself as you want to be and then begin to work toward it. With a will and a way, and with laughter, with humor, with strength, with passion, with compassion, with style, and with love.

From "On the Pulse of Morning," delivered at the inauguration of President Clinton, her presence lifts us again in the final words of this book:

> Here, on the pulse of this new day,
> You may have the grace to look up and out
> And into your sister's eyes,
> And into your bother's face,
> Your country,
> And say simply
> Very simply
> With hope—
> Good morning.

She elaborates the wish and goal of this work, that readers may be inspired by the presence of a new day and shared writings to take a risk and "see themselves Free."

Sustenance for Living

The organization of this book's selections begins and ends in world conflict and the peaceful resolution that comes between individuals much more easily than nations. At age 105, Naomi Shihab Nye's grandmother on the West Bank, looks out across her "difficult" land and reflects that "one moment on top of the earth is better than a thousand moments under the earth." As with other authors throughout this chapter, she explores how the inner self is sustained by the nurturing of basic needs. The sharing of food, human relationships, the essence of nature, and home gives substance to life.

We move into another house, far from the Palestinian world, where Janice Brazil's grandmother nourishes others with food while sustaining herself with memories and pictures of her "Cadet" lost in World War I and her son in Viet Nam. Yet, as in Nye's piece, she is supported in a world of love by a granddaughter. She too is able to say, "Life is good."

Stories and songs also provide cultural sustenance. Indicating that the distance from the West Bank to Mississippi may not be so far after all, Demetrice Anntía Worley's "little brown children" reflect on the stories of ancestors who stood their ground so others could live. Next, Wendy Barker relates Helen's escape from Menelaus, prompted by women's stories of drudgery that finally sent Helen to her lover, Paris. And in Waldron's poem, we see the Magdalen Laundries as prisons for "promiscuous" women and mothers of children born out of wedlock. It is a Druid song that feeds this young mother's resolve to protect her own life and that of her unborn child.

But Nature provides another critical thematic sustenance. Echoing throughout this chapter are Willa Cather's words about returning to our "real home." In *The Song of the Lark* (1915), protagonist Thea Kronborg's observations of her respite in Arizona's Panther Canyon set the stage for our authors Susan J. Tweit and Joan Loveridge-Sanbonmatsu. Cather writes,

> Here everything was simple and definite, as things had been in childhood. Her mind was like a ragbag into which she had been frantically thrusting whatever she could grab. And here she must throw this lumber away. The things that were really hers separated themselves from the rest. Her ideas were simplified, became sharper and clearer. She felt united and strong.

Our chapter ends with profound revelations of courage of the spirit, a theme marked throughout. Ruth Kessler depicts phenomenal strength during the Holocaust and afterwards, where silence is the only logical and emotional way to handle the unspeakable.

During the most difficult of times, others express their longing and humanity through the arts. Paula Cooey's mother nourished the human spirit by teaching dance to Appalachian children during the Depression. Maya Angelou continues to underscore the critical nature of nurturing the spirit in the self. In her remarkable "Art for the Sake of the Soul," she writes,

> The strength of the black American to withstand the slings and arrows and lynch mobs and malignant neglect can be traced directly to the arts of literature, music, dance and philosophy that, despite significant attempts to eradicate them, remain in our community today....When a larger society would have us believe that we have made no contribution of consequence to the Western world—other

than manual labor, of course—the healing, the sustaining and the supporting roles of art were alive and well in the black community.

Art as sustenance for the soul.

This first chapter underscores courage as coming from a unique intertwining of the arts, including stories and songs of ancestors, the land, and most importantly, our ability to sustain each other through powerful relationships. The literature within is organized to demonstrate this flow of sustenance for the inner self.

Faith in the Unknown

The theme of our next chapter, Faith in the Unknown, is supported by Werner and Smith's (1998) longitudinal research studying factors that support resilience in overcoming adversity and in reaching our potential. Sometimes this belief is religious, other times personally spiritual. A faith that the future will be as good as or better than the present can provide a powerful pillar for our willingness to take risks.

As a young woman with no one else willing to make choices for her, Valerie Bridgeman Davis is forced to trust her intuition as she looks inside her own soul. Meanwhile, the brilliant passion God sends Bárbara Renaud González in "La Diosa" stirs her faith in her own writing, taking her beyond the powerful fears of living her immeasurable desires. She writes,

> Want my stories to be the bread of thousands
> each word a bomb, a machine gun piercing
> those walls of stone we call the heart
>
> Yes, satinsheet bullets, perfume-throated seducing
> my enemies so even the preacher amens
> my sermon
>
> Want my words howling baptized
> born again not afraid
> of dying either, laughing at the ropes and
> inquisitor's stake a testament to the story as I,
> woman, know it, to hell with
> the consequences, the damning
> because I dared to say it

Writers such as Muske (2000) earlier explored negative outcomes of women's diversion from their own needs into consuming relationships with men. In poet Wendy Barker's "Ithaca on the Landing," Penelope holds back her desires for the young men guarding her, having faith in Ulysses' return. But her temptations make her very human, very real. A modern-day Joan Shalikashvili risks her future on an intuitive love that forces her into a similar faith that her own feelings will guide her future. That faith sustains her journey throughout unfamiliar territory.

This poignant humanity becomes part of Terri Jones' profound fear, handled only by equal faith, in her essay, "Hints of a Cancer Victor." She writes, "My God is not a vengeful God," and Jones is sustained by the professionals and friends who surround her, as well as an impenetrable faith. Not only did she elevate her own spirit, but with her physician, Dr. Kathy Safford, she went on to create the WINGS organization ("Women Involved in Nurturing, Giving, and Sharing") to fund treatment for breast cancer victims without health insurance.

It is with both irony and love that we include the poems of Dr. Amy Freeman Lee, who died shortly after submitting these amazing pieces. Approaching her ninetieth birthday, she wrote of her "lions," the faith that gives her

> ... courage for the jump
> Into the only place where the future lies.

She concludes her poem "Why Wait?" with the words

> I fly!

Similarly, Gail Hosking Gilberg follows the pull of the "tiger" that envelopes her to immerse herself in her own voice and take it forward into unknown places. We wonder if their kindred spirits are regenerated into poet Barbara Lovenheim's subsequent painful move forward to her own future:

> I stepped out of my fragile self
> And buried my sins in the yielding earth.

This chapter ends with another type of regeneration, a faith in others that extends beyond most of our capabilities. Diane Graves writes of the Salvadoran birth-mother who gave up her daughter for adoption, filled with a faith that the child's future would be better than knowing only war and hunger. Indeed, Graves expresses great hope that her adopted daughter, Elena, will show the promise of the future that was born from such tremendous sacrifice.

The Courage of Choice

Our third chapter, *The Courage of Choice*, depicts the decisions Walton (1986) believes are the essence of courage: "(1) careful presence of mind and deliberate action, (2) difficult, dangerous, and painful circumstances, and (3) a morally worthy intention." As such, our writers are aware that the outcomes can be negative and often severely punitive. Yet, they choose action over apathy, mirroring Kingsolver's (2002) observation,

> In the long run, I find it hardest to bear adversaries on the other end of the spectrum: those who couldn't care less, who won't or can't fathom the honest depths of love and grief, who opt out of the bull-ride through life in favor of the sleeping berth. These are the ones who say it's ridiculous to imagine that the world could be made better than it is. The more sophisticated approach, they suggest, is to accept that we are all on a jolly road trip down the maw of catastrophe, so shut up and drive.... In the long run, the choice of life over death is too good to resist. (250–51)

Many of the decisions of these authors were years in the making, very different from the common view of courage as a daring rush into action. The lives in this chapter are woven together by the time and deliberation of making huge choices.

As a national leader in the movement for humane treatment of animals, Amy Freeman Lee finally agreed to address the most difficult audience of her career, a prestigious but hostile group of animal laboratory scientists. She proceeded with the lecture because of her "personal belief as a nondenominational theist that all creatures are part of the divine creation and, therefore, are sacred."

Catherine Kasper's beliefs also allowed her to proceed after years of delay by parents' overwhelming illnesses and disapproval of her desires to attend graduate school. As with Amy Freeman Lee, she too risked rejection by a traditional academic world that might be unwelcoming to her non-traditional goals.

Both she and Professor Demetrice Anntía Worley turned to writing as a full engagement of themselves. In "The Dark and Gray of Morning Light," Dr. Worley depicts the lonely process of moving beyond the painful ending of a relationship as she doubts herself and "questions her words." Only with the choice to "lift the veil" of her aloneness can she find her own strength to dream and write.

Aloneness also permeates the lives of those in cultures outside mainstream society. Isaura Barrera's courage is "born of *corazón*, not guts." Finally accomplished as the result of painful personal reflections and experiences, hers is a story of risk and choice to synchronize these often dissonant worlds. Additional authors also use experience as the source of their courage to choose. Tragically scarred by physical abuse, the woman in Mitsuye Yamada's poem, "The Club," "felt a slight tremor" through the wood in the statue used to hit her. Therein, she found the power to leave "forever." This same life flow immerses Joan Loveridge-Sanbonmatsu in the summer song of the tiny tree frog, the *coqui*. Filled with a strength to overcome fear, she can now move forth into the darkness outside.

Doris Sage and Mitsuye Yamada explore the courage of being an activist, dispelling even concerns of imprisonment to support moral governmental justice. Sage goes to prison for her beliefs and once there gives voice to the inmates. In reflections on similarly incarcerated friends, Yamada's voice explains to her traditional Japanese mother,

> If we put people who want to do the right thing in prison
> it keeps other good people who want to do the right thing
> from doing it.

Sage exposes us to the plight of women forced by life's situations to make alternative choices, such as going to prison rather than testifying against their men. But these incarcerated, often poverty-stricken women "helped each other; they taught us the unwritten rules ... The women were magnificent!" She brings to light the reality of so many of a forgotten underclass.

Similarly, Biblical scholar and poet Bonnie Lyons brings humanness to courage and removes the sense that choice is restricted to wealth or entitlement. Through exploring Rahab's choice to betray her people to Joshua's spies, she presents the irony of a prostitute exploring a moral dilemma:

> I could not have saved the kingdom;
> it was already doomed.
> I saved what I could.
> The same logic that allowed me
> to survive as a harlot.

Gaynell Gavin also explores the bravery of the impoverished. Instead of writing of her own activism as an attorney in choosing to represent low-income families, she says, "It's about Ruth." Agonizing over the bureaucracy that prevents a sexually abused child, Laura, from being adopted by Ruth, her courageous aunt, Gavin reflects in personal frustration: "I also did not want to believe that black children received less care and attention from the Department than other children, but how could I know ... if the delay in Laura's sex abuse consultation was due to overwork, honest skepticism about her ability to give information, racism, laziness, or other reasons that hadn't occurred to me?" Despite near hopelessness, she and Ruth both choose to help this child.

This saga of powerful women agonizing over choice spans across time. Bonnie Lyons poetically explores Eve's decision to leave the protection and boredom of the Garden and enter into human time and death, but also "adventure, change, possibility," while a modern day Valerie Bridgeman Davis feels the lure backwards of her lover and also decides

> if she does not go
> this time,
> she will never
> leave

As with Nora in Ibsen's *A Doll's House*, each of the women in this chapter would hear a figurative door slam behind them as they choose life and risk over the familiar.

Seams of Our Lives

As Muske (2003) and Gilligan (2002) observe, a woman is not totally her own person, but is intricately bound to a community of others. In addition, she is part of a life cycle and universality based on relationships with nature, life, and death. Authors write of the expansiveness of this tapestry of realities in the chapter, *Seams of Our Lives*. The edges of the tapestry's seams are sometimes smooth, other times jagged, and occasionally ripped apart. Some are permanent while others are basted together as a temporary hem during times of celebration or tragedy. But often it is this connectivity that shapes women's ability to risk the journey.

Through her writing, Gail Hosking Gilberg connects with the world of kindred authors who "carry around" her words as treasures. She discovers that she is having a significant impact on the world outside. Only by another discovery, that of the bond between life and death, was Bert Kruger Smith able to manage her immeasurable grief at the death of her young son, Jared. In a personal conversation with this book's first editor, Dr. Smith related, "Writing Jared's story was my therapy. It pulled me back into the world around me." With terrible sadness, we report the subsequent death of Bert Kruger Smith, a brilliant writer and mental health activist. Yet, her reflections in this work remain as a testament to the continuity of her words that unite us even in her passing.

Nanette Yavel writes of Sarah, who was unable to sustain this fragile connection with reality, and poignantly explores the jagged edge of mental illness. Sarah relates far better with the inner selves of fellow institutionalized patients than does the arrogant, but powerful, medical community. Similarly, poet Ruth

Kessler explores how this very type of heart is viewed as untrustworthy, pushed aside in order to worship the "False Prophet" that envelopes our world. Both authors rely on the individual's connectedness to intuition and inner knowledge as basic to the human condition.

Within wonderful imagery, Janice Brazil allows us to glimpse a snapshot of age observing youth, along with a memory tying the present to the past. Relationships and a lifetime of seams also stitch together Hilda Raz's *Stock*. As in Brazil's poem, memories support a life flow of connectedness with loved ones. For Raz, this involves a mother relating to a daughter who is now her son, and to her critically ill father-in-law. But her own desperate health crisis initiates a stream of consciousness that causes reflection on past and future, Christianity and Judaism, illness and death, friendship and forgiveness, women as nurturers. As Raz's reality evolves in a dream-like quality, Wendy Barker's Venetian traveller cannot sleep with her desire to pull away the tight masks that have kept her from the "lightness" of "her own sun and moon."

The tie of relationships is also profound in a woman's life. Four subsequent poems move from love's connectedness and initial simplicity through its complex growth, and finally, its dissolution. Amy Freeman Lee explores the pain of loneliness as a loved one enters our life briefly to "eat, and talk / And laugh," and then to depart. The ache of losing the precious "Now" moments to time and distance underscores the heart's pain without the presence of those we love.

Barbara Lovenheim artfully weaves us down the dual paths of the innocent wedding ceremony, from the rehearsed aisle to the final moment when future paths will never again be so simple and predictable. In a setting far removed, for three days Rosemary Catacalos' lovers "learned abandon / and rose out of ourselves / and became one overwhelming thing." Circumstances separate these lives, and despite love and joy, they must part again.

The parting is final for the Plaintiff in Demetrice Anntía Worley's "Judgment of Dissolution—Found Poem." Life's simplicity in Lee's initial connectedness and in Lovenheim's wedding ceremony is long gone, along with the passion of Catacalos' lovers. Worley writes, "Efforts at reconciliation have failed."

In our final stories of the chapter, connections span across oceans as Estelle Shanley and Naomi Shihab Nye remain tied in heart to family and international roots. Shanley is torn by professional and family pulls known to so many women. She cannot give up her Irish roots and desert the women of Belfast who need her journalism skills. Nor can she put her family through the daily turmoil of worry over her safety in a life-and-death situation. Nye's grandmother is also tied to her land. She fights to maintain with dignity the normalcy of a routine that sustains her. While, as with Shanley, she cannot control a world gone mad, she can still "stitch the mouth / in the red shirt closed."

The Real Self

While a woman's relationships with others, the land, life, and death form an inescapable connectedness, for many it is the discovery of the "real self" that establishes her courage. In this next chapter, poetry and narratives are bound together by the presence of an inner strength that allows a woman to claim and control her life and interactions. In *Walden*, Thoreau reflects,

> Let us settle ourselves, and work and wedge our feet downward and through the mud and slush of opinion, and prejudice, and tradition, and delusion, and appearance ... till we come to a hard bottom and rocks in place, which we can call reality, and say 'This is, and no mistake' .... Be it life or death, we crave only reality.

Our chapter begins with the power of mothers to give strength to their sons to battle racial prejudice. In her award-winning poem "When I Am Asked," Valerie Bridgeman Davis' role in the social revolution is to raise strong black sons by "instructing the saplings / Of the next revolution in the school of my experiences." Both she and Joan Loveridge-Sanbonmatsu must "reclaim the stolen esteem /And broken spirit" of offspring who have committed no offense other that being born within a racial minority. In "Two Warriors," Loveridge-Sanbonmatsu writes,

> Raising two warriors
> to stand undiminished
> hearts full
> with *gambaru*
> to meet this world
> giving them a shield
> to deflect racism,
> a shield with tensile strength,
> This has not been easy.

Gambaru, Japanese for *courage and energy*, brings us back to Isaura Barrera's courage born of *corazón*, or heart, rather than of the "guts" viewpoint of a majority society.

Kim Barnes models another message for her children: that danger can be overcome with bold actions. As Walton (1986) notes, "Both fear and calmness are contagious." While Barnes has a life-long give-and-take relationship with the river, she respects its power. Her seeming foolhardiness is the meat of future family stories. But so is her modeling of risk and confrontation of her fears.

Poets Pat Mora and Janice Brazil erase the image of older women as powerless. With physical stamina and inner strength, the widow and childless Doña Feliciana builds a house for herself, announcing, "Es mi casa. I am my family...." Brazil's woman, her face chiseled by time, possesses "Power and perception / from a lifetime of living."

In "Swallow Wings," Rosemary Catacalos' young woman from the "hood" is immersed in gaining that lifetime. She proclaims, "I grew up, folks, and I been down 'til I couldn't / get no more down in me." But still her world keeps saying "and, and, and, and / and." Similarly, Valerie Bridgeman Davis claims that her courage to dare to live comes from "a wide open heart / Full of power, unafraid / Of inescapable pain." Surviving a heart attack, she returns to run a marathon. Both she and Catacalos demonstrate the power to continue despite the past.

With the inner strength of the goddess Diana, Nanette Yavel's "Eve" begins our authors' poetic trilogy of Biblical women. Burdened by the Devil, she is given her freedom, allowing her to withstand the weight of evil. But Bonnie Lyons' Lilith claims that she was the first woman, not Eve. Banned from history as a witch because of her feminist claim that God created her at the same time as, and equal to, Adam, she exalts

> But the boundless ecstatic
> desire to mate
> with the world itself
> is the source of my power.

Lyons' Biblical Judith's life is also ruined because of the danger of her power and independence. As Lilith notes in the poem, each of these women is punished "for curiosity."

Vincent van Gogh reflected, "What would life be if we had no courage to try anything?" Yet, how little times have changed across the ages. Modern-day Ginger Purdy was similarly spurned for her desire to initiate a Woman's Chamber of Commerce. Despite disdain by others, she developed skills as a motivational speaker and created women's networking opportunities for personal and professional ties. Both she and Demetrice Anntía Worley learned that silence abdicates power and maintains women's status quo. Worley writes,

> In the end, we might as well
> speak for ourselves,

> hold the positions
> we want,
> love ourselves
> with wicked glee.

But can this power within, this need to sustain our real selves, become deleterious to our emotional and physical well-being? With Nan Cuba's "Confessions of a Compulsive Overachiever," we complete this chapter's cycle of personal courage with her evidence that, even with the best of intentions, in giving voice to other women we can risk putting our own needs aside. Cuba created the "Gemini Ink" writers' guild to help her family financially through difficult times. But when she became swept up in the success of "giving speech to women's silence" (Muskie, 2000), her own pain and needs emerged. We learn that woman's power within must be nourished continually.

Crossing Borders

More transparent but also often more impenetrable, the borders that we face can appear immeasurable at times. This final chapter explores some of these boundaries, including societal conventions, racial and religious discrimination, and acceptance of cultures far different from our own. Writers also consider the process of aging and crossing the border between life and death. Once we have established ourselves in new places, we move on to a promise of tomorrow, of the future to come. Naomi Shihab Nye reflects in "Eye-to-Eye" (1980),

> For one brave second
> we will stare
> openly
> from borderless skins

as we finally come to know each other while accepting the limitations and promise of our human condition.

Our initial pieces deal with the impact on the lives of children when parents sway far from convention. They realize that their daughters and sons may face ostracism and even physical danger because of decisions made by adults. In Ruth Marantz Cohen's *vie exceptionelle*, she breaks with conventions and goes beyond the traditional to seek out and enjoy those things most important to her personally. Yet, she shares herself unconditionally with the students in her world, simultaneously modeling self-creation for her daughter, Rosetta.

Joan Loveridge-Sanbonmatsu explores racial and job-related discrimination: If she can move beyond racism and marry a Japanese-American, how can she explain to her sons why her own parents never attended her wedding and have refused to see their grandchildren? How can she gauge the impact of subsequent family disruptions though six years of intense time spent in legal battles as she fought to overturn discriminatory nepotism rules across the nation, impacting positions and salaries of women university faculty? She models the pain and triumph of our writers,

> There is a certain knowledge
> that in the end
> we will be able to recall and
> say that
>
> once in our lives
> we gave all that
> we had for
> justice.

Gail Hosking Gilberg crosses religious borders after similarly painful reflections. In her conversion to Judaism from a traditional Christian family, we see a woman with the courage of her convictions who also impacts profoundly the lives of her children and future grandchildren.

A strong sense of justice permeates Connie Curry's essay, "We Who Believe in Freedom." In 1965, Mae Bertha Carter and her husband decided to send their younger seven children to previously all-white schools. When Curry visits them, "their house had been shot into, credit had been cut off, their crops were plowed under, they were being evicted, and their children were suffering terrible treatment from both teachers and students." But they prevailed, as did author Demetrice Anntía Worley, as she describes her bridge between cultures. Pat Mora writes of the pain of exclusion caused by language barriers, and the humiliation in learning English. Yet, potential outcomes of not pushing forward elevate these women to a new level of courage.

Jean Flynn crosses many borders: poverty, salary discrimination, battles for adequate schooling, all based on a need for human respect and dignity. As with the other authors, the outcomes of her work grace us all. But there is the human factor of anger, one that must be acknowledged and allowed as these authors spend their lives seeking basic rights. Janice Brazil's "Questioning" voices this anger as one of "the rites of passage / a woman bleeds through / in order to feel." Another barrier is crossed: Women giving themselves permission to express their voices.

The subsequent poems follow the journey of illness and the final crossing of death's border. Karen Waldron relates her mother's lengthy passage from life's concerns to another level of consciousness that envelopes her. The cross-ing continues as Ruth Kessler poignantly elaborates the pain of those left behind, and Naomi Shihab Nye respects her grandmother's dignity in death. Each poet intimates that there are things about the lost life that we living will never know. Nye suggests that there are parts that they

> Wouldn't let us see
> because every life
> needs a hidden place.

The chapter winds from death's passage to Ruth Kessler's weeping Angel of Love and our need to recover from human errors. Within a realm of poten-tial physical danger, Karen Waldron struggles across cultural barriers by gain-ing personal understanding of the needs of Iraqi women and their children. Barriers of hatred and personal attack must be peeled away for commonalities to arise.

As it opened, the cycle of the book also closes with the words of Dr. Maya Angelou. Reflecting that each of us has gradually become "a bordered coun-try," she proclaims the words of "A Rock, A River, A Tree" to put war aside. Her words are music to the writers of this book, as they have crossed so many bor-ders and long for a peace to finally be themselves.

Umberto Eco noted, "The reader completes the text." We hope that you, our readers, will complete the text of your own life by following the journeys of these courageous women.

REFERENCES

Bauhn, P. (2003). *The value of courage.* Lund, Sweden: Nordic Academic Press.

Cather, W. (1915). *The song of the lark.* Boston: Houghton-Mifflin.

Gilligan, C. (1993). *In a different voice.* Cambridge: Harvard University Press.

Goleman, D. (1995). *Emotional intelligence.* New York: Bantam Books.

Griffiths, M. (1995). *Feminisms and the self.* New York: Routledge.

Heilbrun, C.G. (1997). *The last gift of time.* New York: The Dial Press.

Kingsolver, B. (2002). *Small wonder.* New York: Harper Collins.

Long, J. (1999). *Telling women's lives.* New York: New York University Press.

Meccouri, L.L. (1999). *"Making it": Resilient women overcoming adversity in defiance of nega-tive predictors of success.* www.dissertation.com/library/1120354ahtm: Dissertation.com.

Muske, C. (2000). *Women and poetry: Truth, autobiography, and the shape of the self.* Ann Arbor: University of Michigan Press.

Rich, A. (1979). Commencement Address, Smith College. In *Blood, bread, and poetry: Selected prose 1979–1985.* New York: W.W. Norton.

Thoreau, H.D. (1854). *Walden.* In *The literature of the United States* (1966). Chicago: Scott, Foresman, and Co.

Walton, D.N. (1986). *Courage: A philosophical investigation*. Berkeley: University of California Press.

Werner, E.E., & Smith, R.S. (1998). *Vulnerable but invincible: A longitudinal study of resilient children*. New York: Adams.

sources of courage

An Interview with Dr. Maya Angelou

She knew poverty and racism intimately as a child in Stamps, Arkansas, hiding her "crippled Uncle Willie" under sacks of onions in a truck to escape his lynching by "The Boys." A brutal sexual assault at age eight, with her attacker beaten to death afterwards, sent her into silence for years as she feared the power of her own words. Yet, Maya Angelou learned that words were the way to set herself free. Encouraged by "Mama," her grandmother who knew that this voiceless child would become a great teacher, she has been awarded 56 honorary doctorates, several Golden Globe awards, and nominated for the Pulitzer Prize for her poetry in *Just Give Me a Cool Drink of Water 'fore I Die* (1971). She wrote graphic accounts of her young years in the award-winning *I Know Why the Caged Bird Sings* (1970), followed by scores of books and dramatic outpourings evidenced by her role as the first African American woman screenwriter and director in Hollywood.

Touring internationally in *Porgy and Bess*, she embodied pure musical tradition, crediting her success to listening to "Mama's voice, like that of Mahalia Jackson," and to the power of "my inherited art"—African American music. Her passion for social justice brought a close friendship with Martin Luther King, whom she memorialized in her lyrics "King: A Musical Testimony." But it was her four years in Africa that allowed her to embrace the vibrant history she felt had been lost by so many in America. She writes, "African culture is alive and well. An African proverb spells out the truth: *The ax forgets. The tree remembers.*"

In this interview, Dr. Angelou reflects candidly on courage, exploring life's dreams to the fullest, and her vision of freedom for all women.

In your life, where have you found the courage to take such phenomenal risks?

DR. ANGELOU: Years ago, I deduced that it costs everything to win, and that it costs everything to lose. So, if I didn't take a risk, if I didn't take a dare, then I would lose everything. And if I did take the dare, if I lost—I'd lose the same thing. But I might win. So since everything is always at stake, I may as well risk everything for the good thing.

So when I was asked if I would conduct the Boston Pops, I said, "Yes, of course." Now it's true I've gone to a few concerts at one time in my life, and I've been conducted, and I've put together choirs. But the Boston Pops with Keith Lockhart as the Maestro?!! I said "Yes" because ten more years might pass before another woman might be invited, and twenty years might pass before another African American woman might be invited. I said "Yes," and I got a book and I read, and I found out what music they were planning to play. I put that on my tape recorder, and I played it all around my house. I played it in my bus. I played it in my car. And on that day in Massachusetts, I stepped up and conducted the Boston Pops.

I sent a message that I enjoyed it so much that I'd be glad to do it a second time. But I was told they'd never invited anyone a second time. They had Ted Kennedy there that evening. So I said, "Well, that's alright then, but I'd be glad to do it." And I was invited the next year to do it again. So, had I not risked, I could always say, "Well, you know I was invited," but not what it felt like. Would I have opened the door for someone else who's coming behind me? No, I wouldn't have. As it is now, I've opened the door and had fun doing it too.

Has this thought that if I don't do it I'll never get there, and if I do it I may get somewhere, been a predominant theme for you in taking risks, then?

DR. ANGELOU: Yes, absolutely, since my early adulthood; yes, in fact, late teens. Yes.

What advice would you give other women about how they can demonstrate courage and explore their life dreams?

DR. ANGELOU: I would encourage women to know first that I don't believe that anyone is born with courage. I think you develop it. And life's inventions can help you or discourage you to develop courage. If you're born in a silk handkerchief and all you ever have to do is wonder about powdering your nose, then of course, you may not have to have courage. Of course you may be a lackey and not know it.

But if life offers you difficulties, that's the time to develop courage. You use each one of the disappointments, each one of the insults, each one of the rejections as a time to develop courage. You don't develop courage, and all of a sudden you just burst out and say: "I have the courage to do this or that." I think you develop it the same way you develop muscles. In the physical muscles, if you want to pick up a hundred-pound weight you don't go there and pick that up. You start with five-pound weights, ten-pound weights, twenty. You continue to strengthen yourself and sooner or later you will be able to pick up a hundred-pound weight.

I think that a woman ought to start with small things. For instance, don't stay in a room where women are being bashed. If somebody says, "Well, you know that little chic? That little blonde chic's a bimbo." Get out! Don't stay in the room where there's racial pejoratives bandied about which are meant to demean or diminish and de-humanize people. Don't stay in a room where sex and sexuality are a mock. "So the gay ... or straight ... " and this and that. No matter what device you have to use: Get Out!

And once you're out, you don't even have to say anything right away. You may not have the courage to say anything. But Get Out! And then you'll like yourself so much more. Once you're out in the street, in your car, on the sub-way—once you're out, Wow! I really got out of there. I lied and said I had to be in Bangkok, but I got out of there. And little, by little, by little, you develop the courage. Sooner or later, and probably much later, you will sit in that room and say: "I'm sorry I don't welcome this kind of conversation."

Do you have a dream or a vision for women?

DR. ANGELOU: Well, I have one great-granddaughter and I have a granddaugh-ter-in-law. I have a daughter-in-law and I have so many daughters. So many ... of every race you can imagine. You think only God could have brought those together! And I'm Mom to a lot of people: Asian, Latino, White, African, and African-American, Jewish. Mostly, I wish each one the vision to see themselves Free.

I was married for about two hundred and fifty years to a builder. It was my best marriage. And he taught me to build. He said, "Building has nothing to do with strength or with sex, with gender. It has to do with insight. If you can see it, you can build it. But you must see it."

So I wish women could see themselves Free. Just see and imagine what they could do if they were free of the national and international history of diminishment. Just imagine, if we could have a Madame Curie in the nine-teenth century, suppose that twenty other women had been liberated at the same time? Is it possible that we would have gotten small pox and chicken pox and measles and other un-social diseases obliterated? Just imagine, try to envi-sion if, in this country, African Americans were not in a holding position because of racism. Imagine if all that energy and intelligence and enthusiasm could be put to the use of the school system, to the economy: If they envision.

So that's what I wish for women: See it. Try to see yourself Free. What would you do? One thing, you'd be kinder. You'd give over gossiping. A plague. Yeah, you'd stop it. If you could see yourself Free, you would know that you deserve the best. And if you deserve the best, then you will give the best and you will only accept the best.

Do you feel that one individual can begin to make a difference?

DR. ANGELOU: Oh, I know that one individual can make a difference. I know it because I know so many people made differences in my life. And then, I have gone on to make differences in a lot of people's lives. And so, some of the people who've made the differences for me were an African American grandmother who'd gone to the fifth grade. An uncle who was crippled, who never left the town because he was ashamed of being crippled. But the difference he made in my life and in the lives of others can't even be computed. We don't go that high.

So, as the one person, first you have to start to be good to yourself. All virtues and vices begin at home, then spread abroad. So you must, women must, be good to themselves. First off, forgive yourself for the stupid things you've done. And then go to the person whom you may have injured and ask for forgiveness. If the person says: "I will never forgive you," you say: "Well, that's your business. My job was to ask for it. And I ask it with all my heart and you can't forgive me. I'm finished with it. I've done what I was supposed to do."

But you have to start with yourself first. Forgive yourself. And then see yourself as you want to be and then begin to work toward it. With a will and a way, and with laughter, with humor, with strength, with passion, with compassion, with style, and with love.

SUSTENANCE FOR LIVING

sustenance for living

She is born of damp mist and early sun.
She is born again woman of dawn.
She is born knowing the warm smoothness of rock.
She is born knowing her own morning strength.

"A Breeze Swept Through"
—LUCI TAPAHONSO

We are reminded of the very sustenance of our being in the birth of this Navajo child, who "kicked tiny brown limbs. / Fierce movements as outside / the mist lifted as the sun is born again." With her spirit connected to the emotional and physical world, we evidence the intricate part of the self that finds the substance to thrive. In this chapter, writers gain courage from their own "morning strength." We begin with the elderly to show how this connectedness with life's nourishment can span the ages.

"In February she was dying again," begins Naomi Shihab Nye's "One Moment on Top of the Earth." The grandmother hasn't eaten in twenty days, but when she hears that "someone who loved her ... flew across the sea" to see her, she wanted soup. Nye writes "being alive was wanting things again." She was a woman who had almost died, but who "by summer was climbing the steep stairs to her roof to look out over the fields once more," flowing into Nye's second piece, "Stain." It is "the simple love of her difficult place" that nourishes the old woman.

Love of family and human relationships also sustains Janice Brazil's "Grandma." Her strength comes from the endurance of hard times. Despite death having stolen her loved ones, her strength of being remains. Emerson wrote, "What lies behind us and what lies before us are very tiny compared to what lies within us."

The theme of endurance shaping one's character continues in "Standing Ground," where Demetrice Anntía Worley writes of the hardships black men and women faced in a place where "unequal was the norm." Yet, they stood their ground and "protected their families with food, homes, education." Not only did they pass along the physical sustenance for survival, but like Brazil's grandmother, they taught the next generation how to endure, "standing with their roots firmly planted."

Legendary stories and songs have always sustained the human condition. In Wendy Barker's "The Face That," Helen of Troy moved beyond "the stories of the old women" about "the stale place that kept women inside." She bowed to love and passion for guidance.

The impoverished young pregnant girl in Karen Waldron's "Down the Dublin Road" has nothing tangible to give her unborn child. Yet, with its fetal kick, "muted resolve awakes a Druid chill" and it is her song that is the sustenance for her baby. For a brief moment, we feel a sense of hope.

In "Walking Home," Susan J. Tweit tries to find harmony and balance in her life. She's been told that she has a disease that soon will kill her. In pain and confusion, she turns to nature, trying to find the sustenance she needs to survive.

> When I am stuck and cannot dig myself out of my problems, I go
> home to nature .... I head for a place where I will be alone and hear
> myself think, where the noise and busyness of humanity can't drown
> out the 'small still voice' of my inner wisdom.

Instead of experiencing a revelation that would banish her illness, on her journey she learns to listen to her body. She hears her own "tangled feelings, a jumble of anxiety, loneliness, confusion, and anger." Within the voices of these emotions she reflects that if she can maintain inner harmony instead of going to war with her body, she "might be able to learn what I need to get a grasp on my illness."

Similarly, nature continues to provide sustenance in Loveridge-Sanbonmatsu's "The Garden of Isabel." It is in the beauty, "the jewel, the emerald, among the flowers," that we find the harmony that beckons our return to the natural.

This courage of the spirit is intertwined in Ruth Kessler's poems. "Unlike Cain Angel-Like" and "In the Language of Silence" both speak of the Holocaust, but acknowledge that it is the silence that we hear the loudest. "Imagine" begins her first piece. Imagine the ordinariness or commonplace of lives, the "twining of common roots." Yet this ordinary woman was no ordinary woman for in "turning a deaf ear to Authority's orders" she exchanged life for death. The letter reads, "State of Israel ... thanks... heroine." In her second piece, Kessler pays homage to another heroine of the Holocaust, one who "looked into the eye of the abyss." Yet, instead of allowing evil to freeze up her being, she tutored her daughter in "the true shape of the heart." The substance she passed along was "patience, graciousness and courage."

We end this chapter with the sustenance of the arts. In Paula Cooey's essay, "That Every Child Who Wants Might Learn to Dance," we observe how her mother shared her talents with impoverished Appalachian families during the Depression. She contributed and enriched their lives through self-expression in dance. Regardless of their children's level of talent, the parents "learned to take pleasure to feel joy" in their accomplishment. Relatively powerless women banded together to organize a barter system, thus nourishing each other.

Thoreau reflected, "To affect the quality of the day, that is the highest of arts." In Maya Angelou's essay, "Art for the Sake of the Soul," she explores the "sustaining and the supporting" roles of art for African Americans across generations. She writes,

> ... Our singers, composers and musicians must be encouraged to sing the song of struggle, the song of resistance, resistance to degradation, resistance to our humiliation, resistance to the eradication of all our values that would keep us going as a country. Our actors and sculptors and painters and writers and poets must be made to know that...it is their work that puts starch in our backbones. We need art to live fully and to grow healthy ...

In these writings, we see that sustenance of living comes from the land, from those who went before us, and from those who believe in something strongly enough to create art to strengthen us during difficult times. It is in the passing on of stories, of talents, and lessons learned, that courage grows.

one moment on top of the earth

Naomi Shihab Nye

— For Palestine and for Israel

In February she was dying again, so he flew across the sea to be with her. Doctors came to the village. They listened and tapped and shook their heads. She's a hundred and five, they said. What can we do? She's leaving now. This is how some act when they're leaving. She would take no food or drink in her mouth. The family swabbed her dry lips with water night and day, and the time between. Nothing else. And the rooster next door still marked each morning though everything else was changing. Her son wrote three letters saying, Surely she will die tonight. She is so weak. Sometimes she knows who I am and sometimes she calls me by the name of her dead sister. She dreams of the dead ones and shakes her head. Fahima said, Don't you want to go be with them? and she said, I don't want to have anything to do with them. You go be with them if you like. Be my guest. We don't know what is best. We sit by her side all the time because she cries if we walk away. She feels it, even with her eyes shut. Her sight is gone. Surely she will die tonight.

Then someone else who loved her got on an airplane and flew across the sea. When she heard he was landing, she said, Bring me soup. The kind that is broth with nothing in it. They lit the flame. He came and sat behind her on the bed, where she wanted him to sit, so she could lean on him and soak him up. It was cold and they huddled together, everyone in one room, telling any story five times and stretching it. Laughing in places besides ones which had seemed funny before. Laughing more because they were in that time of sadness that is fluid and soft. She who had almost been gone after no eating and drinking for twenty days was even laughing. And then she took the bread that was torn into small triangles, and the pressed oil, and the soft egg. She took the tiny glass of tea between her lips. She took the match and held it, pressing its tiny sulfuric head between her fingers so she could feel the roughness. Something shifted inside her eyes, so the shapes of people's faces came alive again. Who's that? she said about a woman from another village who had entered her room very quietly with someone else. She's lovely, but who is she? I never saw her before. And they were hiding inside themselves a tenderness about someone being so close to gone and then returning.

She wanted her hair to be washed and combed. She wanted no one arguing in her room or the courtyard outside. She wanted a piece of lamb meat grilled with fat dripping crispily out of it. She wanted a blue velvet dress and a black sweater. And they could see how part of being alive was wanting things again. And they sent someone to the store in the next town, which was a difficult thing since you had to pass by many soldiers. And in all these years not one had ever smiled at them yet.

Then the two men from across the sea had to decide what to do next, which was fly away again, as usual. They wished they could take her with them but she, who had not even entered the Holy City for so long though it was less than an hour away, said yes and no so much about going, they knew she meant no. After a hundred and five years. You could not blame her. Even though she wasn't walking anymore, this was definitely her floor. This voice calling from the tower of the little village mosque. This rich damp smell of the stones in the walls.

So they left and I came, on the very next day. We were keeping her busy. She said to me, *Marhabtein*—Hello twice—which is what she always says instead of just Hello and our hands locked tightly together. Her back was still covered with sores, so she did not want to lie down. She wanted to eat whatever I had with me. Pralines studded with pecans, and chocolate cake. They said, Don't give her too much of that. If it's sweet, she'll just keep eating. She wanted cola, water, and tea. She wanted the juice of an orange. She said to me, So how is everybody? Tell me about all of them. And I was stumbling in the tongue again, but somehow she has always understood me. They were laughing at how badly I stumbled and they were helping me. It was the day which has no seams in it at the end of a long chain of days, the golden charm. They were coming in to welcome me, Abu Ahmad with his black cloak and his cane and his son still in Australia, and my oldest cousin Fowzi the king of smiling, and Ribhia with her flock of children, and the children's children carrying sacks of chips now, it was the first year I ever saw them carrying chips, and my cousin's husband the teller of jokes who was put in prison for nothing like everybody else, and the ones who always came whose names I pretended to know. We were eating and drinking and telling the stories. My grandmother told of a woman who was so delicate you could see the water trickling down her throat as she drank. I had brought her two new headscarves, but of course she only wanted the one that was around my neck. And I wouldn't give it to her. There was energy in teasing. I still smelled like an airplane and we held hands the whole time except when she was picking up crumbs from her blanket or holding something to eat.

And then it was late and time for sleep. We would sleep in a room together, my grandmother, my aunt Fahima, my cousin Janan of the rosy cheeks, a strange woman, and I. It reminded me of a slumber party. They were putting on their long nightgowns and rewrapping their heads. I asked about the strange woman and they said she came to sleep here every night. Because sometimes in such an upsetting country when you have no man to sleep in the room with you, it feels safer to have an extra woman. She had a bad cold and was sleeping on the bed next to me. I covered my head against her hundred sneezes. I covered my head as my father covered his head when he was a young man and the bombs were blowing up the houses of his friends. I thought about my father and my husband here in this same room just a few days ago and could still feel them warming the corners. I listened to the women's bedtime talking and laughing from far away, as if it were rushing water, the two sleeping on the floor, my grandmother still sitting up in her bed—Lie down, they said to her, and she said, I'm not ready—and then I remembered how at ten o'clock the evening news comes on in English from Jordan and I asked if we could uncover the television set which had stood all day in the corner like a patient animal no one noticed. It stood there on its four thin legs, waiting.

Janan fiddled with dials, voices crisscrossing borders more easily than people cross in this part of the world, and I heard English rolling by like a raft with its rich r's and I jumped on to it. Today, the newscaster said, in the ravaged West Bank ... and my ear stopped. I didn't even hear what had happened in this place where I was. Because I was thinking, Today, in this room full of women. In this village on the lip of a beautiful mountain. Today, between blossoming trees and white sheets. The news couldn't see into this room of glowing coals or the ones drinking tea and fluffing pillows who are invisible. And I, who had felt the violence inside myself many times more than once, though I was brought up not to be violent, though no one was ever violent with me in any way, I could not say what it was we all still had to learn, or how we would do it together. But I could tell of a woman who almost died who by summer would be climbing the steep stairs to her roof to look out over the fields once more. Who said one moment on top of the earth is better than a thousand moments under the earth. Who kept on living, again and again. And maybe an old country with many names could be that lucky too, someday, since at least it should have as much hope as invisible women and men.

Reprinted from Never in a Hurry (University of South Carolina Press, 1996).

stain

Naomi Shihab Nye

She scrubbed as hard as she could
    with a stone.
Dipping the cloth, twisting the cloth.
She knew the cloth much better than most,
having stitched its vines of delicate birds.

The red, the blue, the purple beaks.
A tiny bird with head held high.
A second bird with fanning wings.
Her fingers felt the folded hem.

The water in her pan was cool.
She stood outside by the lemon tree.
Children chattered around her there.
She told the children, "Take care! Take care!"

What would she think of the world today?
She died when she was one hundred and six.
So many stains would never come out.
She stared at the sky, the darkening rim.

She called to the children, "Come in! Come in!"
She stood on the roof, tears on her face.
What was the thing she never gave up?
The simple love of her difficult place.

Reprinted from 19 *Varieties of Gazelle: Poems of the Middle East* (Greenwillow Books, 2002).

grandma

Janice H. Brazil

The old woman
face lined,
hair thin and wispy,
fingers knarled, bent by arthritis,
back stooped ever so slightly,
looks up from her plate and asks,
Care for another piece of pie?

Holding my stomach with my hands,
I chuckle. *You still make the best pies.*

She laughs and I see
not a 95-year-old woman,
but an image in an old photo.
Wearing the gown she wore
to a West Point military ball,
a beautiful seventeen year old
smiled into the camera,
ready to drink in life.

Can't make good crust anymore though,
she says, rubbing her crooked fingers together.

What were your dreams then, Grandma?
Dancing that night did you know you were holding
a ghost whose memory would be captured
in the name of another man's son?
Swirling, your cadet dies in France
in a war to end all wars.
Who could predict
fifty years later you lose

another soldier in a country you know nothing about?
Would that seventeen-year-old
have danced long into the night
if she had known war would be so jealous
as to strike out twice against her?

It's been downhill ever since I turned 90.
She laughs at her own joke.

The image fades and the face
of a frail old lady stares across
the table at me.
It is still beautiful.
Life is good, Janice,
she says and loses herself
to memories for a moment.

My voice cracking, I answer,
Maybe one more small piece.

the face that

Wendy Barker

She didn't launch anything. Only herself,
when she left Menelaus, snoring, every
couple of weeks grabbing her, poking
a jagged fingernail, stinking ale. Always
she had known, from her swan-feather youth,
she herself made only half a broken egg.

The loveliness of the one who had come
for her. Black eyes like meteors, peonies.
He didn't say he was a prince. Come down
from the high mountains where he had slept
with the wind that swept through the trees
like desire, like the way she wanted him.

So they left. That simple. She chose to
leave the stale place that kept women inside,
kept tedious track of children's last names.
She remembered the stories of the old women
who spoke from their tapestries of a time
when it hadn't mattered who fathered a child

as long as there had been delight. After their
first pleasure, couldn't they have returned
to the mountain, arms around arms, unnoticed?
Couldn't they have launched a new people,
lovely as black and white swans, fire-red
shooting stars, whole unbroken eggs?

In Greek legend, Helen eloped with Paris, son of King Priam of Troy.
Helen's husband, King Menelaus of Sparta, waged the Trojan War to
re-gain Helen.

Reprinted from *Way of Whiteness* (Wings Press, 2000).

down the dublin road

Karen A. Waldron

Judged sinners by the Church, thousands of Irish women were locked behind the walls of the Magdelen Laundries for bearing children out of wedlock, leaving abusive homes, or just living in poverty. Most had their children taken away forever, spending their own lives in harsh, spartan conditions, laundering for often-abusive Sisters of Charity.

The child inside her young body
    shakes in violent fear,
borne as woman's grim burden
      to a Laundry down the Dublin Road.

Her feet carvery-sliced and bleeding,
    at last numbed to chiseled rocks,
swollen belly and sickled-back crushed together,
    her unborn's awakening to hatred's scorched flesh.

Behind, she drags childhood and shattered heart
    in a tattered, dirt-clogged sack.
Mum's tired frown and Da's grave sigh abandoned,
    as must be this quaking globe inside.

Rosaries in hand, strangers will tear it from her sullied body,
    weeping eyes and leaking breasts denied their painful prize.
Both orphans, she to cleanse raw in a laundry of abuse
    and her child to know no Magdalen Mother.

As powerful kicks alert to the solemn gate ahead,
    muted resolve awakes a Druid chill.
Her unseasoned hand pensively circles taut belly-skin,
    a mother-child song surprising hoarse lips.

Sing hush-a-bye loo, la loo, lo-lan,
Sing hush-a-bye loo-la-loo.

Bring no ill-wind to hinder us,
    My helpless babe and me,
Dread spirits of the Blackwater,
    Clan Owen's wild banshee,
And Holy Mary pitying us
    In heaven for grace does sue.

Sing hush-a-bye loo, la loo, lo-lan,
Sing hush-a-bye loo-la-loo.*

Spitting rain sinks into impending dark,
    as she rips skirt-rags for bloodied feet.
Two mortal sinners slipping silently to Life or Death,
    past a Laundry down the Dublin Road.

*"October Winds" (traditional Irish song)

standing ground

Demetrice Anntía Worley

Little brown children, hear the elders' wise
voices. They have earned the privilege to sit
on porches, to tell, what you call *stories*,
but what they name *life*—black men and women

farmed poor Mississippi soil; weighed down their
tongues with *no sir* / *no ma'am*; separate but
unequal was the norm; as janitors,
maids, factory laborers, they protected

their families with food, homes, education.
They survived so we could live. They stood their
ground. We create our tomorrow when we
heed our elders' / ancestors' shrewd proverb—

"Standing, with their roots firmly planted, is
the reason why Balboa trees don't fall."

walking home

Susan J. Tweit

One sunny morning in August two decades ago, I stood at a trailhead in northwest Wyoming's Absaroka Mountains. A green backpack towered over my head, stuffed with food, clothing, compact stove, sleeping bag, tent, and other essentials. Sadie, a German Short-haired Pointer, sat next to me, her dog packs strapped on, quivering with excitement. A shutter clicked. David, my friend Joan's teenage son, handed my camera back to me.

"Well," he said dryly, eyeing my bulging pack, "I hope you've got everything."

"If I don't," I replied with a small smile, "it doesn't matter—I can't carry another ounce."

I handed him the keys to my pickup. "The truck's yours until I get back. And there better not be a scratch on it!"

David grinned, got into the truck and gunned the engine. "Be careful," he said through the open window. "See you in a week or so."

I waved as he pulled the truck onto the highway. The pickup grew smaller and smaller, then disappeared around a bend in the valley. The noise of the engine died away and all was quiet except for the wind in the trees and the river rushing under the wooden footbridge. I shivered, a wave of goose bumps marching across my skin, and then shook myself. It was too late for doubts or fear. I was on my own now. A dipper warbled as it flew upstream.

"Okay, Sadie," I said to the quivering dog, "let's go."

By the time I turned, swaying a little under the weight of my heavy pack, she had dashed across the footbridge and was waiting on the other side, tail waving.

I was twenty-five years old and running away from my life. Two years before, I had been diagnosed with Undifferentiated Connective Tissue Disease, an illness related to rheumatoid arthritis and lupus. In these illnesses, the immune system turns on the sufferer's own body, producing antibodies that destroy our connective tissue, the stuff that cushions joints and links muscle to bone, nerve fiber to muscle, and cell to cell, allowing us to feel, to think, to walk, to talk, to make love. I lived with a near-perpetual chill that turned my skin yellow and jaundiced-looking, my toes, lips and fingertips numb. Most mornings, my joints ached fiercely and creaked audibly, snapping and popping like Rice Crispies in a bowl of milk. Some days, I dropped things without knowing why. From time to time, my finger and toe joints swelled, flushing red and hot to the touch. Now and then, I would wake at night, drenched with sweat and wracked by unexplained fevers. My energy went in spurts: whole days vanished in a fog of fatigue. There was no cure for my illness. I was told I'd live two to five years, or perhaps, on the outside, ten.

As my connective tissue disintegrated, my life came unglued as well: my marriage fell apart, I left my career in field ecology, and I moved away from my home, leaving northwest Wyoming and detaching myself from nature. Finally, lonely, sick and confused, I decided to return on foot to the mountains I love.

I borrowed Sadie, a friend's dog, and planned to hike more than 100 miles through some of the wildest country in the Lower 48, a region that belongs more to the resident grizzly bears than to humans. The trek would take around seven days, depending on my stamina. Sadie and I would climb two passes, cross the Continental Divide, wade numerous streams, and cross a major river. There'd be no roads, no phones, no flush toilets, no grocery stores, no emergency rescue.

When I am stuck and cannot dig myself out of my problems, I go home to nature—whether just a rock on the edge of a mesa overlooking town or a remote wilderness. I head for a place where I will be alone and can hear myself think, where the noise and busyness of humanity can't drown out the "small, still voice" of my inner wisdom. Silence is an undervalued resource, a rarity in landscapes where the myriad human-generated sounds—car engines, thumping stereos, jackhammers, cellular phones, video games, and televisions— overwhelm mind and spirit. Yet silence—not the total absence of noise, but restful quiet—is critical to our spiritual lives. It is in silence where we meet our inner selves without distraction, where we tune out the trivial and focus on what is at the core of our lives.

I needed that kind of silence, so I headed home, making a beeline for the mountains I knew intimately from my years as a field ecologist. Walking across them, I thought, I might find the wisdom I needed to live with my illness.

The night before I began the trek, I stayed with my friend Joan. I told her about my planned walk as we sat drinking wine in her comfortable living room. "I really need to get off by myself," I finished. "But I'm taking Sadie for company."

Her anger hit me like a slap in the face before I heard the words. "A week on foot and alone in that country with your health—that's just stupid!" she exclaimed. Her eyes flashed. "Not just stupid, it's dangerous!"

She paused, as if expecting me to defend myself, but I couldn't.

"You won't listen to me. You'll go anyway, won't you?"

I tried to joke away her concern, but we both knew she was right. I could fall and break a leg; I could be attacked by a grizzly bear, drown fording a creek, be struck by lightning on a ridge; the stress of the trip could trigger a flare-up of my illness. The list of dangers was long. I'd be on my own, miles from anywhere in a maze of roadless mountains, with no way to let anyone know I needed help, much less how to find me. I could die out there and no one would even know or find my body before the flesh eaters devoured it. Thinking about the myriad dangers put knots in my stomach, so I forced my mind away. There was no point in scaring myself. I had to go, and I had to go alone. And if I was going to survive the trip, I had to be tough. I had only myself to depend on.

I didn't sleep much that night, besieged by fears. The next morning, Joan agreed to let her son David drive me to the trailhead. She hugged me before she went to work, but she didn't say anything. She didn't have to. I knew I was wrong. But I had to go.

When I reached the other side of the bridge, Sadie set out up the trail in front of me. Her dog packs jiggled and her feet raised small puffs of dust as she trotted along. The sun was warm on my face, the air perfumed by pinesap. A red-tailed hawk circled high overhead, then screamed: Ki-yeer!

"We'll be okay," I said out loud in the quiet, and followed Sadie up the trail.

That afternoon, Sadie and I came to our first creek crossing. High runoff from the previous winter's unusually abundant snow pack had swollen the normally small creek to a silty torrent. I eyed the water doubtfully, and then lowered myself carefully to the gravel bank to change from my hiking boots to the old running shoes I'd brought for creek fording.

I sighed.

Sadie whined.

"It's okay, girl. It's running high, but we can make it."

Shoes on, hiking boots slung around my neck to keep them dry, I hauled myself upright.

"Ready?" I asked Sadie. She wagged her tail.

"Okay," I said, "in we go."

The water temperature was a shock. Bone-chilling cold. The cobbles of the streambed were slippery, the current stronger than I expected. Sadie, pacing the bank behind me, whined again.

"Come on, girl!" I said impatiently, struggling to keep my balance as I inched forward against the current. I heard her splash in, but couldn't turn back to look. I was in past my knees. The bones of my feet and legs ached with the cold. Up to my thighs, and I was halfway across. I couldn't see Sadie, and it took all I had to keep going. Inching forward, my legs and feet numb, rubbery, I was nearly there.

An arm's length from the bank, I slipped into a hole in the stream bottom, invisible in the opaque water. My legs flew out from under me. My pack pulled me down. I grabbed a tree root protruding from the bank. For a long moment, I hung on the balance, the current tugging at me, my arms clinging tight to the rough root. Finally I pulled myself out, soaked and shaking.

I remembered Sadie, and willed my numb lips to purse and my tongue to whistle. To my immense relief, she appeared a ways downstream. She scrambled up the bank and galloped over, packs flapping, water streaming off her skinny body, tail wagging.

I hugged her close, and she licked my face enthusiastically.

"We made it!" I said, and realized that even my voice was shaking.

Raynaud's Phenomenon. "Damn!"

Raynaud's Phenomenon, a frequent companion of some connective tissue diseases, is a circulatory ailment in which the blood vessels in one's extremities—fingers, toes, nose, lips, and ear lobes—constrict spasmodically, restricting or eliminating blood flow to these areas. In a severe Raynaud's attack, the extremities go numb, and the sufferer is likely to injure herself, since nerve connections shut down in the circulatory freeze. The chill of Raynaud's is as dangerous as hypothermia, making thinking difficult and logic fuzzy.

I couldn't let myself be weak now. My brain clicked on and I began what would become an automatic routine after every stream we forded. Take off my cumbersome pack. Peel off my wet fording shoes. Dry and massage my numb feet and legs. Check for injuries. Put on my socks and force my hiking boots on. Eat a handful of trail mix. Stand up—ignore the wobbling! Move around. Swing my arms vigorously. Examine Sadie. Haul on my pack and get back on the trail—quickly, no time to feel—before the chill of Raynaud's shut me down.

Several days later, our first pass and its vertiginous snowfields safely behind us, Sadie and I sprawled on the grassy banks of the Thorofare River, dogged by clouds of whining mosquitoes. It was lunchtime, and I was starving. I munched my crackers and cheese, trying not to inhale mosquitoes, and scanned the lush green expanse of meadow across the river. Not far away, a sandhill crane nearly as tall as I was probed the wet soil for food. A large, furry animal crept along behind it, belly low to the ground, the way a dog stalks a magpie. When it was just a few feet away, the stalker launched itself into the air, leaping for the bird. At the last possible moment, the crane lifted off on wide wings and flew away. The stalker thudded to earth. The crane circled, bugling its resonant call, then landed and resumed feeding. The furry one resumed its creeping approach. I sat motionless, fascinated, until my brain belatedly registered the stalker as a grizzly bear.

I rose quietly, lunch in hand, heaved on my pack, and motioned Sadie to follow. I tiptoed backward, silent, eyes on the bear, all the way to the trail. It was all I could do to keep myself from breaking into a run. The bear raised its shaggy head and looked across the river. Sadie and I froze. Sweat trickled between my shoulder blades. After a minute, it looked away. We reached the trail and walked oh-so-casually into the cover of a grove of spruces before I thought to breathe. Once we were safely out of sight, I couldn't stop shaking. I forced my legs to hike on, cursing myself steadily under my breath. I was guilty of relaxing my alertness, of forgetting the reality of this very wild outside and who eats whom. In a world with grizzly bears, Sadie would be merely a mouthful, but I would be just the right size for prey. I was out of touch.

I had walked into the wilderness to grieve, mourning my losses: my marriage, my home, my place in science, and my intimate bond with nature. I was alone, ill, facing my own personal winter. I knew I had choices, but I couldn't see what they were. Anger at the fate that had struck me with a deteriorating illness kept me prisoner, like Persephone, the daughter of the goddess Demeter, confined in the underworld by Hades. Demeter's desperate search for her lost daughter plunged earth into winter. Only when grieving Demeter rescued her daughter from the Underworld did life-giving spring return. I was searching for a way to return spring to my life, to reconnect to the wild I had once claimed as kin, to thaw my heart, to remember how to live.

That evening, Sadie and I came to our last major creek crossing. I followed the trail to the ford shown on the topographic map, arriving just as the sun's slanting light gilded the landscape. The shadows of the lodgepole pines lay like logs across the trail. I walked up to the creek bank—and there the trail ended. At the base of a steep, newly eroded bluff, the creek roared by, high and deep. We'd never make it across. I put my pack down, whistled to Sadie, and hiked upstream for perhaps a mile, looking futilely for a crossing. I hiked back downstream, tired now, still searching. No luck. There was no crossing spot. If we couldn't ford this creek, we had to turn back. Blue with Raynaud's, shaking, I pulled myself together. I pitched my tiny tent, lit the stove, fed Sadie, and boiled water for my own dinner. As I ate my bowl of noodles, I pulled out the map: upstream were impassible cliffs; downstream the deep Thorofare River. In front, the creek we could not ford.

I studied the map, searching for a solution, until darkness erased its fine, undulating lines. Then I crawled into my sleeping bag, near tears. Sadie curled up next to me. I was exhausted but could not sleep. The creek roared in my ears. Large animals—I hoped they were only moose—crashed through the forest. My mind circled and fretted. Sometime in the night, I unzipped the tent door and poked my head out to scan the sky for stars. The night was overcast. I peered intently, searching for a glimpse of the constellations. The heavens were blank.

In looking to the night sky for enlightenment, I was following an ancient human tradition. Astrology, the study of coincidences between human lives and the movements of the stars and planets, began with the cultures that inhabited the fertile crescent bounded by the Tigris and Euphrates rivers around 1400 to 1000 BC, in what is now Iraq. Picked up and modified by the Persians and Egyptians and later synthesized by Greek, Chinese, and Indian cultures, the body of knowledge grew and changed with each succeeding contact. Astrology and astronomy were one discipline until the European Age of Enlightenment separated them, embracing the study of the observable movements and features of the stars and planets and condemning the unexplainable concurrences of astrology to the realm of myth and speculation.

More recently, psychologist Carl Jung delved into astrology early in his career. It was, he felt, a powerful part of the human myth, the stories we create to understand who we are. Jung saw universal symbols or archetypes— from the Greek *arche*, meaning "primal," and *typos*, "imprint or pattern"—in the stories assigned to the constellations and planets. Those tales, he believed, helped us to know ourselves. Later, Jung turned away from astrology, perhaps under pressure from the scientific establishment, which couldn't swallow wisdom so dependent on intuition, so contrary to the straight-line, incremental path of logic.

Yet science does itself a tremendous disservice to dismiss the wisdom borne on intuition: some of the greatest scientific leaps, from Newton and his perhaps apocryphal falling apple demonstrating the law of gravity to Watson and Crick "seeing" the double-helix form of DNA, have come through intuition. Such an "ah-hah!" moment, the unconscious linking of connections half-glimpsed, inspired immunologist Polly Matzinger of the National Institutes of Health to develop a profound new model of how the human immune system works. Our immune systems, Matzinger believes, protect us not by simplistically searching for foreign bodies to destroy, but by responding to signals of danger emitted by our cells. Matzinger explains her model with an analogy to her Border collie Annie. When guarding a herd of sheep, Matzinger says, Annie doesn't waste her energy casting about for invaders; instead, she rests, watching the sheep. When they show signs of unease, she leaps into action, ready to find the problem and defend the flock. Dendritic cells in our bodies, says Matzinger, act like Border collies. These cells' fingerlike projections touch from 50 to 500 neighboring cells. As long as this "flock" acts normally, the dendritic cells snooze. As soon as one of the cells does something abnormal, however, such as spewing its potentially toxic contents after being infected by a virus or leaking cell fluids after sustaining a physical injury, the dendritic cells leap into action like so many Border collies, triggering the process we call the immune response.

It may seem like splitting hairs to move from seeing the immune system as a search-and-destroy process to seeing it as a watchful Border collie. But the difference between the two models has profound implications. For one thing, Matzinger's model explains many important "exceptions" to the conventional immune system model, including why the immune systems of pregnant women do not attack and destroy the "foreign tissue" that comprises normal fetuses. For another, her model opens the possibility that the immune systems of sufferers of connective tissue diseases are responding to danger signals generated by the cells of our connective tissue, rather than turning on us in an attack from within. Despite its potential, the scientific establishment has not yet embraced Matzinger's model. It is too radical, too intuitive.

I was raised in the logical culture of science, but I have experienced the insights born of intuition. I never miss a chance to read my horoscope in the daily newspaper, and when I am outside at night I look to the heavens to read the stars, searching for comfort and connection in their timelessness, wisdom in the stories they carry.

The next morning, I rose early in a golden dawn, the forest around me sparkling with crystalline frost. Too miserable to admire such beauty, I ate a quick breakfast while pacing the bank above the creek. I looked at the map again, and then admitted defeat. Sadie and I started off down the trail, headed back to where we'd begun.

About half a mile along, we met a backcountry ranger. I stopped to chat, my voice rusty with disuse. He asked where we were going and I poured out my frustration.

"Yeah, that crossing washed out this spring," he said. "Bad luck for you." He thought a moment, and then said, "You know, there's a place down the creek that might be shallow enough for you to cross, just above the confluence with the river. I've done it on horseback."

A glimmer of hope lightened my mood. I pulled out my map, and he pointed to the spot. "Good luck!" he called as we walked away.

My spirits rose as Sadie and I headed off cross-country. Soon we came out onto a broad gravel bar, and there was the creek, rushing past in a channel nearly twenty yards across, far wider than any stream we'd attempted so far. I paced up and down beside the flow, scanning the current and reading the creek bottom.

Sadie sat, waiting.

Finally I decided. We could do it. I plopped down on the gravel, took off my boots, and slipped on my fording shoes. Then I looped a piece of nylon cord around the straps on Sadie's dog packs and tied the end to my waist. I didn't want the current to sweep her into the river.

In we waded. The icy water had already reached my mid-thighs when Sadie, afloat and paddling frantically, hit the end of her cord. I willed my legs to hold and kept going, leaning upstream to counter Sadie's weight. The water reached my crotch. I hitched up my pack and kept going. My legs and feet were numb, but I made myself inch along, step by step. Finally, soaking wet and shivering, we made it across. I grabbed Sadie and twirled her in a dizzy circle of joy before my legs collapsed under me.

Two noontimes later, I sat in the shade of a fat Douglas-fir tree above the Snake River. The path behind led into the wilderness we'd hiked through; a few miles ahead lay the end of the trail.

"We made it!" I said to Sadie. I groped in my dusty pack and celebrated by sharing the last food with her. I carefully smeared four crackers with peanut butter, crumbled the end of the cheese over them, and dotted each with hard raisins. I set two crackers in front of Sadie. She gulped them immediately and then delicately licked her jowls. I ate one cracker slowly, savoring this final backcountry meal, leaving the other balanced on my knee. A breeze whooshed through the branches overhead, the river tumbled by far below. A white-breasted nuthatch called Yank! Yank! Yank!

I had gone to the wilderness in the hopes that I would hear a voice speaking from the silence. I had imagined receiving a revelation that would lift me out of my misery and banish my illness. Instead, what I had heard were my own tangled feelings, a jumble of anxiety, loneliness, confusion, anger. Where was the light of revelation in these dark emotions?

Sadie whined, breaking into my thoughts. I leaned over to pet her. The breeze pushed a small cumulus cloud over the sun, its shadow sweeping the ridge like a giant hand. It passed, and the sun's warmth returned.

Perhaps, I thought, the voices of my emotions were just what I needed to hear. Since my diagnosis with an illness that I was told was the result of my "dysfunctional" immune system attacking my own tissues, I had felt I was at war with myself. I had believed that I could not trust my body and my own intuitive wisdom. I had tried to be tough and self-sufficient, running my life with logic and objective detachment. Perhaps the chill of Raynaud's, the physical shutting down of my blood flow, reflected the metaphorical freeze I had imposed on my body's voice, the insights I had no data to explain and the emotions I was afraid to feel. Perhaps I had forgotten how to listen.

The sense that we call "hearing" involves both physical ability, the workings of the nerve endings that receive sounds and transmit them to our brain, and discernment, the mental processing necessary to focus on and interpret a particular sound from the welter of signals that bombard us. If either fails, our hearing suffers. I think of listening as the latter, the attentive part of hearing. Listening only to the logical, rational side of myself, I had been hearing only some of the signals, interpreting only part of the message. No wonder I felt lost and confused.

Polly Matzinger believes that the immune systems of sufferers of connective tissue diseases haven't turned on us, destroying our tissue from within in some twisted self-harming response. Instead, she suggests our inner defense systems may be responding to danger signals that we cannot discern. Like coal miner's canaries, the cells of our connective tissue may be dying from some as-yet-unidentified threat; our dendrites and the other immune system cells simply clean up the damage. If Matzinger's theory is true, sufferers of connective tissue diseases should listen to the responses of their immune systems, rather than suppress those signals.

If I listened more carefully, I might be able to learn what I needed to get a grasp on my illness. First though, I needed to know myself better. Walking through the days alone but for Sadie, fording icy creeks, experiencing the terrors of night noises and the benediction of golden dawns had renewed my intimacy with the wild that lives deep inside all of us. That was a beginning. It could start a new, or renewed, understanding of my self. After the solitude and hardships of my trek, I wondered if I knew myself at all. It was time to start listening.

Sadie whined again. Then, with an audible *gulp!* she reached forward and ate my remaining cracker—so much for contemplation.

I laughed and ruffled her ears. "You're right. It's time to go."

I picked up my pack, lighter now than it had been a week ago, and settled it one last time on my shoulders. I stood up and turned for a final view of the trail we'd come on. Then I headed in the opposite direction. Sadie pranced in front of me, her feet raising small puffs of dust as we walked on out of the wilderness.

garden of isabel

Joan Loveridge-Sanbonmatsu

A tiny bird, brilliant green,
perches on the branch of a fig tree.
In Cuernavaca, Mexico, where it is always
spring, always spring.
She sits among the blossoms,
white, fuchsia and rose,
and lemon trees laden with fruit.

A different vista draws this
small green bird away for a moment.
But the beauty of the garden beckons her:
come back, come back, you are the jewel,
the emerald, among the flowers.

For Isabel Muñoz Escobar,Cuernavaca, México 1999
Reprinted from Winged Odyssey (Hale Mary Press, 2002).

el jardín de isabel

Joan Loveridge-Sanbonmatsu

Un pequeño pájaro, brillante y verde
se posa sobre la rama de un árbol de higo.
En Cuernavaca, México, siempre primavera,
siempre primavera.
Ella se posa entre las flores
blancas, fuscias y rosas
y árboles de limón llenos de fruta.

Una vista diferente distrae este
pequeño pájaro verde por un momento.
Pero la belleza del jardín lo atrae:
Regresa, regresa, tú eres la joya,
la esmeralda, entre las flores.

Para Isabel Muñoz Escobar,Cuernavaca, México 1999
Translation: Ziomara Reyes Feliciano de Jiménez y Tracy Karl Lewis 2000.
Reprinted from *Winged Odyssey* (Hale Mary Press, 2002).

unlike cain angel-like
Ruth Kessler

There's a certain race of men
(now I know my brothers and sisters)
who harbor in their breast a bit of trembling,
naked water . . .
Race of ill-omened tenderness, of Abel
returned to life

ROSARIO CASTELLANOS

Imagine
Passover eve.
A foreign country.
A small apartment in Paris.

Imagine
welcome: chopped liver, matza, sweet wine.

Imagine
history's records
banging on memory's door, crying,
pointing a blaming finger.

Imagine
suspicion.

Imagine
the hosts:
a Jew and a Polish gentile married after The War.
And The War even now madly scattered
charred puzzle pieces.
How did hers fit in?

Imagine
in one living room corner
distant relatives' acquaintance-talk of the husbands,
twining of common roots.

Imagine
in another, the forced small talk of wives—
an eager hostess, a wary guest.

Imagine
Polish fare on the table
dressed for the Jewish occasion.
Imagine
the hideous wallpaper
its thick orange stripes, its huge orange eyes.

Imagine
in the tiny kitchen the faucet dripping.

Imagine
the drawn-out meal:
The overcooked meat.
The small silences.
The awkward tiptoeing of people
who never met

Imagine
the Untouchable Subject
stealing   in an unguarded moment
between the main course and the salad
into the room.

Imagine
the intent scraping of forks and knives on the plates.

Imagine
the host suddenly turn toward his wife:
Show them the letter.

Imagine
an old tin cookie box.
Imagine inside
a folded sheet of paper
lying humble and pale as a *matza*.

Imagine
official yellowed stationery,
fading typescript

Imagine words throbbing:

State of Israel ... thanks ... heroine ...
... Righteous among the Nations ...
... saved ... saved ... Jews ... saved ... saved ...

Imagine this receipt of the heart
now quickly refolded, now quickly put back
into the tin box.

Imagine
the hush.

Imagine
not the unimaginable:
a young, powerless woman
turning a deaf ear to Authority's orders,
hearing only what's human and groans;
exchanging death sentences of strangers,
of Jews,
for her own

But imagine
the bus driver not waiting for her;
the snow falling no differently on her coat, frayed at the cuffs like ours;
a fine for an overdue library book imposed on her as on us;

the one rose in her living room vase
lasting no longer than ours.

Imagine
the young man waiting behind her   dyed-haired, frail
to pay for the evening paper
having no notion ...

Imagine
her walking among us—
unlike Cain
angel-like—
unknown, unmarked,
masquerading as you or me.

Imagine
our host now say softly
She has always been a good-hearted woman.

That's all.

Imagine
the words fall on the table between us
plain and homely as the boiled potatoes.

Imagine
in the tiny kitchen the faucet continues to drip.

Imagine
the orange stripes of the wallpaper closing in
on his words   then the silence
like the columns of some ancient temple,
half-destroyed half-unearthed.

Imagine
the bells of a distant church beginning to toll.

Imagine
the night standing outside the window,
a dumb, indifferent witness
ready to swallow this story
like so many others.

Imagine
Passover eve in a foreign country.
Imagine
a small apartment in Paris.
Imagine
not having a proper *Seder*.
Not telling stories of the coming out of Egypt.

in the language of silence

Ruth Kessler

In memory of my mother, Blima Kluberg Traubner

Not because in your language the word *Holocaust* does not exist
you wore a noose of silence around your heart,
or when you spoke the words *War, Occupation, Camps,*
they flickered softly on your lips,
muffled gunshot blazes
fearing to injure me.

How to collect the shards to piece
up that other image
concealed from me—
the steel curtain of The War
having slammed over
your youth, your famous beauty
irretrievably buried under the harrowing Siberian winter,
turning all present and future tenses of your life
into past continuous.

To stitch your life from the drab patches
of deprivation, disappointments, illness,
you used such artistry of
patience, graciousness and courage,
the original materials were
lost to the beholder's eye.

All your life having so little—
having looked into the eye of the abyss,
even the gray stones in life's narrow corridor,
even the chipped beads on the abacus of years,
were miracles enough—
your inexhaustible giving.

Quietly,
you tutored me in small lovely things:
the true shape of the heart,
and how to escape jealousy's claws—
that rare gift
only the aristocrats of the spirit are rich enough to bestow.

Your whole life flickered
like the evanescent flame
of this *yahrzeit* candle,
almost imperceptibly.

To be truly yours,
this poem should be written
in the language of silence.

Reprinted from *Common Intuitions Anthology*(Palettes and Quills, 2005).

that every child who wants might learn to dance
Paula M. Cooey

Before she married, Polly Miller Cooey, my mother, was a talented and accomplished dancer. During the late forties, when I was about three years old, she began teaching dancing and baton twirling. She traveled throughout rural north Georgia, holding classes in the public schools—a sort of itinerant dancing teacher. Unlike other teachers who charged much higher fees, she charged $1.00 per student per hour for weekly classes in ballet, tap dancing, and acrobatics. For those who wished to take private lessons she charged $2.00 for half an hour. For baton twirling she charged $.50 for half-hour classes. Every spring, just before school closed for the summer, she held a colossal recital. All students performed at whatever level they were capable of.

My mother believed that every child who wanted lessons should have them and that every child, no matter how poor, should be encouraged to want them. Though highly talented herself, she never let lack of talent exclude a potential pupil. She reasoned that knowing how to dance and actually performing gave one confidence in public, no matter how clumsy and graceless the performance. She also had extraordinary imagination and choreographed elaborate productions, my most vivid memory being her production of the Nutcracker Suite, performed in the sweltering pre-summer heat of rural Georgia. She spun fantasies of fairies and elves like no one I have ever known since, and she lured even the most cynical little boy and girl into participating in her illusions. I grew up pirouetting, tapping, tumbling, whirling, and twirling to all kinds of music, while immersed in frothy nets, satins, taffetas, laces, tassels, and feathers. I grew up surrounded by children, some of whom could leap through the air like gazelles and whirl like dervishes, others of whom lumbered and flopped about like beached whales, with big toothy grins on their faces, but with no physical grace whatsoever.

Most of these children came from lower middle class, working class, and rural families. Until the sixties, all of them were white.[i] The working class and rural kids often came from large families with more than one child wanting lessons. With some exceptions, their parents worked as farmers, mechanics, clerical and secretarial staff at Lockheed, factory workers in Atlanta, school teachers, and support staff for Dobbins Air Force Base. Though most of my mother's students came from families with two parents, some of them, including me and my sister and my brother, were reared by single working mothers. Contrary to popular nostalgia in regard to "stay-at-home moms" in the fifties, most of the mothers, whether with their husbands or without them, worked outside the home. Even at $1.00 an hour, once a week, most parents could hardly afford to pay for one child, never mind two or more. So my mother and the other mothers worked out a barter system, trading home grown produce, transportation, hair care, and an array of other services in exchange for lessons.

The most elaborate example of this system was Ola Thomas and her four children. Ola was married to an independent truck driver who was often out of work. Ola herself worked as a seamstress on the assembly line for the Lovable Brassiere Company in Atlanta. Ola wanted dancing for all four children and baton twirling for three of them; she further wanted private lessons as well as classes. My mother and she worked out a deal whereby Ola fed my sister and me one night a week, supplied us with "seconds" in undergarments, and on occasion made me and my sister absolutely beautiful party dresses from undergarment taffeta and satin out of remnants purchased from the Lovable Brassiere Company. In exchange, Ola's children received both private and class lessons in dancing and baton, and Ola also made many of the costumes for mother's recitals. Incidentally, Ola's three daughters were outstanding dancers, two of whom became highly accomplished acrobats, though Ola's son predictably lost interest once he reached junior high school. Without such a barter system there would have been far fewer, sometimes very talented, students taking lessons.

My mother and the mothers of her students understood clearly that children needed confidence and that this confidence could be acquired through bodily discipline and practice. They knew well this confidence was much more important than talent. They also valued the experience of enjoying one's physicality for its own sake and sharing that joy through performance with both other performers and an audience of doting parents. So my mother inspired confidence in gawky children and spread joy like an epidemic across north Georgia for about two decades. Some of her students grew up, prospered, and brought their children to her for lessons—still at $1.00 an hour and so forth. And my mother would work out payment with anybody, in some cases just plain giving lessons away—when so-and-so got laid off at Lockheed, was ill and had to quit work, or was wiped out by flood or drought. We ourselves had a few flush years economically and mostly a succession of extremely lean years.

My mother was not wild about the poverty, but she loved her work with a passion I used to suspect was reserved only for her work, to the exclusion of the rest of us. Now, looking back, I think, So what if it was! So what if she loved her work as much as life itself. Her work was one long sustained act of extraordinary generosity; her imaginary world was one in which every child who wished for it might learn to dance. And all of this work took place against a backdrop of rural poverty, economic instability for working class and lower middle class people, and the personal family tragedy of my father's alcoholism.

What makes this story more than simply a nostalgic memory? There is no doubt in my mind that the collusion of these women around dancing lessons for their children, a collusion of joy, was necessary to their own survival, as well as for the future betterment of their children. Furthermore, this community of women, conspiring to link children's bodies to dance, food, and clothing, in its own small way and in its own small location, temporarily subverted oppressive social structures.

Certainly we learned as students that joy was an acceptable feeling to accompany the discipline and performance of dance. This feeling was driven by and companion to physical exertion—ironically sometimes quite painful; at the same time performance itself could and often did produce an ecstasy that bears a family resemblance to *jouissance*.[ii] Our parents, mostly our mothers, learned to take pleasure, to feel joy, in our accomplishment. For many of us were provided an opportunity that few of our parents had as children, an opportunity that might give us polish, helpful to the upward mobility to which our parents aspired in this heavily classed society, in which class difference was masked by a rhetoric of democracy, but never absent. Both performers and observers learned joy, the effect of which was liberating.

This joy and the dance that was its object of cognition varied even within the context in which I lived. While the culture in which I grew up for the most part found dancing socially acceptable, some of its communities in fact prohibited dance altogether, never mind taking pleasure in it. To my Southern Baptist friends, for example, dancing meant the eternal damnation of the immortal soul. Both my mother and I had to contend on more than one occasion with the evangelically exuberant concern of some of my schoolmates and their parents for our future state.

Because much of the culture of the time regarded sexuality at best with ambivalence, even the appropriateness of joy depended to some extent upon not acknowledging the full implications of the sensuality of dance, especially in regard to the younger children. It further depended upon "gendering" the bodies of the dancers: While the culture accepted teaching dance both to female and to male children, dance itself was feminized and most males moved on to other kinds of physical activity by the time they reached adolescence. Thus, little girls of my generation were taught early on that it was acceptable to want to be ballerinas when they grew up, though this accomplishment was extremely unlikely for almost all of them; little boys, however, were discouraged from pursuing dance as a future calling or career. As a feminized world that accepted but did not go out of its way to encourage male habitation, the world of dance created by my mother and her friends and clients provided its inhabitants with a serious, if not unambiguous, female-centered alternative to the aggression of male sports. One could celebrate femininity, within certain fixed restrictions; one could experience joy with relatively little male intervention and dominance.

Ballet, for example, has tended to be viewed in this country as "high art"—in contrast to tap dancing, which owes its origins to folk dancing from a variety of different cultures, both African and European. Acrobatics, until gymnastics, was associated predominantly with the circus—hardly high art. Baton twirling, comparatively new to the world of performance, has never achieved the status of ballet or tap.[iii] That my mother put them all together reflected her own class status, namely, rural and working class. That she would make lessons readily available to the rank and file, outside the context of the dance studio, for almost two decades, was remarkable. That the public school system thought nothing of allowing her to pull students out of class to teach them a non-academic hodgepodge of physical movement, for which their parents paid her directly, is a tribute to her astonishing powers of persuasion. As far as I know, it had never happened before, nor has it happened since in the school systems in which she taught. As she bent these various systems to suit her goals, she extended the context in which students might encounter a range of arts to whole classes of people to whom such advantages had been previously unavailable. In short, my mother simply didn't know she was transgressing class-defined aesthetic categories.

This little world of dance, however feminized, was a world where gender definition itself blurred. Though most of the males left as adolescents, some did not. Of those who remained, some later identified themselves as gay, but most did not. Among the female students, their relationships with each other and with the male students reflected a highly amorphous sexuality. We touched one another and expressed affection without reservation and irrespective of gender, though not in overtly sexual ways. We openly appraised one another's bodies, yet never engaged in genital relations, at least as far as I know. We were

without sophistication, yet erotically aware. That such a world, internally char-
acterized by the blurring of gender distinctions, was culturally marked "femi-
nine" illuminates how power is asserted and maintained by the use of gender
distinction to regulate status.

Joy is revelatory in ways that are not so much explicitly religious as they are
parable-like. By this I mean that the narrative of the dancing lessons works as
a parable. The story of my mother's dance classes, for example, though peo-
pled by families that for the most part identified themselves as Christian, has
little, if anything, to offer that is conventionally religious in meaning. But then
neither do the parables attributed to Jesus in the gospels, properly appre-
hended. Taken at face value, the gospel parables narrate commonplace, ordi-
nary events in a largely agrarian society—farming, cooking, shepherding,
losing money, mending, throwing dinner parties, family conflicts, squabbles
over labor and wages, even assault and robbery. What makes them revelatory
lies not in their reducibility to a single ethical or religious teaching, but con-
sists instead of a constellation of features and interactions. Chief among these
features is a characteristic inversion of political power that further subverts
conventional expectations. This characteristic of inversion and subversion may
produce in the hearer a mature joy, by which I mean a joy that is not innocent
of pain.

How does this transaction take place? The inversion of power ("the
Kingdom of God is like a mustard seed ....") generates surprise, a surprise that
usually depends heavily on foiling the expectations of the hearers (one does not
normally associate great power with tiny seeds), compelling them to wonder,
creating a disturbance to their conventional ways of thinking about God, the
world, and themselves. One could say that good parables turn the hearer
upside down, inside out, and backwards. So, in the case of the gospel parables,
many depend for their richness of meaning upon an inversion of the ordinary
relations of power, both secular and religious. So, for example, in the parable
of the good Samaritan, rather than working through control from the top
down, God takes on the life of a despised ethnic and religious minority minis-
tering to an elite and thus works in and through human life from the bottom
up. Similarly, in the case of my mother's dance classes, poor and low-income
families get dance lessons for the children that are usually reserved for middle-
income and affluent families, because relatively powerless women infiltrate
and modify a public school system and organize a barter system.

These inversions are disturbing, and as such are not innocent in regard to
pain. Consider, for example in the case of the gospel parables, the implications
of the seed that falls upon the rocks or the dismay of the prodigal son's good

brother. Or ponder the host's rejection of the elite guests who refused to come to his dinner party. In the case of the dancing lessons, consider the backdrop of poverty and personal family tragedy against which the lessons occurred, circumstances for which all the dancing lessons in the world could not ultimately compensate.

Nevertheless, while these inversions no doubt disturb, either because they are so enigmatic as to be incomprehensible or because their full implications are painfully clear, the occasion for such disturbances is also at bottom, an occasion for great joy. Thus in parables, hosts throw dinner parties and ultimately invite the outcasts, the maimed, the poor and the reprobate; likewise a dancing teacher goes out and finds students who want to learn to dance, without concern for whether the children have talent or their parents have money to pay for the lessons. Thus, whether joy over finding a lost coin or a lost sheep, or joy over the discovery that a single seed could grow and flourish, producing shade for birds, or joy over the return of a lost child, or joy over figuring out how to arrange dancing lessons for four children—the joy of a central character or characters of a parable becomes the signifying mark for a hearer that what has occurred, however ambiguous, unexpected and disturbing, is good.

Far beyond the limits of the pages of the Hebrew and Christian scriptures, one may seek and find parables, not only in a text, but also in a childhood memory, or for that matter, in one's own immediate relationships with others, one's work, a visual image, a film, indeed throughout all of social and natural life. Thus, to my mind, the narrative of my mother's career as a dancing teacher performs as a parable, in that it reveals God's grace at work in the details of mid-twentieth century southern U.S. rural and working-class life, sustaining an oppressed people, who sought to be faithful to a vision of the future for their children, however limited and immediate—a vision that in its execution, subverted, however temporarily, some of the economic and educational structures of oppression themselves. Moreover, this joy, in all its corporeality and generosity, that this transitory band of mothers made, took, and shared in the midst of an otherwise often grim existence, discloses a deep and abiding good will and delight that identifies their work as *God's* ongoing work in and through material, often tragic, human existence. It reveals God making and repairing a world in and through human joy—God's love compounding itself from the bottom up.

Joy is in and of itself ethically ambiguous. It may be generous, selfish, both, or ecstatic, though by virtue of its potential to expand the self, it tends to direct the self outward toward others in some way. Thus, the context in which joy occurs largely determines its ethical implications.

In the case of the dancing lessons, the mothers took joy in part because they felt they were giving joy to their children, in part because they enjoyed watching their children dance. My mother, the teacher, and Ola Thomas, the seamstress, found great joy in their work of teaching and sewing and the beauty both produced. We children, their beneficiaries, enjoyed learning to dance and to perform in recitals, although practicing was another matter. In short, the mothers' good will toward their children produced a reciprocating delight or joy in the children that refracted back as further the delight or joy of the mothers. Thus, we see joy compounding and reverberating.

What strikes me as curious about this joy is how little focused it was either on self-sacrifice or on self-fulfillment. Surely both were involved, but selves were simply not at the forefront of consciousness. Rather the focus was on the dance—taught, learned, staged, costumed, performed, watched, and usually paid for in some fashion. Looking back, I now see dance as a profound metaphor for love, both human and divine, for which the language of self-sacrifice and self-fulfillment is impoverished at best.

One of my mother's primary motives was to give dancing lessons to as many children as she possibly could, irrespective of talent. It was so important to her that she went to great lengths, beyond normal human effort, to make dancing as available as possible. Likewise, the joy she experienced in seeking to realize this commitment further fueled her generosity. Furthermore, her joy was contagious across its time and place in ways, unforeseen and unpredictable at the time, that would enrich future generations of children and parents.

What my mother refused to take for granted proved to be one of her strongest virtues. She did not, for example, assume that all the children she taught shared the same circumstances. Had she made this assumption, she might have insisted that all families pay for lessons with cash. She did not assume a single definition of good, or she might not have accepted the untalented. She took her students as she found them in their highly varying range of skills and interests, encouraging them to do their best for their sakes. Her aim was to share her own gifts with everyone. She further assumed that everyone should share their own unique talents. Her respect for particular differences allowed her to become a particular manifestation of a universal love.

... (A)lthough joy is crucial to survival and carries within it enormous potential to subvert oppressive structures, other profoundly important qualities of embodied imagination interact with joy, sending us into the world day after day as well—among them, courage, hope, faith, righteous anger, and the memory of suffering. I also want to stress that joy guarantees no happy endings, no absence of pain. Nevertheless, to paraphrase an ancient poet, while weeping may tarry for the night, joy comes with the morning, that our grieving might turn to dance and our souls might sing in praise (Psalm 30).

This article was originally presented as a keynote lecture for an international conference on "Corporeality, Gender, and Religion," sponsored by the University of Groingen and held at Nieuen Schwans, the Netherlands, on December 17–19, 1998. It was later published in extended form in *Crosscurrnets*, 48:2, summer, 1998, pp. 185–97. It currently appears in Cooey, *Willing the Good: Jesus, Dissent, and Desire* (Minneapolis: Augsberg Fortress Press, 2006) pp. 2–8. Reprinted by permission of the publisher.

[i] Prior to the sixties my mother would not have been allowed into the black schools. She went to work for the YWCA in the early sixties in order to stabilize her income. While at the "Y," she instituted a program for dancing in the local black schools. Later, her classes at the "Y" became a primary means of attracting blacks into racially integrated programs.

[ii] My mother's only criticism of this essay was to wish that I had spent more time talking about the ecstasy produced by performance.

[iii] As my colleague Diane Neal points out, baton twirling and, in some contexts, tap dancing are associated with nationalism in this country.

art for the sake of the soul

Maya Angelou

miss rosie
when i watch you
wrapped up like garbage
sitting, surrounded by the smell
of too old potato peels
or
when i watch you
in your old man's shoes
with the little toe cut out
sitting, waiting for your mind
like next week's grocery
i say
when i watch you
you wet brown bag of a woman
who used to be
  (the best-looking gal in Georgia)
used to be called the Georgia Rose
i stand up
through your destruction
i stand up.

That poem was written by Lucille Clifton, an African American poet who teaches in universities all over the United States. It seems to me the perfect explanation of how we human beings have managed to stand erect—how, often brought to our knees by our own greed, chicanery or ignorance, we manage to pull ourselves up to a standing position.

Miss Clifton has suggested miss rosie, a beleaguered, battered and lonely old woman as her inspiration, and using the same poem, in each instance I insert the word "art," for "miss rosie," for I believe that art encourages us to stand erect and stretch upward toward the higher ground.

I believe that without the presence and energy of art in our lives, we are capable of engaging in heartless activities without remorse and cruelties with clear consciences. We become base because we think of ourselves only as base. We find no delight in immaterial things, and address ourselves and each other in the cruelest terms, for we believe we are deserving of nothing better.

I grew up in an Arkansas that seemed to me to be a place on no one's planet or, for that matter, on no one's mind. The relentless poverty of the Depression, allied with the virulent racial prejudices of the time, had the power to grind the spirit into submission and pulverize the very ability to dream. Yet, I, as well as others, survived those lean years and those mean Arkansas roads, and I think we survived particularly because of the inheritance of black American art, an inheritance left to us by our forebears as surely as steel magnates left massive fortunes for their heirs.

In Stamps, Arkansas, when parents on their way to the cotton fields left small children too young to work in the care of others too old to work, they knew that the baby tenders would recite Paul Laurence Dunbar's poems to their children. Thus, even if a father was twenty miles away, his son would know of his father's love for him because the older person would recite and act out:

> Little brown baby wif spa'klin' eyes,
> 　　　　Come to yo' pappy an' set on his knee.
> What you been doin', suh—
> 　　　　　　　　makin' san' pies?
> 　　　　Look at dat bib—you's ez du'ty ez me.
> Look at dat mouf—dat's mearlasses, I bet;
> 　　　　Come hyeah, Maria, an' wipe off his han's.
> Bees gwine to ketch you
> 　　　　　　　an' eat you up yit,
> 　　　　Bein' so sticky and sweet—goodness lan's!
> Little brown baby wif spa'klin' eyes,
> 　　　　Who's pappy's darlin'
> 　　　　　　　an' who's pappy's chile?
> Who is it all de day nevah once tries
> 　　　　Fu' to be cross, er once loses dat smile?
> Whah did you git dem teef?
> 　　　　　　　My, you's a scamp!
> Whah did dat dimple com f'om
> 　　　　　　　in yo' chin?
> Pappy do' know you—
> 　　　　　　　I b'lieves you's a tramp;

Mammy, dis hyeah's
                    some ol' straggler got in!
Let's th'ow him outen de do' in de san',
            We do' want stragglers
                        a-layin' 'roun' hyeah;
Let's gin him 'way to de big buggah-man
            I know he's hidin' erroun' hyeah
                        right neah.
Buggah-man, buggah-man, come in de do',
            Hyeah's a bad boy you kin have fu' to eat.
Mammy an' pappy do' want him no mo',
            Swaller him down f'om his haid to his feet!
Dah, now, I t'ought dat you'd
                    hug me up close.
        Go back, ol' buggah,
                        you sha'nt have dis boy.
He ain't no tramp, ner no straggler,
                    of co'se;
He's pappy's pa'dner an' playmate
                    an' joy.
Come to you' pallet now—go to yo' res';
        Wisht you could allus know ease
                    an' cleah skies
Wisht you cold stay jes' a chile
                    on my breas' —
        Little brown baby wif spa'klin' eyes!

The strength of the black American to withstand the slings and arrows and lynch mobs and malignant neglect can be traced directly to the arts of literature, music, dance and philosophy that, despite significant attempts to eradicate them, remain in our communities today.

The first Africans were brought to this country in 1619. I do not mean to cast aspersions on my white brothers and sisters who take such pride in having descended from the Pilgrims, but I would remind them that the Africans landed in 1619, which was one year before the arrival of the *Mayflower*. We have experienced every indignity the sadistic mind of man could devise. We have been lynched and drowned and beleaguered and belittled and begrudged and befuddled. And yet, here we are. Still here. Here. Upward of forty million, and that's an underestimate. Some people swear there are more than forty million black people in the Baptist Church. They're not even including other denominations or backsliders or black atheists in the world. How, then, have we survived?

Because we create art and use our art immediately. We have even concealed ourselves and our pain in our art. Langston Hughes wrote:

> Because my mouth
> Is wide with laughter
> And my throat
> Is deep with song,
> You do not think
> I suffer after
> I have held my pain
> So long.
> Because my mouth
> Is wide with laughter
> You do not hear
> My inner cry
> Because my feet
> Are gay with dancing
> You do not know
> I die.

When a larger society would have us believe that we have made no contribution of consequence to the Western world—other than manual labor, of course—the healing, the sustaining and the supporting roles of art were alive and well in the black community.

An incident that occurred years ago informed me of the power of African American contributions. I was a member of the opera company performing *Porgy and Bess*. I was the first dancer, very young, blitheringly ignorant. I never called myself first dancer, but, rather, referred to myself as premiere danseuse or prima ballerina. I sang the role of Ruby, but I sang it by heart. I had trained as a dancer, not as a singer, but I had sung in church, and so I had learned to sing, somewhat. But I was no threat to the singers, of whom there were forty-five and who among themselves had 120 degrees in music. There were so few places for black singers trained in classical music to work that the company could afford to get a person who had one degree from Curtis and another from Julliard just for the chorus.

We traveled throughout Europe and arrived in Morocco while the company sent the sets on to Spain. Black opera singers, white opera singers, Native American opera singers, Spanish-speaking opera singers, Aleut opera singers,

Asian ... all opera singers are one people, much like New York taxi drivers. They're all cut from the same cloth.

The singers were informed by the conductor that since the sets had been sent on to Spain, they were obliged to perform in a concert. They were ready. They had their portfolios, I am sure, on microfiche, jammed up in the heels of their shoes. They were ab-so-lutely ready.

I said to the conductor, "I'm sorry, I have no aria. That is not my field." He was Russian with masses of Russian artistic temperament. He fell back two whole steps and clutched his hair and said in a heavy Russian accent, "But don't you at least know one spiritual?"

I didn't say this to him, but I thought to myself, Is grits groceries? Do I know a spiritual? I grew up in church. Sunday, all day, and every evening of the week found me and my family in church, and at all those gatherings we sang. So, of course I could sing a spiritual. I looked at him and said, "I will try to think of something."

The other singers went out that evening and delivered beautifully the important arias in the canon of European classical music, and they were very well received. Near the end of the concert the conductor beckoned me onto the stage.

I thought of a song my grandmother sang in that little town in Arkansas. Every Sunday for ten years, I had gone through the same ritual: We would gather in church. Fifteen minutes after the service began the preacher would say, "And now we'll be privileged with a song from Sister Henderson." Each Sunday, my Grandmother would respond, "Me?" Then she would take her time, look up at the ceiling as if she was considering: What on earth could I possibly sing? And every Sunday she sang the same song.

In Morocco, all alone on the stage, I sang her song:

> I'm a poor pilgrim of sorrow.
> I'm lost in this wide world alone.

I sang the whole song through, and when I finished, forty-five hundred Arabs jumped up, hit the floor and started to shout. I was young and ignorant. I had no idea of the power of this, my inherited art. I didn't know what to do. I looked stage right and stage left at the singers who had always treated me as if I were a mascot because I offered them no competition as a singer. Every night, one or another of them would come out and almost pat my head and say, "Maya, sorry to tell you, you flatted the E," or "Oh, Maya, mmmm, you sharped that G!"

But I looked at them now. I looked stage left and stage right, where they were crowded together glowering at me. I said, "I'm sorry. I'm sorry. I'm sorry that I have the glory ..." They had sung Respighi, Rossini, Bach, Bloch, Beethoven, lovely lieder and lovely Britten art songs, and they had been well received. And I had sung what Dr. Du Bois called a sorrow song, not written by the free and easy, not written by anyone credited with being creative, and forty-five hundred people had leaped into the palm of my hand.

"Why?" I walked alone that night in Morocco, my first time in North Africa. I thought, Oh, it's because they feel sorry for the poignancy of my slave history. I later learned that the people in the audience had no idea of my slave history. Why, then?

Great art belongs to all people, all the time—indeed it is made for the people by the people.

I have written of the black American experience, which I know intimately. I am always talking about the human condition in general and about society in particular. What it is like to be human, and American, what makes us weep, what makes us fall and stumble and somehow rise and go on from darkness into darkness—that darkness carpeted with figures of fear and the hounds behind and the hunters behind and one more river to cross, and oh, my God, will I ever reach that somewhere, that safe getting-up morning. I submit to you that it is art that allows us to stand erect.

In that little town in Arkansas, whenever my grandmother saw me reading poetry she would say, "Sister, Mama loves to see you read the poetry because that will put starch in your backbone." When people who were enslaved, whose wrists were bound and whose ankles were tied, sang,

> I'm gonna run on,
> See what the end is gonna be ...
> I'm gonna run on,
> See what the end is gonna be ...

the singer and the audience were made to understand that, however we had arrived here, under whatever bludgeoning of chance, we were the stuff out of which nations and dreams were made and that we had come here to stay.

> I'm gonna run on,
> See what the end is gonna be ...

Had the blues been censored, we might have had no way of knowing that our looks were not only acceptable but even desirable. The larger society informed us all the time—and still does—that its idea of beauty can be contained in the cruel, limiting, ignorant and still current statement that suggests you can't be too thin, or too rich, or too white. But we had the nineteenth-century blues in which a black man informed us, talking about the woman that he loved,

> The woman I love is fat
> And chocolate to the bone,
> And every time she shakes,
> Some skinny woman loses her home.

Some white people actually stand looking out of windows at serious snow falling like cotton rain, covering the tops of cars and streets and fire hydrants and say, "My God, it sure is a black day."

So black people had to find ways in which to assert their own beauty. In this song the black woman sang:

> He's blacker than midnight,
> Teeth like flags of truth.
>
> He's the finest thing in the whole St. Louis.
> They say the blacker the berry,
> Sweeter is the juice ...

That is living art, created to encourage people to hang on, stand up, forbear, continue.

I suggest that we must be suspicious of censors who say they mean to prohibit our art for our own welfare. I suggest that we have to question their motives and tend assiduously to our own personal and national health and our general welfare. We must replace fear and chauvinism, hate, timidity and apathy, which flow in our national spinal column, with courage, sensitivity, perseverance and, I even dare say, "love." And by "love" I mean that condition in the human spirit so profound it encourages us to develop courage. It is said that courage is the most important of all the virtues, because without courage you can't practice any other virtue with consistency.

We must infuse our lives with art. Our national leaders must be informed that we want them to use our taxes to support street theatre in order to oppose street gangs. We should have a well-supported regional theatre in order to oppose regionalism and differences that keep us apart. We need nationally to support small, medium and large art museums that show us images of ourselves, those we like and those we dislike. In some way that is very important to us we need to see those we dislike even more than those we like because somehow we need at least glancing visions of how we look "as in a mirror darkly."

Our singers, composers and musicians must be encouraged to sing the song of struggle, the song of resistance, resistance to degradation, resistance to our humiliation, resistance to the eradication of all our values that would keep us going as a country. Our actors and sculptors and painters and writers and poets must be made to know that we appreciate them, that in fact it is their work that puts starch in our backbones.

We need art to live fully and to grow healthy. Without it we are dry husks drifting aimlessly on every ill wind, our futures are without promise and our present without grace.

Reprinted from *Even the Stars Look Lonesome* (Bantam Books, 1997).

FAITH IN THE UNKNOWN

faith in the unknown

Daini reflected, "True faith is to follow the tiniest light in the deepest of dark, trusting that it will guide you to safety." For some, faith is an assurance that things will work out, even during the worst of times. For others, it is a religious belief, or perhaps a spiritual awakening, that carries them through their daily encounters and experiences. While the authors in our previous chapter turned to the inner self to sustain their courage, the writers in this chapter rely on faith to light their way.

Valerie Bridgeman Davis surrounds her poem, "The Soul's Source," with the words of Thomas Moore: "The soul is its own source of unfolding." Her piece is about trusting one's instincts and developing a faith in oneself for answers. Bridgeman Davis writes, "in your soul are answers / to questions you've never asked."

Also looking within, the voice in Bárbara Renaud González's "La Diosa" delves into her worst fears: of love, of writing, of being alive. She pleads to her God for "the courage to tell the story." As with the voice in "The Soul's Source," she wants the easy answer. God responds, but not in the way González envisions. This brilliant poem pours forth a passionate struggle between faith and action.

A studied passion envelopes Penelope in Wendy Barker's "Ithaca, on the Landing." She trusts in the love of a man so much that she is willing to forego her own pleasure although he has been away for years and "she could not know / who he would be / becoming in those years / of sailing...." Her faith is tempted by the men guarding her, especially "the lean one with the flute, / long thighs relaxed / in sleep...." Indeed, her own human needs make her faith the more difficult.

Joan Shalikashvili took that step beyond safe parameters by marrying a man she barely knew and by going with him to a country where she could not speak the language. Trusting her intuition, she could not have foreseen that he would become a renowned military leader in modern-day history and that their life together would take her to unbelievable places. Young and trusting in love, she writes, "what a loss it would have been for me if I had been too afraid to make that initial move from my very safe environment in a town where I had lived all my life to try that adventure with a new husband in a new country." Her faith sustains her even through unforeseen circumstances that threaten her subsequent happiness.

Terri Jones was forced to leave the safety of her personal world. In "Hints from a Cancer Victor," she writes that as an adopted child she always believed that she was chosen and that bad things could never happen to her. Yet, when she discovered that she had breast cancer, she had to look to her faith to give her strength. Jones writes, "Sometimes, in the dark of night, faith is all you have to hang on to." Having faith that "God really doesn't send you any more than you can bear" is one of a number of survival hints she has for her audience. "No matter what shape your faith takes, you gotta believe."

Faith in a higher being also plays an important role in Amy Freeman Lee's poetry. Both pieces deal with the elderly moving "into the only place where the future lies." She asks for courage and dignity in dealing with her mortality and death. In "Hoops of Fire," she hopes she "will hear / The applause of God...." And in "Why Wait?," Lee opens with "When I was in a golden cage, / I decided to wait." Each verse substantiates her inertia. But the pull of the night's wonder finally moves her to fly so that she can find the answer to "who pierced the sky / So the light could sparkle through."

We see this movement forward in Gail Hosking Gilberg's poem, "The Tiger." Emily Jong wrote that "Everyone has a talent. What is rare is the courage to follow the talent to the dark place." The tiger, or Gilberg's talent, "got me believing /I have a taste for the journey" while giving her "no false promises." She would have to follow it to her own dark place.

Another spirit awakens in "Red Dirt Road." As Maya Angelou advised in this book's introduction, Barbara Lovenheim forgives herself and forges ahead. Unsure that the sins she has buried will really be "dust to dust," faith tinged with human fear permeates her being.

Finally, in Diane Graves' essay, "Of Birth-Mother and Daughter," a Salvadoran mother gives up her child for adoption. Forced to have faith in the unknown, she could not know what life her daughter would have; yet, she knew it had to be better than that of a female child growing up in the midst of poverty and war. Graves writes, "Elena's birth mother was courageous, and she took the ultimate risk: She placed her child for adoption, to be raised by people she did not know, in a nation she will never visit." She believed that her little girl would grow into womanhood without fear of her future.

The poet Tagore wrote, "Faith is the bird that sings when the dawn is still dark." Each of the authors in this chapter took enormous risks without substantiation that they could actualize their dreams. The courage to listen to Tagore's bird singing gave them hope that the future would be better than the present.

the soul's source

Valerie Bridgeman Davis

"The soul is its own source of unfolding."
—THOMAS MOORE

You are looking for an answer,
she said, knowing I was looking
to her for an answer,
but she smiled that gentle
knowing that tells the student
the teacher will not bite

this is your test, she said
yours to discover
you to unrobe, and know
it is your body to feel
your mind to ponder
your heart to dream
and you may not
pass the task along

that would be easy,
she said, knowing I was searching
for the easy way out,
but she smiled that gentle
knowing that tells the student
you're on your own

look inside, she said
in your soul are answers
to questions you've never asked
and parts of you are in the open

in the closed regions of your
soul, if you would dare
to wander into the place
that you've closed off
and labeled "no access"
you will discover
Thomas Moore is right:
"the soul is its own source of unfolding"

Reprinted from *Communitas* (Austin Presbyterian Theological Seminary, 2006)

la diosa

Bárbara Renaud González

She
did this to me when
I finally laid down my
pride fatter than *orgullo* and
wrote her a letter

Begging for the courage to
tell the story, something that really
mattered

God laughed the first time.

Just who you think you are, girl?
dreadlocks tossing a heavenly
cloud of perfume, Chanel
No. 5, of course

Then *La Diosa*, serious, says, haven't
you been listening to the stories I send
you daily? You want email
tonta?

What about the wheelchaired-boy on the 92, la
Puerto Rican flag dangling from those
broken spokes, listening to music louder
than tattoos blue-inked on his shrinking
back, coming, I'm sure, after
the dreams the months of
hospitals

God sighs.
Where you been mi'ja

See that little girl, her face
a velvet punching-bag in the shadow
of your girlfriend's *feminista*
murals on Presa and St. Mary's, her father
watching from Mr. Tacos alongside
la otra. The niña a crayon-box
of beatings hoping you'll notice her at the laundry
La Terry painted day and night one long
and lonely summer remembering
Her own father's fist

God won't stop *regañandome!* And what about
the *viejito* box-man under San Pedro's
sky sleeping on cardboard pillows talking
to himself and what about *la crazy* on
Hildebrand the one with Goodwill sneakers slashed
into homemade *guaraches,* earphones connected to nothing but
the voicies singing in her head, what dirty hands she has guarding
the purse made from trashbags, *que no?*

While you're rushing home to a glass
of wine or the swimming pool at the Y?

Let me explain,

SHUT UP, God says.
You want to write? Don't
be afraid! Surrender
to me

It's the only way, she whispers,
popping a cinnamon mint into her mouth, frosted
lipstick

Now then.

Her tiger-eyes become a cobalt-*cielo*, hot
and wild like a brown woman when she listens to
Celia Cruz

Passion.

It slipped out
ohmyGod

Avergonzando my late mother who surely
made it to heaven dying
a virgin after eight *niños*, her virtue
intact after the divorce with Daddy and
Si, me voy a morir una virgin, y que?

Now you're talkin!
God yelling 'bove the Sunday guilt get
down on your knees girl and
just sayit like nobody will hear you like it's not a sin like
what you got to lose like you have breast
cancer stage four and your *chichis* gone and
it's your last day on earth and

Then it happened

I want my ink to turn into blood
Someone peeped in my voice

Want to get drunk on it, falling down
a voice smelling of whiskey, cheap

Want my stories to be the bread of thousands
each word a bomb, a machine gun piercing
those walls of stone we call the heart

Yes, satinsheet bullets, perfume-throated seducing
my enemies so even the preacher amens
my sermon

Want my words howling baptized
born again not afraid
of dying either, laughing at the ropes and
inquisitor's stake a testament to the story as I,
woman, know it, to hell with
the consequences, the damning
because I dared to say it

I want my own fucking chapter, God

She prayed for me then.
And I got my passion alright

★   ★   ★   ★   ★

Brought me the black man on Sunday
at the park throwing a football calloused
as his working-hands

It was like he was perfectly spinning
my *destino*, I was caught sure,
Cupid's arrow going Fed-Ex
and I was playing again like before
with my Daddy before he left us, and
I had to be the father to my brothers, the man
to my mother

Until I forgot how to be a woman so
afraid of being me

Confess all this a few nights later to
the football player massaging my
jammed show-off fingers
bruising purple but his eyes worse, a broken-down
café, *terrible things I've done in the past, baby*

Two sons abandoned so the boys' mother packed
left him for San Antonio who finds good husbands knowing

that years later he'd return, desperate to be
the father different than the one
he never knew

And I see arrows stabbing, twisting into his lost-
penny eyes, rusting now but once pure
silver, a running back with his four-minute
mile not fast enough to escape
his *pasado*, not fast enough from fear, of falling
in love

And I'm afraid to tell him
terrible things I've done in the past, my
lies where to begin, the ones
to my husband or the ones with
the lover or the pretending to
my mother

This fear bringing us together
so that I want to scoop his
brown into sugar rubbing his wounds with
mine into sweet
verdad

★   ★   ★   ★   ★

La Diosa *cabrona* answered
my prayers, gave me the whole
shebang.

Valentine-baby, football-player calls me, he's
not just any old heatwave-frying eggs into
cascarones kind of weather, my
Diosa gave me a police-brutality kinda riot, 911
emergency, Mexico City 9.8 on the Richter scale where
thousands died and that's how panicked I was when
football-man reached for me

That's when the rains came, a miracle
in Texas, stuff fell out, wriggly
musty fire ants from the Goliad Mission where
I was born near the killing
grounds of the Texas Revolution, rattlesnakes tumbling
from the cotton fields and peach-cobbler vomit smelling up
the cafeteria where the gringos pushed away
my Spanish, some forgotten horny toads
in my pockets, now endangered once
native and that baby chick I stepped on when
I was five on the rancho and the kittens jumping
off the roof where I took them, playing despite
and Mami said that God would punish
me forever

I'm dizzy, a carnival of past like
the time drinking too much tequila hoping
for Zapata to save me in a Morelia hotel
room, only this time out came the bottle's
clay-earth, the agave's sea-green ferment
bubbling, distilling pure to a word
I can't forget even when there are so many
others in front of it like starched
manteles and ice-pink aprons, and
this passion is going to
hurt me

That's why she sent me the football player working
double-shifts on the railroad who supports
his children, his mother, his world
a limbo of custody, a motorcycle racing
at one hundred and forty miles per hour, his
time to rest

Swore he couldn't forget me, checking
under my bed for voodoo dolls sure
I put a spell on him, checking
I know how you women are, he said that

I was more dangerous than the gun
he trusted

Promised to take me on a midnight picnic, playing
on the merry-go-round, slow-grind
dancing on the Eastside, swimming
naked while he told me stories about the minister
And his wife

My Rwanda massacre he is
only way for a machete to crack this puny
heart wide open, pulsing like those Aztecs must
have devoured on the pyramids only this time I sacrificed
myself, because She answered

*   *   *   *   *

See how tricky God is?

And then he disappeared
I love your body and your mind, baby
We belong together
But I'm afraid of what this means

La Diosa caresses my palms
soothing like my mother used
to before dying without finding
love in all her telenovelas, budweisers
drinking herself to sleep until
one night she didn't wake up

And Daddy ashamed, wasn't he
Of not being a good-enough man working
and working and working and working and still
no money and that's the only way
to be a man isn't it until he couldn't
anymore and left us

Just so you understand, Honey
Diosa takes my hand into her blazing
red and polished absolution
smears *sangre* from between her legs to
my fingers

Touches my lips with the crimson
stain, returns my pen, then sits
down beside me, crossing
Her long legs, admiring
Her Manolo platforms, snake-skin

See how I gave you everything you wanted?
See how many broken hearts there are in the world?

Begin.

ithaca, on the landing

Wendy Barker

How was it Penelope waited
upstairs all those years,
before he finally

found his way back?
Every night unravelling the weave,
her fear of fixing to the wrong one

knitting her nerves.
But the wool kept the shape of the warp,
she could not straighten the strands

after so many nights.
All day weaving with more and more
wrinkled skeins, all night pulling out

threads with her fingers,
all that winding
and rewinding, back and forth

across the loom after breakfast,
the sound of the soft
contact betwen wool and wood,

the rhythm, meshing
color upon color, and then
at night the whole thing in reverse,

everything pulled apart
until blue and silver
strands turned dull, lost their sheen.

Sometimes she would stop, try to see
beyond the window's flat shadow.
She could not know him

through that space, she could not know
who he would be
becoming in those years

of sailing, slipping into fern—
lined coves, dashing his prow
against headlands so splashed

with sun and spume
that at first he couldn't even tell
who lived there.

And who was it
he would come home to
after all her nights unravelling?

Sometimes during those
unfinished years, sometimes under
the weight of a blunt moon,

she thought she heard music,
one of the men on the ground floor
singing, so softly singing,

and once she leaned down
over the upstairs landing to see
how they lounged in her chairs.

She travelled their faces:
not brutes, not swine, but men,
beards curled across their cheeks.

Some young, smooth
as the rubbed wood of her loom.
And the lean one with the flute,

long thighs relaxed
in sleep, smiling in his sleep.
What if, at night,

she left her weaving alone?
Let it grow, become whole?
What might the tapestry become

if she stopped saying no
over and over, refusing
the downstairs of her own house?

Penelope, faithful wife of Ulysses, was courted by many men during his absence. They were asked to wait until she completed her weaving, but each night she unravelled that day's work.

Reprinted from *Way of Whiteness* (Wings Press, 2000).

risks and challenges: facing the unknown
Joan Shalikashvili

Although I never thought of myself as a risk-taker, a friend once said that when I married and moved to a foreign country, I was taking a risk. Years later that same person would have the opportunity to tell me that I had a "baptism by fire" in learning how to face challenges head on.

But I'm jumping ahead too quickly—back to that summer long ago. I had been on a vacation with a friend who taught school in Kaiserslautern, Germany, and she introduced me to the "special soldier" who would become my husband. Although at the time I was a very happy, single school teacher with no desire to get married, all of that changed that summer.

I had met my future husband the latter part of June, and by the time we were married on December 27 of that year, we had seen each other for little more than two weeks. I have to admit that now I realize having a daughter move to a foreign country to marry someone she hardly knows would probably stop the heart of any mother, but at the time it didn't seem unusual. When you're in love, you probably don't think about anything as a risk, and I certainly didn't think twice about moving to Germany where he was assigned with the military.

That move was the beginning of a real change in my lifestyle. Prior to that, I had lived in Portland, Oregon, all my life. During those years, I had gone to Seattle on the train, to San Diego on a bus, and as far east as McCall, Idaho, also by bus. When I flew back to Germany for the wedding that December, my mother, my sister, and a good friend came with me. By the first of the year, though, they had all departed for Portland, and I was left alone in a new country, unable to speak the language, with a husband who always seemed to be at work.

But there were classes I could take to learn the language, and I only had to step outside our door to find a friendly face (either German or American), so it wasn't long before I felt very much at home. Other wives encouraged me to get out and shop at the markets and go on trips to other towns. The weather was similar to what I was used to on the west coast—not too cold with just a bit of snow in the winter, snow in the nearby mountains for skiing, and in the summer pleasantly warm days with cool evenings—so I didn't really have any adjustment on that score.

Sometimes it was hard to realize that I wasn't living in the States—but then I learned about German food! To this day, I can't imagine what life would have been like without having had an authentic German schnitzel or a Nurnberger bratwurst or a schwienelenchen or a big plate of spaetzle—and to be on familiar enough terms with the gasthaus owners that they knew not only what table we wanted but exactly what I'd order for my meal.

I can no longer remember what it was like to live in one place for the first twenty-five years of my life. Over the course of our marriage, my husband and I have lived in four countries other than the United States—Germany, Korea, Italy and Belgium (a total of over ten years overseas)—and have visited probably twenty others. I have lived in a chateau, met a queen, attended ceremonies to welcome heads of state to our country, had dinners at the White House, and even spent a night in the Lincoln bedroom. I've met people from other countries who will be life-long friends. And I have wonderful friends from our own country who were stationed with us at one time or another. I don't know what I would do without these people in my life.

As I write this, we're back on the west coast, living in a sleepy little town called Steilacoom, and the time when I took that original risk is just a fond memory. Yet, life continues to hand us trials and challenges that test who we are.

An event occurred on August 7, 2004, that initiated the most challenging chapter thus far. On that date, my husband suffered a massive hemorrhagic stroke. Like the rest of my life, his stroke was simply something that I faced because it was in front of me. However, I have to admit that it has thrown us into the most emotional time we've ever experienced. We continue to make our way through the slow and often painful recovery process.

After nearly one month, John left the hospital to go to a stroke rehab center in Seattle, and I fought to keep some semblance of normalcy in my life. John struggled to overcome the effects of the stroke with three kinds of therapy. To date, he continues to have paralysis on his left side. My own therapy included aerobics, counseling, and weekly massages.

Nearly three months after the stroke, John came home. Adjusting to the change in his life was very difficult for both of us. Needing help with almost everything dealing with personal hygiene was hard for him to accept, especially because previously he had been so independent. Even with constant caregivers, we had many frustrating moments that put a great strain on our relationship. The weeks of physical therapy taught me that I had to stand back and watch, not try to be his therapist. John began to turn away from me, often not talking for days at a time. I felt so isolated and ignored. It was hard to even imagine how he was feeling.

Then, in November 2005, John had a seizure so intense that his right hip fractured. He spent another six weeks in a rehab center and came home shortly after the start of the new year. His recovery has been slow, but he continues to make progress, as does our relationship. We've learned that we have to talk when things bother us, that we can't lapse into silence. We try not to shut each other out. And I've learned to rely on my faith, family, and friends.

I credit the people in the town of Steilacoom with "saving me." They have been the "pieces of God" in my life. People I knew only slightly supported me and made me know that I could get through this. They were my haven when John was struggling with his own problems and couldn't include me in his life. Through this tragic experience I have learned the true value of friendship.

Looking back, I realize that I never really saw the choices in my life as risks. When I was young, there were so many other women who were already doing what I had only begun. They had left their families and the comfort of a country where they knew the language to move to another country strange to them.

Those many years ago, when I ran off to Germany to marry the man I had seen for a little over two weeks, I promised I would be with him for better or worse. Facing the obstacles of John's stroke and fighting to stay by his side were my only choices. And challenging as it has been, we've been together through it all for over 40 years.

★ ★ ★

During the years 1993–1997, General John Shalikashvili was the Chairman of the Joint Chiefs of Staff, in charge of all military operations for the United States.

hints from a cancer victor

Terri Jones

I am NOT a cancer SURVIVOR—I am a cancer VICTOR. It wasn't enough for me to *survive* cancer. I wanted to triumph over it. In my mind, there was very little doubt that I could do it. You see, I have been blessed in my life and *bad things do not happen to me.*

This strength and self-assurance were instilled in me from birth. As an infant I was adopted by two loving and incredibly devoted people. I was a chosen child ... picked out from all the other babies. I knew I was loved and wanted. One thing about being adopted. You have no medical history. Knowing this I was especially vigilant about my health care. I never missed a scheduled doctor's appointment. I routinely performed breast self-examinations. When I was 38, I decided to have a baseline mammogram. I did everything right.

After living on the East Coast for eight years, I moved back to San Antonio and wasted no time in locating a new butcher, baker, candlestick maker. And gynecologist. My first appointment was only eleven months after my last annual check-up. I thought I was well within the "margin of error." My appointment was scheduled for April 22. I remember it was a Thursday. In early April, I had noticed that my breasts were tender and enlarged—especially my right one. But, I was consumed by the demands of my new job and believed that anything wrong could certainly wait another week or two. Anyway, two things were working in my favor. One, I had cleavage for the first time in my life—even if it was slightly lopsided. And, two, I've always heard that cancer doesn't hurt.

Was I ever wrong!

After taking one look at my right breast, my doctor wasted no time in sending me three floors down to Dr. Kathy Safford's office. As I recall that afternoon, I am struck by the eerie stillness I felt as I faced the inevitable. My certainty was confirmed a few days later after a surgical biopsy when Dr. Safford said, "It's cancer."

Well, I *already* knew that. I think all cancer patients do. You may hope and pray that you are wrong but, in your heart, you know you are right. In no time at all, I was processed through the cancer survival system. First, a battery of tests and scans; then a catheter surgically implanted in my chest wall for the administration of chemotherapy drugs. I listened intently as my oncologist recited the odds for a person with my kind of cancer.

"Stage III," he said. I didn't want to know how many stages there were.

Over and over during those weeks, I appreciated the value of having no medical history. It makes filling out forms and the interminable sessions with hospital admissions people a snap. However, for you unadopted folks, here is a helpful survival tactic I hope you never have to use: *Xerox the information.*

One of the most common stories you hear about chemotherapy is that it makes you so sick you believe the cure is worse than the disease. I grew up on Mexican food. I eat corny dogs at the State Fair. How bad could this be? Anyway, *bad things don't happen to me.* Within hours of the catheter surgery and the start of my first course of chemicals so toxic they are known only by letters and numbers, I was happily chowing down on a double Sonic burger. The next morning, before my home health care nurse arrived, I went out for breakfast tacos and was mentally savoring the chili cheeseburger that I planned to have for lunch. This was a habit that was to earn me a certain amount of infamy within the nursing service corridors.

I think it's really important to remember that—no matter what you hear, no matter whom you hear it from—if it didn't happen yesterday, it's been improved. In the years since my treatments, there have been numerous advances in care. Ten years ago chemotherapy may have been dreadful but, today, there are drugs to counteract the drugs. Faced with this, you should ask for everything available to make you feel better. Even if it is an order of french fries. Let me tell you something else about chemotherapy, radiation, surgery, and all the conventional treatments: A friend said to me one day, "How awful." My reply to her was "How wonderful." To a person with cancer, these are miracles, albeit mostly unpleasant, but miracles nonetheless.

Another side-effect people talk about a lot is hair loss. I was prepared. Shortly after I was diagnosed, I purchased three wigs that looked nothing at all like the short blonde hair I'd lived with. If I was going to have to wear a wig every day, then every day was going to be a good hair day! What people don't tell you is that your hair doesn't fall out all at once. It's not like waking up with a pillow more full of hair than feathers. *You shed.* I wasn't going to spend my time picking strands out of my salad so I took matters into my own hands— realizing it was probably the last time during the course of my treatment that I would be in control. I headed off to the wig shop to have my head shaved.

Having your head shaved is not a particularly easy thing to do. There is a certain confirmation of just how really sick you are. Let me tell you something about looking like a human Chihuahua. Without hair you have *really big ears!* For several minutes I thought I might be the illegitimate daughter of Ross Perot! After it was all over and swept up, I walked out a red head.

Here is my helpful hint number two: *You must maintain a sense of humor—no matter how hard it is.* You've likely heard the expression "laughing in the face of death." Well, that's exactly what you have to do. Norman Cousins wrote a whole book about the healing power of laughter. The other adage is "Laughter is the best medicine." I watched a lot of Nick at Night.

Throughout my treatment, there were moments of high comedy. I found humor in just about everything I encountered. There was a time when I was admitted to the hospital with a high fever and terrible, terrible sores in my mouth. I thought that I sounded like Elmer Fudd, but Dr. Safford insisted it was more like Baba Wawa. So, there I am. I talk funny. It hurts too much to eat. And all the hospital kitchen keeps sending me are baby lima beans. I hate baby lima beans, but there didn't seem to be any way to stop their ceaseless flow. Eventually, I had a rubber stamp made saying, "I hate baby lima beans." After a few of those stamped on hospital menus I never saw them again!

Not only could I laugh but I could make those who loved me laugh, too. That was a gift—for all of us. There can't be anything worse than seeing your child suffer or knowing a friend is in pain and you can't help. So, for those minutes of gladness, we forgot where we were and what was going on.

There was only a split second between my diagnosis and my first phone call. I raised the stock price of AT&T single-handedly. I told everyone. And that is my third survival hint. *Tell everyone you know.* First of all, the more people who know increase the odds that you will get a lot of presents! You will have a tremendous amount of support in reserve when you most need it and least expect it.

I read a book called, *Where the Buffalo Roam*, written by a fellow with terminal renal cancer who underwent experimental treatment at Duke University Medical Center. He chose the buffalo as his talisman because it was a species which was almost extinct, but now flourishes. A dear friend of mine helped form a loose confederation of other friends we called the "possums." Possum is the Latin word for "I can."

And, as you might imagine, I engaged in rank self-promotion. Just before being admitted for my bone marrow transplant, I sent out nearly 100 postcards to let people know the hospital address and 800 number of the transplant unit. I was touched by the non-stop outpouring of encouragement and support of close friends, acquaintances, and business associates. I received hundreds of good wishes from people whose lives I must have touched in unnoticed ways but whose generosity of spirit leaves me with a profound sense of humility. Joseph Conrad wrote, "The purpose of the journey is compassion." And, I can assure you, that's a lesson I learned early, and often, during this trip to hell. But, I knew I had a round-trip ticket.

After my surgery, when I was told that a bone marrow transplant was my best hope for survival, I felt like the world had slipped from beneath my feet. How can this be happening to me? *Bad things do not happen to me.* Throughout that year, I felt like providence was guiding many of my decisions. I knew then that my responsibility was to learn as much as possible and trust my doctors. If I couldn't be in charge, I was going to be prepared. It was in that frame of mind that Dr. Fred LeMaistre entered my life to save my life. Or so it seemed to me.

The bone marrow transplant is the scariest thing I ever faced. I am fortunate to have a strong sense of self, parents who adore me, and friends who wanted me to stick around for one more glass of wine. Even with all that, there were stabs of savage, petrifying fear. One night I remember wondering how brave, strong, clever me was going to make it through the night. The trick is not to let the fear show, or conquer or rule your life. And that is easier said than done when someone is explaining that you will receive near-lethal doses of chemotherapy and then, just before you die, you will be rescued by an infusion of your own stem cells.

I took comfort in knowing nothing really good is accomplished in a vacuum. Whether it's closing the big sale or vanquishing the cancer infidel. There is always something more, Something greater: greater than my sense of self, greater than the talents and skills of the medical professionals. I was raised a Roman Catholic and have an unshakable belief in God. Throughout my trip along the cancer highway, I never stopped to raise my fist to the heavens like Job and to curse my fate. My God is not a vengeful God. I just don't believe that in April of 1993, He sat in heaven and said, "You know, that Terri Bronocco... she really ticks me off. I think I'm gonna give her breast cancer." But, my God is not totally capricious, either. He had something in mind. Only now do I know what it is.

In the last few years, there has been much talk about angels. How they appear in unexpected forms. I had many angels on this pilgrimage, but none more important than a fellow traveler, Cindy Dennis. Cindy was in the waiting room at the Cancer Therapy and Research Center on my first visit there. Neither my parents nor I figured her to be in the midst of cancer treatment. On my next trip to the center, she was there wearing a fabulous scarf and straw hat. When I asked her how to tie the scarf, she not only gave me fashion advice, she gave me her phone number. She was six months ahead of me and had just come through her bone marrow transplant. At that time, I didn't know how important she would be to me. Do I believe in angels? You bet I do!

Sometimes, in the dark of night, faith is all you have to hang on to. But you get nourished and sustained without even knowing it's happening. For the capacity of people to reach out to strangers, for the countless prayer chains, I am truly grateful. God really doesn't send you any more than you can bear. And, to make sure, He sends you the help you need to get through it.

And so, I offer you survival hint number four: *Have faith.* No matter what shape your faith takes, you gotta believe. During World War II, Winston Churchill delivered one of the shortest commencement addresses on record. He said, "Never, never, never give up." And, in his own way, so did Dr. Seuss:

> I'm afraid that some times
> you'll play lonely games, too.
> Games you can't win
> 'cause you'll play against you.
> And when you're alone, there's a very good
> chance
> you'll meet things that scare you
>   right out of your pants.
> There are some, down the road
>   between hither and yon,
> that can scare you so much
>   you won't want to go on.
> But on you will go
> though the weather be foul.
> On you will go
> though your enemies howl.
> Be sure when you step.
> Step with care and great tact
> and remember that Life's
> a Great Balancing Act.

I kept the words of Churchill and Seuss with me during my treatment. While there were scary times, there were many days filled with more hope and more joy than I'd ever known before.

Someone once said that second marriages are the triumph of hope over experience. In my case, long-range vacation planning was a triumph of hope over the odds. I remain hopeful about my future, a future that now includes a wonderful husband. I once said that I wanted to live just long enough for medical science to discover a cure for breast cancer. Now, I plan to live long past that. In April, I ran in the Susan G. Komen Race for the Cure with 27,000 women all sharing the same vision and hope. Together we will see many years pass, many babies born, and all breast cancer specialists put out of work.

If you want to survive, remember hint five: *Have hope.* If you want to make it to the end of the tunnel, you have to let someone else light your way. Charity comes in all forms. It is generously given and doesn't require repayment. My mother, silently sitting day after day in the bone marrow transplant unit in an uncomfortable chair with the air conditioner blowing down her neck. That's charity. My father, bravely overcoming his dislike of needles and blood standing resolutely by through all the procedures. That's charity. The research nurse who shepherded me through the transplant process with good cheer and encouragement. That's charity.

Our current pop philosophy is "practice random acts of kindness." I can't even begin to recite the concerted acts of kindness extended to me during all these years. The very best of our humanity was given to me. When I felt that I couldn't take one more step or endure one more assault on my body, these people were truly the wind beneath my wings. I'm reminded of the story of the man who was suffering much travail. When his life was over and he was looking back, he saw only one set of footprints in the sand.

He said to God, "How could you leave me alone during those terrible times? Why weren't you walking with me? Where are your footprints?"

God replied, "In those times of trouble, I was not walking beside you. I carried you."

That this goodness and understanding can come out of something so bad, so evil, is a treasure beyond value. Should we live every day as if it is our last? You bet. Should we live each day as if it may be the last for someone else? Absolutely. This odyssey reminds me of something Ralph Waldo Emerson said about ourselves: "What lies behind us and what lies before us is nothing compared to what lies within us."

Only now do I know what God had intended for me. Dr Kathy Safford and I co-founded WINGS (Women Involved in Nurturing, Giving, and Sharing) to help countless other women who, regrettably, will follow in our footsteps, but who do not have health insurance or adequate income to pay for breast cancer treatment. We ensure that no woman will ever have to choose between life-saving medical treatment and feeding her family. As breast cancer victors, we know exactly what St. Luke meant when he wrote: "To whomsoever much is given, much is expected." There must be easier ways to discover this truth but, for me, it came the hard way. Yet learning this lesson proves what I've always said, *Bad things do not happen to me!*

hoops of fire

Amy Freeman Lee

I have not seen lions
Since I saw them jumping through
Hoops of fire in the circus.
I can hear the crackling flames
And smell the fragrance of burning
Set aflame by lightning,
But last night they roamed
Throughout my house.
Could it be because they knew
That is where they'd find
The circle of fire?
For now it is my turn to leap
Through the fiery hoop
Of real and surreal steel.
To loan me their dignity
And courage for the jump
Into the only place where the future lies.
Then they can take back
Their flaming zero
And return to the applause
Of the crowd
While I hopefully will hear
The applause of God
Perhaps in the disguise
Of thunder.

why wait?

Amy Freeman Lee

When I was in a golden cage,
I decided to wait.
There was no point
In bruising my wings
And hurting the heart
Of the giver of the golden cage.
    I waited.

One day, the death of the
Giver of the golden cage
Opened the door and released me.
What a strange irony I thought;
Someone's end is another's beginning.
The seesaw of paradox never stops.
    I waited.

Octavio, I said,
Carve me a waiting figure.
He did in pink limestone;
The color was right,
But the figure remained trapped
In my imagination.
    I waited.

Later on, I found a woodcut.
Rockwell Kent had placed a woman
In a doorway waiting in the night;
She had one heart but two roofs,
One belonged to her small house,
The other to the goddess of Heaven.
    I waited.

Now, every day I place
Food and water under the flowering tree
For Solo vino, a big, black tom,
Who comes torn by the lightning of battles
To eat and rest a bit in the sun
Only to return to self-made storms,
      I wait.

I place another feeder
High up in a tree beyond all cats,
It's for the wild birds—all of them.
Their flight patterns and songs
Are more varied and engaging
Than those of the caged birds.
      I wait.

My feet are on the ground,
But at night, I look toward the moon
And wonder who pierced the sky
So the light could sparkle through.
The answer belongs to those who are free.
It's past time to spread my wings.
      I fly!

the tiger

Gail Hosking Gilberg

In watery hues
a tiger came to me,
half wild, half domestic
and vivid as a bowl of oranges
on a summer windowsill.
He gave me no false promises
only the feel of his thick thighs,
the rhythm of his pace,
his tight naked muscles.

If I tell you I became that tiger,
could actually feel
the measure of his ways,
could you re-imagine our lives?
We are in great need
of getting away
from the familiar.

He had no urgent sense of time.
When I stopped, he stopped.
And when the crow flew into the picture
the four of us stood there,
still,

waiting.
It could have been a savage moment,
or you could have told me
I was on some errand of madness.
But those commanding thighs,
too alive to argue
got me believing
I have a taste for the journey.

The big black bird
like a messenger
devoid of a voice
watched me walk ahead
with the tiger. Only for a while,
I said as I looked back.
Only for a while.

red dirt road

Barbara Lovenheim

On Red Dirt Road where it crosses Upper Terra,
I stepped out of my fragile self
and buried my sins in the yielding earth,
fingers flecked with bits of soil:
dust to dust.

I counted out stones for a miniature cairn
marking time and space
watching as a beetle gingerly made its way
through the burial ground.

Sitting on my haunches, feet flat to the ground,
I wondered if spirits could rise from the dead
to haunt the heart of the now alive.

# of birth-mother and daughter
Diane Graves

When Karen Waldron first approached me about this essay, she asked me to write about the adoption of our daughter. As I considered the assignment on and off over the following weeks, I realized that in adopting a child, I had shown very little courage and taken few risks. Yet, two others had shown tremendous courage and taken overwhelming risks, and I shall write about them. They are my daughter's birth-mother, and the daughter we share.

Here is what I know about my daughter Elena's birth and her mother. Elena was born in Chalchuapa, in the Santa Ana province of El Salvador on Mardi Gras day 1993. Our daughter's birth-mother was 30 years old when Elena was born. She was unmarried and illiterate. She had placed one other child, another daughter, for adoption four years before.

I know this about her life, too: She was part of a population that had no opportunities for education, personal and professional growth, or decent medical care. It is very likely that she lived with Elena's birth father, but perhaps because marriage licenses cost money, and they had none, they were not married.

She was a member of El Salvador's huge underclass—those who are neither among the ruling families nor the professional classes that support them. She had witnessed one of the bloodiest civil wars in twentieth-century history, and she had seen her nation's infrastructure gutted by it. She had very likely lost family members to the war and unrest. She had probably been prevented from voting by a power structure that was more secure if she was disenfranchised.

Elena's birth-mother had made an adoption plan prior to the birth of this baby. She worked through her parish priest, who in turn contacted a Catholic church-run convent orphanage in San Salvador. Within three days of Elena's birth, she was placed with a foster mother—a wet nurse—and we were told that she was ours. The foster mother cared for her until Elena was four months old. After that, Elena moved to the convent orphanage, a bare-bones but loving facility where she stayed until my husband and I came to pick her up. She was there three months.

About a month before we traveled to El Salvador, the adoption was final-ized in the Salvadoran courts. At that hearing, Elena's birth-mother had to appear in court and state under oath that she was relinquishing this child for adoption. Baby Elena was there, now six months old, accompanied by one of the sisters from the convent orphanage. She saw Elena, her baby daughter, and had to turn and walk away, because she knew what was best for that infant girl. That took strength and courage.

Elena's birth-mother was courageous, and she took the ultimate risk: She placed her child for adoption, to be raised by people she did not know, in a nation she will never visit. She showed enormous courage by putting the needs of her tiny daughter ahead of her own.

I have never met her, so I can only surmise what she thought as she made this incredibly difficult decision. However, in my mind's eye, I imagine these things: I imagine that she wanted her child to know how to read. She did not—she had to sign all of the legal documents with a thumbprint. She wanted her child to have good nutrition and medical care. She wanted her child to be edu-cated, and to live in safety. She wanted her child to be able to vote, and to express herself without fear. She wanted what every mother wants for her child—happiness and the opportunity to blossom. I don't doubt that she wished she could come to el norte herself, and raise her child here. Even though she was uneducated, she knew that the best way to ensure these things for her little daughter was to place the child for adoption by a North American couple. When I think about her, I cannot imagine the strength and power of such a per-son. I feel an incredible obligation to raise our daughter to be the best she can be, and to honor her heritage.

Our daughter, Elena, is also a person of strength and courage. When we brought her home, we were living outside of Chicago, Illinois. Elena came home with a bad cold and had a miserable flight. When we changed altitude over Cuba, her ears hurt terribly and she screamed from the pain. Within a few days of our arrival home, she developed chicken pox. Elena quickly demon-strated that she was a fighter, and she impressed our pediatrician and his staff with her strength when they tried to give her a shot. She was underweight, slightly anemic, and small for her age. But she put up a struggle!

As Elena has grown, she has faced her own challenges. We noticed that she had reading difficulties, and when she was 10 we learned that she is dyslexic. For two parents who read constantly and both majored in English, this was a significant revelation. It has been humbling to watch a child strug-gle, but persevere, with something that comes as naturally to us as breathing.

As we have lived with Elena, we have learned some wonderful things about her. She is an artist. She is visually gifted, loves dance and theatre, and has learned basic guitar and violin. She is active and coordinated in ways I envy. She is easy with other children and is a good friend. She loves animals, and they love her. She is particularly crazy about stuffed animals; in our collection of critters, each has its own individual name and personality. Elena is stubborn! When she refuses to do something, it is a battle. When she makes up her mind about something, a freight train can not slow her down.

She faces one of the toughest challenges a child can deal with. She is a beautiful brunette being raised in our still-segregated culture by parents with northern European ancestry. Fortunately we now live in a region that is almost evenly Hispanic and Anglo, and there are many mixtures of families all around us.

Still, Elena knows she is an adopted child. She must often think and wonder about who she is, who her birth-parents are, what her life would be like if she still lived in El Salvador. She must wonder if her birth-mother would make her pick up her room the way this Mom does. She must wonder where she got her strong appreciation for color and pattern. She must wonder if she will ever meet anyone from her birth family, if she will ever know any biological relatives.

These are big questions for a child growing up in early twenty-first-century America. And yet she seems to be a pretty darn self-confident person. I'm not sure I could have done as well, and I admire her courage every day when she goes out the door. She is so determined, and so sure of what she wants in life, that she is an inspiration to me, her dad, and our extended families. I'm not the one who is courageous. Elena is. And we know that she got her courage from her mother.

No parent knows what is in store for her child, and I am the same. My hope for Elena is that she will continue to push herself to do her best. As we face the beginning of high school, I worry about what that experience will bring. Many friends of slightly older children have warned that adolescence is a phase to tolerate, and that all three of us may be stunned by how mean the girls are to one another. I worry that Elena's otherness and her reading disability will make these tough years, and could well undermine her resolve and self-confidence.

However, I try to take the long view and think about what kind of grown woman she could become. I hope that whatever she chooses in life, it will involve her creative side. I hope that we can help her nurture her vivid imagination in the face of standardization and "teaching to the test." Elena will have to risk failure to reach her goals. The educational system tends to reward people like her dad and me, but it will very likely be an ongoing challenge for Elena, and it will require her courage and resolve to master it. The rewards offered by that system may not intersect with her talents and abilities. I can imagine that she will often feel frustration and be discouraged. If we are fortunate, she will benefit from that experience and become a person who can meet a challenge head on and stick with it. The risk is that she will become timid and leery of trying new things for fear of failure's pain.

Like all parents, my husband and I wish Elena to be happy in life, and to be a person who will be honored and respected both in our own culture and in her native one. We hope Elena will be a responsible, caring person with a strong work ethic and a sense that one should always give something to those less fortunate. We have a wonderful role model in an unusual place. We have a friend and correspondent in El Salvador with whom we have kept in touch since we were there in 1993. Astrid Lopez worked as a hotel receptionist when we traveled there, but her work situation has been difficult since that time. The economy is quite poor and jobs are not stable. Still, Astrid has time to volunteer with orphaned and very poor children, and seeks to make their lives happier and more comfortable. She often writes to us about her experience and has shown us that even in a very poor country, people find ways to help those less fortunate.

In El Salvador, families are important, and children are treasured in a ways that are rare in the United States. When we traveled to pick up Elena, we were astonished by the number of people who offered to help us. Even the cabbies would hold her while I was situated in their cars, or while I gathered my things to get out. I can't imagine such a thing in the United States. I hope the love of family and the value of children will always be central in Elena's life. Raising her in San Antonio, we are glad that she is exposed to a culture that emphasizes family so deeply.

At some point, we will have to talk to Elena about the realities of her native country—about the deadly civil war there and what role the United States had in that conflict. We will need for her to understand that even though terrible things happened there, she should still be proud to be Salvadoran. In some ways, understanding her nation's recent past may help her comprehend her birth-parents' decision to place her for adoption, and it can show her that courage and resolve can lead to good things. Her country has gained a democracy (though still fragile) and better rights to free expression by taking the ultimate risk.

My husband and I have talked about taking her to El Salvador when Elena is an older teenager—mature enough to comprehend the realities of the situation, but still young enough to allow us to visit together. That visit could require enormous courage on her part, as she will see the realities of life in a third world country and open up even more questions about what her life might have been. But it will let her see the lush beauty of her native land, and possibly help her understand herself even more—the origins of her creative side, the parts of her that are uniquely Salvadoran.

Our experience together, as it is with all families, is one of ups and downs, with the parents worrying about and trying to foresee the future as we make key decisions about Elena's education and upbringing. In spite of those concerns, our daughter is a gift and an inspiration to us. Her presence in our family is a reminder of our own responsibilities as global citizens, of the kinds of courage that exist in the world, and of the risks we all must take to give our lives meaning.

THE COURAGE OF CHOICE

the courage of choice

Not to choose is to have already chosen.
—JEAN-PAUL SARTRE

As we hear from our authors' voices, courage has a cacophony of sounds. While not bold in its immediacy, the courage to choose a path or action may demonstrate a considered willingness to move forth despite one's fears. Many of these authors considered their decisions carefully and over time before acting. In accepting societal responses ranging from ostracism to punishment and incarceration, our writers in this chapter choose to move forward in the face of overwhelming obstacles.

In "Fire Walk," as an activist in the Humane movement, Amy Freeman Lee prepares to address a hostile national audience of animal laboratory scientists. Her profound belief that it is morally, ethically, and spiritually wrong to use animals in experiments demanded that she accept the invitation. She writes, "I have never worked harder on a speech in my whole life." It wasn't physical danger that she was concerned about, but "the risk to the mind and spirit in the form of ridicule and false accusations."

While also having strong beliefs, Catherine Kasper had to put them aside. She had always wanted to go to graduate school, but gave up her dream to take care of her parents. For fifteen years "there was no time to think about other choices, and no one to offer them." Then her father died. She writes, "I could work at a meaningless job until I died, like my father. Or I could learn how to live.... I chose the latter." In "Begin Again," Kasper chooses to follow her dream. Despite negativity and a lack of others' belief in her, she risked applying to doctoral programs. Afterwards, nothing else seemed as daunting. She writes, "The price of risk varies, but the ability to take one opens up a world of new possibilities."

Both Catherine Kasper and Demetrice Anntía Worley found both struggle and fulfillment in their writing. In Worley's poem, "The Dark and Gray of Morning Light," the voice asks "From where comes strength to lift the veil, to dream, to write?" Carl Sandburg notes, "Poetry is an echo, asking a shadow to dance." In Worley's room, candles burn despite the dark light, consuming another's power over her. Buoyed by prayer, she is now ready to "dance." Her strength to write returns, along with her dreams.

Isaura Barrera is also alone in a mainstream culture that opposes so many of the values of her home. In "Sacred Space, Stage Setters, and Miracle Makers," she writes that courage is the journey. It is "primarily about the path that we walk and only secondarily about the places where the path may take us." She looks at her parents and sees that they had a courage that wasn't reflected in her school curriculum, but a courage "rooted in the heart" that was linked to their "deepest longings and most cherished dreams." Suffering for years with the "disjuncture between the paths of my lived-in 'home' world and those I read in my 'academic' world," she was forced to devalue this courage of heart in favor of an unfamiliar, majority view. In the process, she learns that "claiming and expressing one's self, one who is 'at heart,' takes courage at any age."

The voice in Mitsuye Yamada's poem suffered as well. In "The Club," the abusive husband pits his ideal woman against his real, and therefore less perfect, woman. She was never to touch "this prized / wooden statue," but after a succession of beatings she found the courage to hold this weapon. She placed it "between my clothes in my packed suitcase." Overcoming one's fear of "the dark" is also a theme in Joan Loveridge-Sanbonmatsu's poem, "Night Is My Friend." A soothing melody emanating from nature allows her to move forth. She reminds us both of our childhood when night was full of frightening objects and also of our adulthood when we still seek the courage to move into the unknown.

But some authors gave up their own freedom to insure justice for others. In her essay, "The Edge: Across Borders, Over the Line, Through Prison Gates," Doris Sage describes how her experiences in El Salvador gave her the courage to find her voice and actively participate in demonstrations to close down the School of the Americas. She chose a path where she paid for her beliefs by going to jail as a Prisoner of Conscience. While incarcerated, she is moved by the plight of still others, the impoverished and degraded female inmates who taught each other the rules of survival. "This was my 'family'— women who were caught up in a difficult situation that they met with grace, good humor, and courage."

The mother in "Doshite Human Rights?" asks "Why you and Maiku go to visit bad people in prison?" As with Doris Sage, Mitsuye Yamada responds: "These friends of ours believe in justice." They chose loss of freedom to protest injustice. They each demonstrate the strength of conviction underpinning the courage of choice. As Benjamin Disraeli noted, "Action may not always be happiness, but there is no happiness without action."

Searching her soul for the best action, Biblical Rahab responds. With the promise of saving her family, she chose to give up the kingdom of Jericho to Joshua. In "Rahab's Scarlet Cord," Bonnie Lyons depicts the complexity of choice among those excluded from mainstream society as well as the balanced decisions in love and betrayal. Is saving some better than saving no one?

Gaynell Gavin grapples with this question as well in her essay, "Choosing." An activist attorney, she writes about the case of Laura and her maternal aunt, Ruth. Fighting to remove a child from a drug-ridden and sexually abusive environment, she and Ruth work to provide a healthy world for this one child amongst the neediest. Despite supreme and time-consuming efforts, they falter under a bureaucratic system designed to help; yet, in effect, it only hurts the child. As she moves on to her future advocacy work, terribly undervalued by our legal system, Gavin admits, "Then, I put my head down on my desk and cry but only a little because I am afraid if I don't stop myself now, I will never be able to stop. I will drown...."

Bonnie Lyons' poem, "Walking Out," is again about choice. She depicts Eve not as "weak and disobedient," but one who chooses life over "a garden / of perpetual plenty." By taking the bite of the forbidden fruit, Eve risks "entering the world / of time and death." She chooses adventure and wonder about the future over the boredom of certainty.

Also moving into a world of pain and discovery, Valerie Bridgeman Davis concludes the chapter with her poem "Free." To be true to herself, the voice in the poem must leave, even though "his words are charms / narcotic antidote / to her first attempts / at freedom—" It will be the courage of choice that will either lead to her being free or chained "to the life she / has come / to long / to leave." As Moshe Dayan commented, "Freedom is the oxygen of the soul." Bridgeman Davis inhales deeply.

Despite their fears, the courage of these women shapes their capacity to be present to life. Whether taking a stand against injustice, fighting for the right to be heard, or dealing with personal loss, by looking within themselves they find meaning in their lives. Only then can they take the risk to move forward.

fire walk

Amy Freeman Lee

The bolts of blazing light
Slash the curtain
Of the night
They are the thunderbolts
Of Zeus.
I tried to snatch them
To catch an upward ride,
But they are reeling
Out of sight
Beyond my grasp.
I must hasten to make
A lasso of my heart
And throw the loving rope
Before they start
To disappear.
The choice is there;
The courage must be mine
To make the fire walk divine.

The greatest risk of all is life itself. From the moment of birth to that of death, human beings are consciously engaged in making choices. We are the only sentient beings endowed with this gift for which we pay the inescapable price of personal responsibility. For example, right now I must make a choice of one experience that represents the greatest risk of my entire life. I have narrowed the field to just three: Shall I decide to risk a surgical procedure followed by a year in a body cast or spend my life in the safety of a wheelchair? Shall I engage in a chance to join a group of citizens to fight the Minute Women during the McCarthy era and risk being branded a communist? Or shall I as a representative of the humane movement face the "enemy" in the form of animal laboratory scientists? While each experience has aspects of the physical, mental and spiritual elements of life, the first is primarily physical, the second essentially mental, and the third is overwhelming spiritual.

I choose the encounter with the animal laboratory scientists to share with you as an example of a major fire walk in my life. Although I am fully aware of the fact that some medical progress has been made through the process of using animals as subjects of experimentations, I have never believed that we have the ethical, moral, or spiritual right to engage in this procedure. This concept springs from my personal belief as a nondenominational theist that all creatures are part of the divine creation and, therefore, are sacred. My love of animals, which is embedded deep in my soul, is life-long.

Frankly, I never held animal laboratory scientists in high regard. Therefore, when I received an invitation from Dr. Harry Rosmiarek, Professor and Director, University of Pennsylvania Laboratory Animal Resources, to speak at a National Convention of animal laboratory scientists in Cincinnati, I was stunned. Later, I learned that he had heard me speak on several occasions. However, it was a brave act on his part to invite me to speak, because at this time his choice would seem radical since it was not customary for anyone from the humane movement to address animal laboratory scientists. I asked him to let me think about it. Then I called John Hoyt, the President of the Humane Society of the U.S., of which I am a Board member. I confess that I had hoped for a way out, but to no avail. President Hoyt informed me that we had been trying to get our foot in these laboratory doors for a long time and here was our chance. My heart sank. I knew I had to give the talk or I would not be able to live with myself again. At this point, I found solace by recalling the words of a friend of mine who was in show business, "I never became a star because I did not have the courage to face the possibility of failure." I've always lived by the principle that if I'm asked to do something, it's for a specific purpose. And whenever I really dread something, when it begins to show on my personal screen, I know that it is about to manifest itself in my life.

I had good cause to dread the experience, because the conference in Cincinnati would not be my debut in this area of lecturing. Several years before, my conscience had made me accept an invitation to address a meeting of military veterinarians who were engaged in animal laboratory science. The conference took place in San Antonio, so at least I would be on home territory. On that occasion, I lucked out by having the advice of my late friend, Mrs. Richardson Hamilton, who was also a Board member of The Humane Society of the United States. She cautioned me about my severe attitude and my thinly disguised anger. When I walked into the lecture hall, the air was crackling with electricity. Everything about me was wrong: I was a woman; I was not a scientist; and to make matters worse, I was a devotee of the humane movement. The members were ready for battle. As I stepped on the platform, I felt the kind of cold associated with winter in the Artic Circle. We call this sensation fear. I had not experienced stage fright since I was five years old.

While I do not claim to have won a victory at the San Antonio meeting, at least a spirited dialogue took place between the scientists and me. As a matter of fact, it was so dynamic that finally the officer in charge of the conference interrupted to inform us that we had talked through the time allotted for lunch and that we would have to settle for a ten-minute break. In Texas, perhaps we could say that the meeting was a success since nobody got shot!

Because I had the weight of the world on my back, I have never worked harder on a speech in my whole life than on the one for Cincinnati. In preparation, I began by being Socratic—I asked myself a question: How is it possible for anyone to be an active member of an organization that violates some of one's major principles? In other words, how could I be a member of anti-vivisection organizations and of The Humane Society of the United States that is not based on the philosophy of anti-vivisection? That question is actually answered by another question. If one wants to really help the animals, doesn't one start with a knowledge and understanding of the status quo and then begin to work from that point? Animals have been used in experimentations, are being used and, no doubt, will continue to be used for some time to come. Obviously, one starts to work in the lab where the action takes place.

However, you do not have to be a Hicksite Quaker to know that before one enters the arena, one has to have the right attitude. Common sense tells one that you cannot persuade anybody by an aggressive, abusive, threatening approach. One must not only know the correct attitude but believe and live it. To me, this demand proved to be one of the gravest risks of all. It was like major surgery without anesthesia.

Fortunately, my friend and colleague, who is also a member of the board of The Humane Society of the United States, Dr. Marilyn Wilhelm, agreed to go with me to Cincinnati. The eve before I was to speak, Marilyn suggested we take a walk in the brisk late afternoon weather and then have an early dinner. During dinner she asked me to tell her what I planned to say at the convention. I began by giving her a summary account, at which point she interrupted and said that she wanted to hear the whole talk. When I finished fulfilling her request, she informed me that if I presented my lecture in its present form, I would increase the enmity between the scientists and us and set the chances for reconciliation back at least a century. She said that my approach was obviously

THE COURAGE OF CHOICE   121

aggressive and that my underlying rage was equally apparent. In summary, she called my attention to the fact that the art of friendly persuasion was nowhere to be found in my presentation. She then excused herself and retired to her room.

It was now 9:00 p.m. I had to be at the Convention Center very early the next morning, and now I had no speech. I panicked! I went to my room, sat at the desk, tore up my notes and started from scratch. Around 3:00 a.m. I went to sleep for two hours, got up and reviewed my new notes, as I never read to an audience but merely use a skeletal outline as points of reference.

At 7:30 a.m., I caught a cab and proceeded to the Convention Center. The doors were locked and the guard would not let me in because I was not wearing the necessary badge. I found a phone and called Dr. Rozmiarek, who rescued me. During breakfast with him and other doctors I asked Dr. Rozmiarek if the CBS crew had arrived. He said that because groups of people were picketing the scientists for having a "nut" like me as one of the speakers and that another group was picketing my colleagues because they had gone over to the "enemy," no press was allowed. I explained that CBS was doing a documentary on my life and that if they were not permitted to film, I could not speak. He jumped up and called a board meeting and CBS was in.

The beginning of the program provided an insight into eternity. When the show finally got on the road, preceding my keynote address, every past president was called on to speak. By the time all the past presidents got through, I was half asleep myself. I was coming to bat with three strikes against me. The situation was impossible and I knew that I was about to lay the biggest egg of my career at a time when I wanted to do the best job of my life. To fail the animals would devastate me!

While I was listening to the innumerable talks by the past presidents, I kept trying to decide how best to begin my remarks. However, I believe that in the main I followed the path of my intuition that came to me during the comments of the past presidents. I always pray before I speak not only to ask for guidance, but also to acknowledge the fact that I am merely an instrument, not the originator of the act. This I believe we call intuition, which originates in higher hands, as do all things. Fortunately, in my inner ear I had begun to hear the construction of a bridge and the breaking of ice floats as they slowly moved under the bridge. My intuition told me that it was time to take the risk that I had prepared to take and at this point I dived into the icy water of the world of animal science.

Finally, I was introduced and given my chance to speak. That day, as I faced the audience, I confessed that perhaps the best-known advice is to begin in areas that one shares in common with the opposition. Since the official biographical material about me that was provided to the scientists told little about me other than my professional life, I wanted them to know that my family owned and operated a cattle ranch, so that I was a devotee of the environment and a lover of nature. I did confess that while I was a native Texan, I was not a typical one. For example, I had made a careful study of rodeos, and I lectured against them all over the country. I told them what I told all my audiences when speaking on the subject of rodeos. I suggested that they not take my word about rodeos as gospel, but to write to the central office of the Rodeo Cowboy Association and request their rule book on rodeos, which states the requirements of the participant in each rodeo event.

Then I said after you have read the rules, tell me how you can qualify without being cruel to these animals. The risk in rodeos is great, because if you repeat a cruel act sooner or later, you do it automatically and without feeling. Nothing is more dangerous to the mind, heart and spirit of an individual than desensitization. This is one way that murderers are bred who can pluck a flower or kill a child and feel absolutely nothing.

I also wanted them to know that I had shown three- and five-gaited American-bred saddle horses all over the United States for years. I told them some stories about the bright and dark side of this glamorous activity. Some of the most exciting experiences of my life occurred when one of our horses would win a grand championship. One of my horses, a black gelding named Midnight Star, was the first American-bred saddle horse to win the triple crown in one year. The triple crown includes the championship at the Kansas City Royal, The Chicago International, and the Kentucky Derby.

As in all human activities, the horse show world is fraught with risks from people who are not engaged in horse shows because they love horses, but because they find shows a social ladder, to those who discover horse shows as a source of unsavory money. The risks of broken bones from accidents are ever present. As for mine, I always considered them my fault. Ironically, if in the opinion of competing riders you had the best chance to win, you were in the specific danger of having an "accident." There is a saying among professional male riders that if you want to remain sound in body do not ride in ladies' classes! By now I hoped the audience members would know that I was no fanatic or box seat horseman.

Then, in the heart of my talk, I related to them how the rules of The Humane Society of the United States relating to the use of animals in laboratory science procedures are a masterpiece of compromise achieved without violating principles. They do not state that no animals should be used in experimentation, but they ask that no experiment should be done that is not absolutely necessary; that experiments should not be repeated unless there is scientific proof of the need; that no more animals should be used than are essential; that substitutes for the experiment should be used if the quality of the experiment is not diminished; and that every animal should be treated humanely before, during, and after the experiment. Any fair-minded person will have to admit that there is no evidence of fanaticism in these rules.

The Humane Society may send you to the battlefield when it is necessary, but never without sufficient ethical ammunition. I explained that the irony is that those of us in the humane movement are equally concerned about the scientists who perform the experiments. I described for the audience how our job is to help them remain sensitive, for the risk for them is to become insensitive and a danger to themselves and society.

That day at the lecture, we did not slam shut the laboratory door, but opened it a tiny crack. Of course, the door had been worked on preceding me by other caring human beings in the humane movement. Gradually, the misconceptions (the scientists as sadists and the humane movement members as fanatics) about each other have lessened, contacts have increased, and dialogues continue.

The fact that I remember this experience so vividly and with such a depth of feeling is proof that I consider it among the most challenging risks of my entire life. Was it physical danger about which I was concerned? Not really, although every public appearance has this potential. The fanatics are always with us, especially when the basic difference of opinion is severe. There is always the risk to the mind and spirit in the form of ridicule and false accusations.

However, not all risks are this blatant, for some are as subtle as poetry. In the case of making initial thrusts into the closed arena of the laboratories of animal scientists, one not only is trying to appeal to hundreds of animal scientists on behalf of millions of animals, but also to expand the policies and acts of The Humane Society of the United States in relation to this gravely needed field of work. Actually, it is a philosophic battle as subtle and complex as chess. Because the goal is obviously far more than personal, the risk is prodigious. To fail would create an irrefutable, severe blow to the mind, heart, and spirit.

begin again

Catherine Kasper

To begin with, always to be doing work that one did not wish to do, and to do it like a slave....

—VIRGINIA WOOLF, *A Room of One's Own*

When I was in my senior year in college, I told my father I intended to continue for a master's degree, and he said, "What does a *woman* need a graduate degree for?"

He refused to fill out financial aid applications, and when my mother was diagnosed with a brain tumor, he asked me to help care for her. That's what I did. I like to think that somewhere in the back of my head I was planning to save up for graduate school, but instead, I was sidetracked by supporting myself and by wanting to help my parents, both of whom would become seriously ill. It was a sidetrack that lasted nearly fifteen years.

I had grown up in a Midwestern working class neighborhood, where I now realize we were taught how to be vital members of the service sector. We could take orders well, polish floors, and serve food proficiently, but had no training on how to work toward opportunities our parents didn't have. I worked in bookstores and restaurants, night-shift at a perfume factory. I babysat, sold newspapers, answered phones. My high school was clear about the careers open to women: nun, mother, primary school teacher, or beautician, in that order. None of those felt right for me. Fortunately, my mother liked to tell us that we could do whatever we wanted as long as we could read. She taught us that answers to our questions could be found in books, in the lines and in-between the lines. I was sustained through stressful times by books like *All of a Kind Family* and *Harriet the Spy*, and later, biographies of Amelia Earhart and novels by Virginia Woolf and Gertrude Stein. When I had time to myself, I would read or write furiously in my journals. I came to learn how lucky I was that my mother convinced my father of the "new world" necessity of an undergraduate degree for young women.

At the university, life seemed nearly miraculous to me. Endless reading material in massive libraries, encouraging professors, and real physical and intellectual freedom was my utopia. There was nothing I wanted more than to spend my life in this setting, teaching and learning for the rest of my life. One of my teachers told me I should apply to Yale, a school I had never heard of and whose location I didn't even know. I only knew that when I brought the application materials home, my father refused to sign them. Then, my mother's seizures began.

After my mother recovered, I joined the nine-to-five work force. I taught myself several computer programs, basic design, and accounting. I moved from various secretarial positions to being a marketing director for an architectural firm. Nothing seemed quite challenging enough. I was trying to renovate a house by myself, but I wasn't ever home to enjoy it. I sometimes worked sixty hours a week, and while I learned much about architecture, my brain withered. During this time, my father became ill.

I spun in place, consumed by the emotional stress and the doctor's visits and care. My father needed to be taken to dialysis regularly and soon two days a week increased to three days, then four. He had a detailed diet that consisted of boiling vegetables two and three times, and severe leg cramps that my younger sister tried to massage out. After he retired, he began to run out of the house to work in the middle of the night, or wander away from the house and forget where he was. My mother couldn't sleep at night, and so her health deteriorated as well. There was no time to think about other choices, and no one to offer them. My father died after seven long, painful years of deterioration accompanied by dementia. After his burial, I decided to put my life in order: I wrote a will and purchased a cemetery plot for myself. I could work at a meaningless job until I died, like my father.

Or I could learn how to live. Although I'm not sure I knew it then, I chose the latter. And I knew what that was, no doubt, because I had read about characters in books who, in the face of adversity, were able to do just that. Before I was in need of my own nursing care, I wanted to do something I loved.

Suddenly, the whirlpool of my father's illness released me. I could think about myself as well as take time for myself in a rare and fortunate time period before my mother's health would take another downturn. I negotiated a one-day-a-week, three-hour absence from work. I made up the three hours in the evenings and on Saturdays. It meant taking the bus to the train as usual, then walking home around ten or eleven o'clock. I applied to the creative writing program at a nearby university.

The echo of my heels on the linoleum floor, the odors of damp, concrete walls and chalk dust in windowless classrooms were my own Proustian *madeleine*. The university campus felt like home; it was the only place I had ever truly been happy. I was thrilled to be an inheritor of the legacy of Woolf and Stein, and all the people who had fought for equal rights and education. Yet, when I was filling out the graduate application forms, I had panicked, and so, promised myself that if I felt too old, I would escape right after the first class. After all, by American statistics I was a freak: a thirty-three-year-old single woman going back to school for her master's degree. Everyone around me had successful careers and families; they were focusing on their *children's* college plans and their own retirement accounts. People my age were at a pinnacle, not starting over again at the beginning. It was even more painful to realize what Yale graduates had already accomplished.

Although everyone seemed much younger, and I didn't recognize any of the writers people mentioned during class, I stayed. I furiously scribbled notes, even when no one else did. I tried to read a work by every author mentioned whom I didn't recognize; I went back and reviewed every one I did. I had a mortgage and a new school loan, but I didn't quit even though it meant I had to find another job with more flexible hours. I held a teaching assistantship, went to classes, did consulting work, and tried to keep my house from falling to pieces.

I worked for a restaurant and catering business, and on weekends, I would schlep great bowls of potato or fruit salad to outdoor events. I carried hors d'oeuvre trays and beer kegs, and washed china in other people's kitchens. I sold cookies and bread from behind the large glass café cases and designed menus and mail-order catalogues.

I wanted to go on for a PHD even though it would mean selling my house and moving to a state with an excellent doctoral program. The job climate for liberal arts majors was at an all-time low, with at least six hundred applicants for each vacant position. And I would have to live an entirely other life, one I couldn't even picture, one preceded by garage sales and donations of most everything but books. It meant the disapproval of my mother, who was in stable, but dubious health, and questioning by family and friends. I could, of course, remain at my job where I was offered a sizable raise, keep my house, and live a familiar, comfortable life. According to the statistics, there was a better chance any English major would be in a restaurant kitchen than in a classroom.

Once I took the risk to apply to doctoral programs, nothing else seemed as ominous. The *Oxford English Dictionary* defines risk as a "hazard, danger, exposure to mischance or peril," or as a "venturous course." I began to notice that people who didn't take risks had my father's sad expression on their faces.

They lacked the exhilaration that follows the fear. The dictionary also offers risk as "a person who is considered a liability or danger, one who is exposed to hazard." Do those people who take risks truly become different? I never felt it was danger or peril I had exposed myself to, only, perhaps, a "venturous course." If anything, it was more like fleeing from a house on fire; it was an act of self-preservation.

Plaster flaked onto the floor when I opened my doctoral program acceptance letters. I was about to move across the country for the first time in my life. I chose Denver, because it offered a highly ranked program and the greatest contrast to the flat corn fields of Illinois.

I earned my PHD in English Literature and Creative Writing. In my final year in the program, I went on the job market as a practice run, but instead, found an ideal position. Both challenging and often exhausting, this work is never boring. As an associate professor, I am required to teach and to write and to publish, which means I am lucky enough to be fully engaged in what I've always loved most.

Being a writer, I was warned, is a career of pure risk. It is, in the end, a career that demands putting some comforts, some material possessions, and the judgment of others aside, for a commitment which is difficult and often lonely. It is rarely glamorous, but always interesting. My brain is continually challenged. I told myself that even if I failed entirely, I could go to my grave knowing I had at least tried. The price of risks varies, but the ability to take one opens up a world of new possibilities. I wouldn't ever have to wonder, "What if?"

the dark and gray of morning light

Demetrice Anntía Worley

Between the dark and gray of morning light,
she questions her words, and asks self, *From where*
comes strength to lift the veil, to dream, to write?

Her meditation replays their last fight—
she stood, eyes open, her anger, so rare
between the dark and gray of morning light,

burning, a phoenix, she rose—he took flight
creating a positive void: *alone.* Dare
come strength to lift the veil, to dream, to write?

In her bedroom five white candles burn bright,
dancing angels, illuminate a flare
between the dark and gray, a mourning light,

they consume his presence, a parasite
feeding on her silence/thoughts/self. With prayer
comes strength to lift the veil, to dream, to write

herself out of a wisteria night;
pen transposes *solace* from *solitaire.*
Between the dark and gray of morning light.
Comes strength to lift the veil, to dream, to write.

sacred space, stage setters, and miracle makers: reflections on courage

Isaura Barrera

I've never thought of myself as either a risk-taker or a particularly courageous woman. The word courage was never used much in my family. We used its Spanish translation of *coraje* only in reference to anger, overlooking its other possible definitions. Courage remained an unspoken reality carried silently in the definite message that we needed to face our fears and "have heart," no matter the circumstances. With this message came a persistent insistence that joy existed, and a continuing encouragement to claim it, elusive as it might seem. Yet, neither message was ever explicitly associated with courage. Rather, both were presented as merely something that we had to do if we were to live in this world, flawed as it was.

As I reflect on this apparently indirect attention to courage, I am reminded of something that I read a few years ago written by Caroline W. Casey. Apparently, the word *sacred* derives from an old Greek word *sacer*, which was posted on signs at the edges of villages and cities to warn that you were leaving safe and familiar territory. The meaning of sacred, then, might be described as "autonomous journeying beyond conventional boundaries." While it was not Casey's purpose to define courage, the phrase "autonomous journeying beyond conventional boundaries" captures core aspects of the meaning of courage as I have come to know it.

Journeying. I believe that courage is primarily about the path that we walk and only secondarily about the places where that path may take us. I cannot clearly trace my journey from the implicit understanding of courage reflected in my home and culture to the more formal understanding I was taught in school, and then to my current more conscious and integrated understanding. But there are stories along the way that I believe mark the territory I've traveled.

The story with the strongest impact relates to my family's cultural and personal history, which is woven into the framework of all my subsequent journeying. This story was a story told in many parts as my parents and relatives spoke of their childhood. It is a story colored, though not dominated, by memories of loss, violence, and persecution, some historical and some personal. Both my parents lost a parent at a very young age; they both experienced floods and the after-effects of revolutions. Living on the frontier—*la frontera*—there was always the threat and often the reality of accidents, raiding parties, storms, and other such disasters. Less immediate and less explicit, knowledge of more global catastrophes like the Inquisition, World Wars I and II and the Depression also seeped through their words as they talked of their lives and those of their parents.

This is not to say that doom and gloom permeated my family's conversations. It is rather to say that all aspects of reality were taken as an inseparable whole; the less positive was never hidden or sacrificed in favor of the more positive. It was actually only as I began to write these reflections that I realized the extent of my parents' courage, both as children and as adults. It was not the courage reflected in my school curriculum, or in the books and movies I enjoyed. It was a quieter, more subtle courage, born of *corazón*, not guts. Courage rooted in the heart has its own distinct character. It is inextricably linked to the hope that underlies our deepest longings and most cherished dreams. But I am only now truly learning about such courage.

Culturally as well as personally, I assimilated my family's history of transition and heart. One of my earliest steps into the unfamiliar occurred at the age of six when I "left" home and entered the academic community. One doesn't usually think of school as sacred space, but perhaps for many of us it is just that: the space where our until-then-conventional sense of self is challenged. It was at school that I first stepped "off the sidewalk" and entered an unfamiliar world with radically different and dissonant language and expectations. For me, it was a world that looked the same and was composed of many of the same people, yet was simultaneously radically different. The two worlds I experienced seemed one, yet remained apart, each with its own distinct social and linguistic expectations.

It would be many years before I could respond to the challenge posed by the dissonance between my two diverse worlds without losing, or at least eroding, the truth of who I truly was and am. Claiming and expressing one's self, who one is "at heart," takes courage at any age. It is especially difficult at age six.

No one referred to attending a school whose curriculum reflected neither my home culture nor language as a courageous journey. No one pointed out that the formal definition of courage I learned in that setting was only one culture's perspective, of no greater, or lesser, value than the one I'd learned in my home. So, in that early academic setting, I learned about courage as I learned about colorful autumn leaves—as real, but somehow unrelated to my everyday experience. Like tracing an object's contours with heavy gloves on, I could apprehend what I was touching, yet not truly identify the nuances and finer lines that defined its true nature. This disjuncture between the paths of my lived-in "home" world and those I read in my "academic" world is exemplified in the following story.

This story is about an experience that happened during my first years of college. I was attending Our Lady of the Lake University in San Antonio, about four hours from home. It was a Sunday and, after having spent some time at home, I was getting ready to catch the bus to return to school. My father wasn't home and I didn't want to leave without saying goodbye. My mother decided that we could drive out to the ranch where he and my brother were working. Just as we approached, the car became stuck in the mud. I don't remember if it had been raining or if the mud came from an irrigation ditch. It wasn't far from where they were working, but far enough that they couldn't hear us if we called. I panicked, because I was sure we'd never get out and I'd miss my bus. It was always stressful leaving home and this was no different in that respect.

My mother, who was in her late 50s at the time, calmly got out of the car and told me to jockey it a bit as she pushed from the back—now I had the added fear that I'd run her over! It was then that she said words that I've carried ever since "Hay veces que tenemos que hacer tripas en corazón." Literally, "There are times when we have to make intestines into heart." Until very recently, when I found this phrase in a Spanish dictionary, I believed that my mother had made it up. I have never heard it from anyone else then or now. When I heard it on that memorable day, I understood it through my "read about" academic lenses. I believed it to mean something akin to "Make lemonade out of lemons," something done through sheer force of will, a type of white-knuckled courage such as that which I'd read about in school and seen in the movies. And perhaps that was indeed part of my mother's message. But I now suspect that she meant something else as well.

My mother's words did not talk about guts, they talked about heart. Here was a clue to a deeper aspect of courage. At the time I could hear it only dimly, dampened by sounds of the larger culture in which I had become quite proficient, a culture that equated courage with strength, not heart. I had not yet learned to reclaim my early understanding of courage and integrate it with my later understanding. The two meanings, like two distinct maps, remained side by side, one apart from the other. I still believed that my journeying required that I choose only one to guide my walking.

The truths lost in that choosing did not, however, disappear entirely. Their imprint remained, re-emerging in various forms. A few years after my stuck-in-the-mud adventure, I discovered a small book by Sr. Corita Kent and Joseph Pintauro, containing a phrase that awakened the echoes of my mother's words. That phrase —"to make believing more than make believe"—remains with me still, resounding in my mind and my heart repeatedly through the years. I had taken a turn in my journeying, seeking to survive and succeed in a larger world that neither recognized nor valued what it deemed outside its own narrow framework. For many years I set aside much of what I "knew" but could not "prove" according to the tenets of that framework. Unable to find a place for that knowing on the map of reality I had come to believe I had to follow, its contours remained shadowed, reflected only in the realm of fairytales and make-believe. The communal distribution of knowledge, interdependence, extended families, "folk" medicine, visions, the wisdom of elders, the intelligence of the heart, nature as something to be respected rather than controlled ... all these realities and more were devalued as myth, superstition, or naïve knowledge, if they were recognized as realities at all. In the turns my journeying had taken, my deep faith in all those realities had been buried, if not lost completely. What remained would gradually prove to be insufficient to sustain me.

Autonomous. In the current dominant U.S. culture, "autonomous" tends to be understood as being about independence and separation. My family's understanding was radically different. As the youngest and only girl, I spent quite a bit of time alone, reading or playing by myself, in response to which my mother "borrowed" children from our extended family. One or another of my cousins lived with us as I was growing up so that, among other reasons, I would not spend so much time alone.

The dominant U.S. culture tends to perceive infants as enmeshed and non-individuated at birth—thus the subsequent focus on separation and individuation. Other cultures, including my Mexican home culture, view infants as separate and asocial at birth—and focus subsequent efforts on connecting them with family and society. My home culture emphasized social engagement and interdependence; one was never truly alone. Being alone was, in fact, seen as something to be remedied. Even as very young children in elementary school, we seldom went anywhere, even to the water fountain, alone. "Miss, can she go with me?" was an ever-present refrain. In my growing up experiences, the saying "It takes a village to raise a child" was not mere rhetoric. Evenings when I walked home with friends after dark, neighbors sitting on their porches often called out "Why are you out so late?" Similarly, the best way to obtain help of any sort was to call someone. To have no one to call was something to be grieved.

Then, quite suddenly it seemed, it was time for me to leave home once again, this time geographically, as I went off by myself to live in a college dorm. My cultural environments switched once more. Without any real preparation I now had to function "independently" in a social network that held quite different beliefs about autonomy. The tension between my two cultural maps resurfaced. I spent many nights fearfully wide awake, envisioning what might happen and how I might deal with it with no family close by. What I did not realize was that even small non-crisis tasks would be a challenge.

I remember quite clearly the first time that I needed a mechanic to check my car. I was at a loss as to how to find one that I could trust. In my hometown, I would simply call my uncle and tell him I needed to take my car into the garage. Not only could I trust him because he was family, but because the entire town would know how well he had helped me, there was also a sort of built-in quality control system based on relationship. However, in San Antonio, I didn't know where to go for help except the yellow pages, and I knew they were not a truly reliable source of information. How could I find the best services when I didn't know the people who offered them? Obviously, the skills that it took to be autonomous at home and those necessary to navigate in the larger, less personal environment were not the same!

Much later, and only after becoming ashamed of not being "independent" enough, I discovered that buried in the roots—"auto" and "mous"—lies a meaning more related to "self-governed" or "self-regulated" than to independent or separate. Defined in this way, autonomy can be measured more by the degree to which we exhibit focused attention and sustained connection with ourselves, others and the world around us than by the degree to which we function alone in less personally connected environments. I slowly began to understand that self-regulated could be understood as regulated by *myself* or as regulated by my *self*.

Though I lived independently after finishing college, it would not be until I was in my forties that I'd find the *corazón* to once more journey in resonance with the visions in my heart and the sounds of my own rhythms. It would take another leaving—to live with my then-husband in New York—before I realized the degree to which I had stopped expressing the self that resonated so deeply to the rhythms of my family and early cultural environment. The deep pain and despair of that realization birthed the courage to once more risk saying, "Here I stand. I may not fit your idea of who or how I should be, but nevertheless, this is who I am."

It's still challenging for me to integrate individuality and community in my life. The loudest messages in U.S. culture continue to equate autonomy with separation and leaving home. There is little recognition that, for some of us, the most courageous task is not to leave home. We did that at age six. Rather, it is to return home. Only then, I believe, can we become truly autonomous: regulated by who we are "at heart."

Returning home for me has been about reclaiming those places in my heart that hold my deepest truths, places that I've felt I needed to hide or shut down in the face of contradictory messages. Perhaps the greatest test and gift of autonomy in my life came when I returned home both geographically and psychologically after my divorce. On my birthday in 1990, I boarded a plane to move to Albuquerque to begin my current work at the University of New Mexico—and to start finding a voice for the self I was starting to remember. I needed to be in communion with myself before I could be in community with others. For that, I needed to step beyond the conventional boundaries that had for so long passed judgment on which aspects of myself were acceptable and which weren't.

Beyond conventional boundaries. My journeying beyond the bounds of convention has not been the stuff of extreme sports, survivor shows, or amazing races. It has been a quieter, step-by-step turning from external conformity to internal alignment. I have read that some African communities believe that every unborn child has a unique song that exists prior to and extends beyond the bounds of convention into which the child is socialized as he or she grows. The notes that shape and color that song are meant to inspire, enrich, and sustain the spirit that is our gift to community. The bounds of society are meant to serve the song, not to silence or control it. These same communities believe that it is only when people forget their song that they violate community.

I have lived "on the boundary"—between cultures, between languages, between countries and between diverse perspectives—for much of my life. For a large part of that time, the messages that surrounded me tended to focus on the dividing and distinguishing function of boundaries. When I was in Mexico, I was seen as too American; and when I was in the U.S., I was perceived as not fully American. When I spoke Spanish, it was seldom judged to be correct enough; when I spoke English, I was reminded that it was not my first language. No one told me then that boundaries serve two functions. To divide and distinguish is only one of those. Boundaries also serve to mark where two distinct and differing realities touch, where they are joined. I have come to recognize that to journey beyond conventional boundaries is to recognize this place of connection for the first time and see it as a place of synergy rather than conflict. It is this place that currently sings to me.

The last years or so of my journeying have focused on learning and teaching others to integrate apparently disparate meanings and realities. The fruits of my work are best reflected in Skilled Dialogue, an approach to respectful, reciprocal, and responsive interactions across diverse boundaries. I developed this approach as I worked to find my way back home (becoming more of who I truly am) while simultaneously achieving tenure (conforming to external academic requirements for acceptance).

One of the primary aspects of Skilled Dialogue is the skill of 3rd Space, which seeks to find the complementary aspects of apparent contradictions—the places where they touch and join—and then use those aspects to create a larger, inclusive space where each aspect's strengths can be accessed. A simple example of 3rd Space is the color green, which integrates blue and yellow without asking either to change or sacrifice its unique tints. A more complex example is the integration of two often quite disparate realities, such as living from the heart and conducting "objective" research.

Part of me is someone who wants to have her cake and eat it too. I do not want to sacrifice one aspect of reality for another. To me, that is something like being asked to paint with only one color instead of the entire spectrum. Looking back, I realize that my mother's memorable saying hinted that one need not dichotomize desired realities, that there is a the place where intestines and heart join to become something greater than either could be alone. I believe with my heart, but I make that believing more than make-believe only when I infuse it with gut-energy. Only then can I, literally, em-body it into space and time.

As I write this I realize that I am approximately the same age as my mother was on that Sunday so many years ago. We did get the car out of the rut that held it fast and continued on to where my father was working, having lost all track of time. What I realize now is that my parents, each in his or her own way, provided me with an experience of journeying into sacred space on that day.

In his book *Synchronicity*, Joseph Jaworski talks about setting the stage for predictable, albeit synchronistic, miracles. Perhaps that can also be said for all true acts of courage. The stage for a miracle was set that long ago day by my father who, in losing all track of time, literally stepped out of its conventional boundaries. The miracle was created by my mother who believed that she needed to get me to my father and made that believing more than make-believe, going beyond conventional boundaries that said that middle-aged women could not push full-size cars out of ruts. I am still learning from their example.

It is said that in those communities that believe that each child has a personal and unique song, the female elders gather around expectant mothers in the months prior to the birth to listen for the baby's song so that they might sing it as the infant is born. In a way, all communities sing to their children, though seldom with such exquisite care and attention to each child's unique notes. Not having lived in communities willing to listen for my song so explicitly, learning to identify and hear its particular notes is more challenging. It is up to me to take the time to listen, and ensure that the notes I take to heart are truly part of my own song and not someone else's. My family sang to me in their words and actions. Then I left home and began to hear other songs with different notes. Unable to find the harmony between the songs and thinking that one was somehow more powerful, I stopped hearing the notes I could not translate. No one told me that there is always only one song.

Oddly enough, I have always been fascinated with the process of ear-training used in teaching music. It strikes me now that, perhaps, making *tripas en corazón* and make-believe into believing requires a similar process. There are notes all around us, woven into all aspects of the creation that births and surrounds us: in the words we hear and speak, in others' expectations and judgments as well as in their loving gazes and tender touch. The universe sings our song in chorus with everyone else's. Perhaps courage is about listening for and giving voice to the notes that ring true for each of us. Many notes can stir our emotions, but only a few resonate with the song that our hearts hold. As I end my reflections, I would like to gratefully acknowledge the courage of the "stage setters" and "miracle makers" who have helped and continue to help me literally re-member the unique melody line of my heart's song.

the club

Mitsuye Yamada

He beat me with the hem of a kimono
worn by a Japanese woman
this prized
painted
wooden statue
carved to perfection
in Japan or maybe Hong Kong.

She was usually on display
in our living room atop his bookshelf
among his other overseas treasures
I was never to touch.
She posed there most of the day
her head tilted
her chin resting lightly
on the white pointed fingertips
of her right hand
her black hair
piled high on her head
her long slim neck bared
to her shoulders.
An invisible hand
under the full sleeve
clasped her kimono
close to her body
its hem flared
gracefully around her feet.

That hem
made fluted red marks
on these freckled arms

my shoulders
my back.
That head
inside his fist
made camel
bumps
on his knuckles
I prayed for her
that her pencil thin neck
would not snap
or his rage would be unendurable.
She held fast for me
didn't even chip or crack.

One day, we were talking
as we often did the morning after.
Well, my sloe-eyed beauty, I said
have you served him enough?
I dared to pick her up with one hand
I held her gently by the flowing robe
around her slender legs.
She felt lighter than I had imagined.
I stroked her cold thighs
with the tips of my fingers
and felt a slight tremor.

I carried her into the kitchen and wrapped her
in two sheets of paper towels.
We're leaving
I whispered
you and I
together.

I placed her
between my clothes in my packed suitcase.
That is how we left him
forever.

Reprinted from *Camp Notes and Other Writings* (Rutgers University Press, 1998)

night is my friend

Joan Loveridge-Sanbonmatsu

Summer coqui sings
at night. No longer am I
afraid of the dark.

Natsu-gaeru
nakeba sono yó wa
waga tomo yo

A coqui is a tiny tree frog. Japanese translation by
Kayoko Natsume. Japanese calligraphy by Yoshiko Fujita-Butler.

Reprinted from Winged Odyssey (Hale Mary Press, 2002).

the edge: across borders, over the line, through prison gates

Doris Sage

Across Borders

During the civil war in El Salvador, refugees fleeing the death squads arrived in Syracuse seeking sanctuary. In 1992, at the end of the twelve-year war, members of our peace community accompanied one of these refugees back to his home in El Salvador. In the mountains near the Honduras border, the Syracuse-La Estancia Sister Community was established. The five villages of La Estancia had been the headquarters for the *Farabundo Marti National Liberation* (FMLN) guerrilla fighters where some of the bitterest fighting took place.

My first trip to La Estancia, with my friend Shirley Novak, was the third year of these annual trips. The war was still very much in their minds. In each village we were overwhelmed with greetings of "*Paz y Amor*" and embraced by the entire community. I had difficulty understanding our warm reception; only three years before, planes and helicopters, provided by our government, flew overhead, dropped bombs, and burned their villages. El Salvador soldiers trained by the U. S. Army School of the Americas at Ft. Benning, Georgia, shot at them with guns and ammunition also provided by our government. But the people of La Estancia seemed more grateful that Americans would come and stand in solidarity with them than they were for the aid we brought—and they desperately needed the aid. There was poverty and malnutrition; they were building one latrine in each village to prevent cholera; there were no roads, no electricity, no potable water. We hiked up steep mountain trails; the campesinos carried our bags.

We were welcomed into each village with a religious service. Part of this ceremony included the reading of the names of people from that village who had been killed in the war. As each name was read, the people responded: "*Presenté*," acknowledging that person as present in spirit. The people wept and so did we. In one village, during the reading of the names ritual, I watched two women. They looked like they might be mother and daughter. I watched them because their faces were so beautiful. A name was read and suddenly, silently, tears streamed down their cheeks ... *and I became an activist.*

Another morning, as we were getting ready to move on to the next village, a tiny woman picked up my heavy backpack. She was not as tall as my shoulders, looked much older than I, and had no teeth. I said: "No!" "Sí!" she insisted. "*Quantos años tiene usted?*" I asked. "*Sesenta y ocho.*" she replied. I was only 65. I knew I couldn't carry that heavy bag. It was all I could do to get my own body up those steep mountain trails and carry my water canteen. I had no choice; the others had already started on up the mountain. I helped her strap the bag onto her back, and she bounded over the rocks and up the steep path ahead of me. When we reached our destination, she handed me my bag, smiled, gave me a big hug, reached into her apron pocket and brought out a handmade *matata* as a thank-you gift to me—and she had carried my bag!

Matatas are the string bags the women make from the heniken plant that grows in the mountains. After they have harvested the plant and processed the leaves into string, it takes them a day to weave one bag. They sell the bags to us for 50 cents; then we sell them in the U.S. for $10. The proceeds are returned to the community to support the daycare programs, and at that time, to provide therapy for the children struggling to overcome the trauma of the war. Again I cried. This gift was more than 50 cents and a day's labor for her; it represented $10 that could go to support their children's program. They shared everything they had with us—and they had so little. They gave us their hammocks to sleep in. I don't know where they slept; there were dirt floors inside their huts and rocks outside. In the fifteen years that our community has been visiting there, they continue to be the most gentle, generous, caring people I have ever met.

In the capital city of San Salvador, I had been frightened. When peace was signed, the amnesty allowed soldiers to keep their guns. There were no jobs and people were hungry. Some survived by robbing people on the street and so there would be no witnesses, shooting their victims. It would be ironic that if I were shot on the streets there, it might be with a gun paid for with my own taxes. Up in the mountains of La Estancia, the guerrilla headquarters where much of the struggle had taken place and where the people were also hungry, I felt safe. I left my bags and money; nothing was ever taken.

On our way back to San Salvador, we visited the village of El Mazote to hear Rufina Amaya tell the story of a massacre there. She said villagers thought they were safe because they had remained neutral all during the war. They had supported neither the guerrillas nor the military, and until that day, had been left pretty much alone. She said soldiers came into the village and rounded up all the people. They put the women in one building and the children in another.

They brought all the men into the center of the village and shot or killed them with machetes. Rufina saw her husband die. Then they brought out the women and began killing them. Rufina fell where she could crawl behind a bush and witnessed the rest. She heard the soldiers say, "What will we do with the children?" They set fire to the building and burned it to the ground. Rufina said: "I could hear my children calling me; I knew their voices: 'Mamma Rufina,' my son cried, 'they're killing us!'" Rufina lost four children that day. She said she believes God allowed her to live so she could tell this story. And she continued to tell the story. Our government said this didn't happen, that she was lying. The El Salvadoran military government said it was the FMLN guerillas who did it. Finally, the United Nations Truth Commission investigated and began exhuming bodies. They verified that 900 to 1000 men, women, and children died that day. One hundred of the victims were children. Further investigations verified that military officers and soldiers trained at the School of the Americas (SOA) were responsible for massacres, murders, and assassinations in Latin America. Ten of the twelve soldiers responsible for the El Mazote massacre had been trained at the School of the Americas. Rufina's El Mazote story gave my activism focus.

Over the Line

People in El Salvador and Guatemala said to us: "Even if the School of the Americas teaches only human rights, its sordid history demands that it must be closed now." And, after witnessing how the lives of these gentle Mayan people had been so tragically affected by the policies of our government in Latin America, supported by my tax dollars, I could not remain silent.

Along with thousands of other activists, my husband and I began to work to close the school. We did all the things we are encouraged to do in a democracy: We wrote letters, made phone calls, visited our representatives locally and in Washington, vigiled on the steps of the Capitol, and circled the Pentagon in a solemn memorial procession. Finally, we gathered at the entrance of Ft. Benning Army Base in Columbus, Georgia, where this school is located. We walked onto the base in solemn religious procession, carrying simulated cardboard coffins containing petitions signed by hundreds of thousands of people from all over the United States who also advocated that this school be closed. And we carried white crosses bearing the names of people killed by School of the Americas' graduates. We were arrested for participating in partisan political activity on an army base, fined $3,000 each, and sentenced to six months in prison.

At that time, Ft. Benning was an open base; there were no guards, gates, or fences. The public was permitted to drive or walk onto the base any time of the day or night. You could visit the School of the Americas and a public relations officer there would give you a guided tour and a video promoting the school. You can speak in support of the school, as do politicians and graduates, and leave as a free citizen and welcomed guest. But it is considered prohibited partisan political activity if you speak against the school....

Through Prison Gates

My six months at Danbury Federal Prison Camp were worth every minute. They expanded my interest in social justice to include issues of women in prison and lent credibility to what I say about our prison-justice system. As a Prisoner of Conscience, I had chosen to risk incarceration, but by being there, I learned of the injustices of the prison system for most women. I became aware of the inappropriateness of incarcerating increasingly larger numbers of women. Most of the women at Danbury were African-American or Hispanic, and poor. Federal prison camps are minimum-security prisons, where people convicted of non-violent crimes are incarcerated. But I soon learned that many of the women were serving long sentences: five, ten, twenty years. This was primarily because of the mandatory sentencing rules associated with the Rockefeller drug laws.

Most surprising to me was the large number of women serving long sentences for conspiracy. Often these women were serving time not for what they *did* or for what they *knew*, but for what they *could* have known. Conviction required that they *could* have known, and if they didn't, they *should* have known. Sometimes a woman's partner made a deal and got his sentence reduced, served his time for the crime, and was back on the streets, while the woman charged with conspiracy was still sitting in prison with a longer sentence remaining. Women, it seems, are unwilling to testify against their men.

As I researched women in prison, I learned that while in 1980 just over 13,000 women were incarcerated, by 2000, almost 92,000 women were in federal and state prisons (Johnson, 2003). And, according to the U.S. Department of Justice, Bureau of Justice Statistics, 75% of the women in custody are mothers and more than 33% of those mothers report having three or more children. Often, women are the sole support of dependent children. Clearly, incarcerating women has an impact on more than just those women who go to prison.

I also found that the U.S. prison system is in violation of international standards that call for female prisoners to be supervised by female guards. Guards at the Danbury Camp were nearly all male. One female officer monitored the visiting room. Many of our guards were former military. Lacking the skills to handle the prison situation, the corrections officers would become angry, verbally abusive, mean-spirited, and cruel to us. They chose the most vulnerable women to humiliate. Male guards roamed freely through the dorms and bathrooms and did the five or six daily counts of inmates in their quarters. In a woman's prison, a male could exercise complete power with impunity. Their authority and decisions could not be questioned. A frequent comment by the women at Danbury was that these guards would never make it in a men's prison because male prisoners would not tolerate the treatment that we received.

When we entered, we were given an orientation manual and told to study it so we would know the rules and would not get into trouble. We were told that three "shots" (a write-up by the guards for not following the rules) could put us in the "lock-up," "seg," also called "the hole." Unfortunately, the rules in the manual were not necessarily the rules the guards chose to enforce. They made up their own rules, enforced them whimsically and arbitrarily, and changed rules at will. They acted with impunity. One woman said the best advice she received at Danbury was from the officer who admitted her. He cautioned her that she would be held responsible for—and punished for—rules she did not know. She thought that was valuable information.

Information is power and much of the tension was created because of lack of information—withheld intentionally or through negligence. When entering prison, I was stripped of all personal belongings except eyeglasses and a small wedding band. We were expected to be on time, but there were no wall clocks. We could purchase a Timex watch ($40) at the commissary if we had outside financial resources, but many did not. While each of us was assigned a job, at 12 cents an hour (about 90 cents a day), it took a very long time to save $40 for a Timex watch to keep us out of trouble. In addition, we had to purchase all personal items such as soap, toothpaste, toothbrush, and shampoo from the commissary. Many a new inmate had to depend on the generosity of the other women to tell her the time and share their personal items until she could save enough to purchase her own. And, it was the women who helped each other; they taught us the unwritten rules and the rules each guard was likely to enforce. The women were magnificent!

Because my husband was serving his six months sentence in a federal prison for men, I was able to compare the experience in our woman's prison with his. While the attitude of the guards at Danbury was generally surly and mean-spirited, the attitude of the guards in my husband's prison was generally reasonable. There were times when it was clear that guards in our prison were intentionally making it difficult for the women. In my case, they blocked approval for visits from friends and attempted to sabotage the one permitted phone call from my husband. (Spouses are allowed one phone call every three months.) The administration at my husband's prison was cooperative and arranged for the phone call, which also coincided with our 51st wedding anniversary. However, the Danbury corrections officer did not inform me that the call had been arranged, and only through the persistence of the officer at my husband's prison was the call accomplished.

Federal prison policy allows for the possibility for volunteers to come into the prison to lecture or teach a class or a recreational activity. There were also procedures that allow inmates with skills to volunteer to conduct such classes or activities. The procedures for volunteering were outlined in the orientation manual. Such programs occurred regularly at my husband's prison. At Danbury, other than the GED (high school diploma) classes and crochet work, there were no intellectual or recreational activities. Megan, the nun in our group of four Prisoners of Conscience, volunteered to hold a Bible study class with a group of interested women; Ann, a psychiatric nurse and Anne, a social worker, volunteered to teach a class in "Alternatives to Violence." Both had been trained and certified to teach this course. I volunteered to teach a story-telling class. All our requests were denied. But the women were eager for stories, so sometimes on Sunday evenings, I held what I called "clandestine" storytelling at the outer edge of the compound.

The men at my husband's prison had a well-stocked library, with carpeting, comfortable chairs, study carrels with tapes, videos, and BOOKS! The library at Danbury was a footlocker that was available only on Tuesday and Thursday evenings from 7:00 to 7:30p.m. We were forced to sit on metal folding chairs, without desks or tables, to answer the dozens of letters we received each day from other peace activists.

Birthday on the Inside

At Danbury, it was against the rules to conduct a business inside, or on the outside. It was against the rules to exchange gifts, or favors, such as a bottle of shampoo as a thank-you for a woman who cuts your hair, as this could be seen as "payment or conducting business." Yet, this is not an issue in men's prisons, because haircutting is done by selected inmates as part of their "job."

Fighting was strictly forbidden, as were homosexual relationships. We were not allowed to hug, touch, or embrace another woman because prison officials said they could not distinguish between a friendly, comforting gesture, lesbian contact, or the beginning of a fight. So touching, embracing, or gift-giving were not allowed; but some women at Danbury did take those risks.

It was also against the rules to purchase otherwise allowable items, such as a pint of ice cream or fresh fruit from the commissary, for the purpose of celebrating a birthday or a woman's upcoming release. (Fresh fruit had to be purchased, unlike the men's prison, where fresh fruit was part of the menu.) We weren't allowed to have parties or celebrations. Therefore, we weren't permitted to give a gift, do a favor, hug or comfort another woman, or to celebrate.

Early on the morning of my 69th birthday, I was brushing my teeth, when a woman leaned down to whisper *Happy Birthday* in my ear. She was gone before I could look up to see who it was. Throughout the day, in the dorm or the hall women whispered this same greeting. As I passed through the breakfast line, Hope, behind the serving table, dishing our scrambled eggs, smiled and softly hummed: *Happy Birthday to you ... Happy Birthday to you ...* The officer standing on duty nearby, snarled at her for holding up the line, although she did not miss a beat in her serving.

The lid of Megan's water bottle was placed in the center of the table, covered with a paper napkin for artistic display. A tiny bouquet of meadow flowers that she picked on her early morning walk stood upright in the straw-hole of the lid. We were not allowed to pick flowers, weeds, or even dandelions, or permitted to bring them into the dining room—but these were so tiny. Ann and the others had purchased fresh fruit from the commissary the day before and made a fruit compote for our breakfast. Fruit was more of a treat to us than cake.

When I returned to my quarters after breakfast, I found a handmade card and a box of Cracker-Jacks under my pillow. They were from my 19-year-old roommate, Tanya. She knew how much I like Cracker Jacks, for I had eaten an entire box in one sitting, and therefore tried not to purchase them for myself. She was the youngest woman in the camp and we believed I was the oldest. She called me "Grandma," because I am the same age as her grandma whom she was close to and who died just before Tanya entered prison. Word is quietly shared with a few special friends: "Tonight, out behind Dorm A, about 8 p.m."

As I entered the dining room to work, the women sang the "Happy Birthday" song loudly and enthusiastically, overriding the Food Service Officer's attempt to silence them. He took it with uncharacteristic good humor; perhaps because he understood that I was the oldest woman in the camp, or perhaps because I had only a few more weeks left of my sentence.

My son Doug and his family visited in the late afternoon. They had visited Grandpa earlier in the month on his birthday and the grandchildren were getting to be old hands at visiting grandparents in prison. Daniel, age seven, had the ragged old deck of UNO cards dealt out at the table before I arrived. He was ready to play. He had also learned on a previous visit about the unreasonable rules of the Bureau of Prisons when he wasn't allowed to replace the ragged deck of UNO cards with a new sealed deck for the use of others in the visiting room.

We women gathered around 8:00 p.m. at a table on the edge of the hill, some distance from the dorm, to quietly recognize my birthday. (We assured ourselves that it wasn't a "party!") Megan made "champagne" punch from guava juice and ginger ale purchased from the vending machine, and placed it in a large cottage cheese container that sat in a plastic tub of ice. They also served popcorn from the vending machine. Given that gift-wrap or ribbons were not available, the gifts and cards were handmade and creatively wrapped. We could purchase pre-stamped postcards at the commissary, but were not allowed to receive them in the mail, or to purchase commercial greeting cards, so Ann, our gardener, had illustrated pre-stamped postcards with her original flower designs in the upper left-hand corner of the card. Megan wrote a poem in her card.

Our other gardener, Louise, made little notepapers and envelopes, fashioned from computer printout paper "liberated" from the GED program. Even though it was forbidden, she had dried and pressed tiny flowers from the fields and grounds, and used three-inch clear plastic tape to secure them tightly and smoothly to the notepaper. She did this without scissors, knife, or other cutting tools that were also forbidden because they might become a weapon. The envelopes were "glued" with toothpaste. Louise did not reveal how she obtained the tape or where she hid her tiny flowers as she dried and pressed them. If they had been found in the dorm or in her locker during searches, the flowers and tape would have been considered contraband.

The final surprise was a large jar of "Karla's Kream." This concoction is her "Jailhouse Recipe," a luscious hand and body cream, made from ordinary items purchased at the commissary and cooked in the microwave. Karla had been released several weeks before, but had made up her special recipe for me. The jar of cream sat in a basket that another woman had crocheted. Karla had left it with Ann to be opened on my birthday. This was my "family"—women who were caught up in a difficult situation that they met with grace, good humor, and courage.

My experiences in El Salvador, which led directly to my incarceration, continue to involve me in other issues of social justice. I came back home to work with Jail Ministry as a prisoner advocate in the local jail and then became involved in the Women and Prison Project, advocating prison reform. This project, which has the goal of repealing the New York State Rockefeller Drug Laws, is sponsored by the League of Women Voters and the American Friends Service Committee (AFSC). Presently, I am most involved with the AFSC and the New York Civil Liberties Union in the Bill of Rights Defense Campaign (BORDC), working to restore the civil rights we have lost as a result of the USA PATRIOT Act.

I have learned from subsequent study and travel to Guatemala and Colombia that the same issues that introduced me to the ills of our foreign policy continue to be prevalent throughout Latin America. We continue to return each November to Columbus, Georgia, where we vigil at the gate of Ft. Benning, opposing the foreign military training that continues there. As of 2006, over 200 activists have become Prisoners of Conscience over this issue.

From volunteer to activist to Prisoner of Conscience, and now to social justice advocate, I found that the path I have taken has followed logically.

REFERENCES

Amnesty International Action, Spring, 1999.

Johnson, Paula C. *Inner Lives*. New York: New York University Press, 2003.

U.S. Department of Justice, Bureau of Justice Statistics, as reported by Justice Works Community, Women in Prison Program, 1012 8th Ave, Brooklyn, NY, 11215.

doshite human rights?

Mitsuye Yamada

Why you and Maiku go to visit bad people in prison?
    They are our friends, Mother, our tomodachi.
Why you have bad tomodachi?
    They are not bad friends, they are good friends.
If they not bad people, why they in prison?
    Because they stand for what is good and decent
    because, Mother
    because they don't like what the government is doing.
If they not bad people why they don't like the president?
He looks like such a nice boy.
    The president is not the government, Mother.
    The president is
    the president is
    well never mind.
Doshite never mind? Doshite yutte kurenaino?
Why you not tell me?

    Mother, remember when we were put into camp
    during World War Two?
    Do you remember that?
    Did we do anything bad then?
    Are we bad people because we were imprisoned?
Nooo
but they must have some good reason
we don't know about
    Yes, they had a reason all right, but it wasn't good.
    It's called
    how do you say it sabetsu—discrimination.
I don't know about those things.
I don't like to think about such things.
    Nobody does, Mother

But we have to
How come I never hear people talk
about your tomodachi in prison?
    Mother, if you did something bad to people
    would you tell everybody about it? Would you?
Nooo, I don't think so.
    That's why we are telling people
    to help get them out of prison.
    That's why Mike and I are telling people
    about their human rights.
Wakaranai. I don't understand.
What is this thing, humanu raitsu?
    Mother, these friends of ours believe in justice.
    Let me see, how do you say justice
    in Japanese?

Hooritsu mamoru?
    No, Mother, that's not it. Not law-abiding.
    Abiding by the law if the government is wrong
    is wrong.
    If we put people who want to do the right thing in prison
    it keeps other good people who want to do the right thing
    from doing it
    Do you understand now?

I don't know.

Hakkiri wakaranai. I don't quite understand.
But these people are your friends, yours and Maiku
so they must be good people.
That I understand.

1992

rahab's scarlet cord

Bonnie Lyons

The stench of despair
oozed from the bodies
of every customer.
Everyone in Jericho
—man, woman, and child—
knew that the Israelites' victory was decreed,
that we were doomed.

I recognized those two men
I let stay in my house
were Joshua's spies.
I brought them up on my roof
and hid them with stalks of flax.
When the King's messenger ordered me
to turn them over,
I told him the spies had slipped out
and urged him to pursue our enemies.

After the spies promised
to repay kindness with kindness,
to spare me, my father, mother,
brothers and sisters,
I let them lower themselves
with a scarlet cord
through my window
on to the town wall.
The same scarlet cord
was the sign which protected my house
during the annihilation.

I could not have saved the kingdom;
it was already doomed.
I saved what I could.
The same logic that allowed me
to survive as a harlot.

Was this betrayal?
Was that dishonor?
You tell me:
is something
always
better than nothing?

In Josh.2 and Josh.6, following the death of Moses, God instructed Joshua to claim the land of Israel for the children of Israel. Joshua sent two spies into Jericho, who lodged at the house of Rahab, a harlot. Rahab had to decide how to respond.

Reprinted from In Other Words (Pecan Grove Press, 2004).

choosing

Gaynell Gavin

I used to think this story was about Laura, the child, but I was wrong. It's about the woman who saved her. It's about Ruth.

Ruth was Laura's maternal aunt. Laura's mother had a fairly long rap sheet in a file buried among twenty other "priority" files stacked on my desk—theft, welfare fraud, bad checks, prostitution, probation violations, other misdemeanors over a twenty-year period. Having been cared for by Ruth for much of her life, three-year-old Laura had returned to her mother shortly before a baby-sitter called Social Services to say she'd had the child for days and didn't know if or when the mother would return.

A conversational child, Laura told the intake worker and examining doctor that her mother didn't love her and wasn't coming back. "She's gone away. I don't know where." Laura said a man had hurt her. Her physical exam showed vaginal tearing, enlargement, and adhesions.

I visited and first met Ruth in the spring after she had gotten temporary custody, and Laura's case had been handed over to me. A slender, attractive black woman in her early thirties, Ruth was home from her job as a hotel maid by mid-afternoon. She led me to a bedroom with Disney character curtains and bedspread where Laura was sleeping, her round face a shade lighter than Ruth's, and framed by braids. "She's had strep, and the doctor told me to keep her home at least a couple more days. The medicine makes her sleep a lot." Ruth's voice was quiet.

We went back to the living room. I liked the way Ruth kept it uncluttered, just a sofa, a couple of end tables, an armchair. Mostly I liked the way light came through the sheer curtain at the front picture window, and I liked the way Ruth talked about Laura. "She's very intelligent. I'm going to get her in preschool." It was the usual story with the public preschool programs—all full. "I'm going to look for a second job so I can put her in a good private one. I want Kindercare, but it's eighty dollars a week." Ruth was afraid. Afraid that her sister—who was again incarcerated—would be released, show up, and snatch Laura; that nothing would be done to investigate the sexual abuse Laura had suffered or to get therapy for her.

Back at the office, among my hours of afternoon phone calls, I left a message for the social worker, telling him to move immediately to set up supervised visits at the department upon the mother's release and a sex abuse consultation to see if Laura could name a perpetrator, to call me regarding the problems getting Laura into therapy, and to discuss licensing Ruth's as a child-specific foster home. I'd been trying to reach him for weeks, and it was about my tenth message, so I made no attempt to get rid of the terse, stop-screwing-around note which I could hear in my own voice. I followed up the message with a letter.

I wanted to believe that the department placed children with relatives when possible solely due to what's best for the children, but I couldn't help noticing that it's much less expensive to place a child with relatives who typically receive an AFDC payment, while foster parents receive twice the AFDC amount. If Ruth was licensed specifically to foster parent Laura—a possibility for someone who had the right advocates, say for example, the right social worker and the right judge, or the right attorney and the right judge—she would get two hundred instead of ninety-nine dollars each month for Laura.

I also did not want to believe that black children received less care and attention from the department than other children, but how could I know? How could I know, for instance, if the delay in Laura's sex abuse consultation was due to overwork, honest skepticism about her ability to give information, racism, laziness, or other reasons that hadn't occurred to me? I couldn't know for sure, but I did know I had to find some way to keep my inability to know from making me completely crazy. So I tried not to think too much, but then I'd find myself thinking, wondering anyway.

Within a mere week of my latest phone message and letter, I actually got a partial response from the department: the sex abuse consultation would be done within another week. At the consultation, Laura said, "A man touched my bottom, and it hurt. Mom hurt me there too." The department's report found Laura's statements "inconclusive, as a perpetrator could not be identified." I wondered. Had the mother participated in the sexual abuse? I was wearing down though, trying to pick my battles carefully because there were so many, and I decided to let it go. I had a hundred other cases, and there's so much in most of them that we can't ever know anyway.

Along came a nice letter from Laura's mother, at her latest Department of Corrections address, chiding me for taking no interest in her child, doing nothing to help her, and "twiddling" my thumbs, whereupon the impassioned letter-writer assured me that "the shit will hit the fan." The good news was that the department had finally made arrangements for Laura to attend

Kindercare and therapy. Ruth asked me not to push the foster care licensing issue anymore so I didn't. "It's enough," she said. "Kindercare and therapy is enough."

Summer began. Ruth's husband assaulted her and not for the first time. He pled guilty to the latest assault, was ordered into counseling, and signed a release authorizing me to be in touch with the counselor. Eventually, the counselor called to say he was terminating Ruth's husband from counseling because he had recently choked her, screamed at her frequently, and refused to attend counseling sessions. "I think this termination could trigger another incident. This guy needs consequences. Like jail time. I'm going to call Ruth and recommend that she go to a shelter for her own safety."

I called her, too. At work. "You have to choose, Ruth. It's him or Laura. I have to ask the court not to leave her with you if you choose him. If you choose her, you find a safe place for both of you to stay tonight, and tomorrow we get a restraining order." I had picked Ruth as the best thing that ever happened to Laura, but I have been so wrong about so much so often. I waited for her answer, and this time I was not wrong.

Next day we sat in the dim courthouse hallway on a bench where I must have sat a thousand times. Beside me, I could feel Ruth shaking, her thin, pretty face anxious. I gently pried the grip of her hand from my forearm, then put my arm around her shoulders. She was between the social worker and me. I had gotten over my anger at the worker when he came through with child care and therapy. Now, he took Ruth's hand, and her smile flashed white across her face. "We've been through a lot together," she said.

I nodded. "Yeah, we have." I tightened my arm around her shoulders for a second and looked at the social worker's large, light hand covering Ruth's small, dark one.

Fall approached. Laura's case was blessedly quiet. In and out of jail, her mother rarely tried to arrange visits at the department. It looked like we were quietly headed for permanent custody with Ruth, which I remained convinced was best for Laura. Increasingly, I turned my attention to more urgent priorities. And then I learned something new. Tired, aching, devoid of her usual energy, Ruth had gone to the doctor. The diagnosis was multiple sclerosis.

I went to see her. She'd had to move a couple of times since the breakup with her husband. A welder, he hadn't made a lot of money, but they'd certainly had more together than she had alone. She kept the new apartment, like her other places and unlike mine, very clean, but it was still dismal—cramped and dark. Ruth poured us Cokes, we sat down at the kitchen table, and I asked how she was feeling.

"Pretty good." She lit a cigarette. "I found a better place, got to get out of here, can't get rid of the roaches. My brother will help me move. My husband wants to know, can he help me move too? He sent me some money and a typewriter. He knows I want to practice typing so I can get a better job. There won't be any trouble with my brother there."

"You miss your husband, Ruth?"

"I do. I wonder why sometimes, but I do." Ruth stood up and started pacing. She had just gotten home from work, and was still in her pink maid's uniform. "I remember I was seventeen, still in high school. This boy hit me, and I broke a bottle over his head, said I will never let any man treat me that way. I did though. I did. Why do they do that?" She sat back down.

"Maybe because they can? Or at least they think they can." I knew what I was supposed to say about this moving business and the restraining order, what I would have said years, maybe even months earlier. I stared through the adjacent living room window—a small square—out at the asphalt parking lot, thinking, feeling my own eyes narrow, feeling like a fool that this woman needed to ask my permission for her husband to help her move. It's taken me forever to learn a damn thing about human beings, about how so often we don't feel what it seems like we're supposed to feel.

I looked from the window back to Ruth. "I think you're the best judge of who you need to help you move. Seems to me if you need to move, you better do what it takes to get moved. One condition though—I take you to lunch after the next hearing."

Winter came, and I tangled briefly but reasonably amicably with Laura's new social worker over the issue of a subsidized adoption. We were both at the courthouse for other cases when I spotted her in the hallway which was crowded with social workers and attorneys. We were in agreement that Laura should stay with Ruth but not about how that should be done. I thought Ruth should adopt Laura, as she wanted to do, and receive a subsidy payment until Laura reached the age of eighteen. It was an expensive proposition but one that seemed warranted to me. The worker, an extroverted, heavyset woman with curly red hair, disagreed.

"Laura doesn't meet the guidelines for a subsidized adoption. That kid's a total card though. She had Ruth take her to jail to visit her mother a couple of weeks ago, went in with her hands on her hips, and said, *girl, you better get off those drugs, they've ruined your life.* Anyway, Laura's completed therapy and done so well that she's no longer a special needs child if she ever was one."

"Right. Like those special needs adoption guidelines aren't manipulated all the time."

The worker shrugged. "Look, I'll keep the case open until next fall when Laura starts first grade. We'll continue paying daycare until then. This family is close with a good support system through church. Ruth's parents and brother are always going to do what they can to help her out. Even Laura's mom gives Ruth a little money now and then. She's coming around to the idea of giving Ruth permanent guardianship, but she is not going to agree to termination of her parental rights so Ruth can adopt. The case is working out okay, but if you push for this subsidized adoption, you are going to turn it into a big contested mess, with us, the city attorney, the mom, and her attorney aligned against you. Otherwise, Laura's going to be okay. She'll do fine."

"What if something goes wrong? Ruth makes seven hundred dollars a month, and how much longer will she be able to do that hotel maid work with her health problems? What if she loses that job or that ninety-nine-dollar a month AFDC payment or Laura's Medicaid? Now she's got you and me and the court if something happens, but what about when this case closes, and we're all gone?"

So we went back and forth in the courthouse hallway with the worker telling me AFDC and Medicaid were in place as ongoing services and that Ruth was not in good enough health to qualify as an adoptive parent anyway, especially in a subsidized adoption of a special needs child.

"Now that is absolutely brilliant public policy. And compassionate. Let's tell her we want her to raise this kid even with her health problems, but she doesn't qualify for the help she might be able to get if she didn't have the problems, even though if she didn't have the problems she probably wouldn't need the help as much. Brilliant." But I knew that to even bring, let alone win, a termination case without department support was impossible, and termination was necessary to free a child for adoption.

The next spring brought Laura's permanency planning hearing in a courtroom with large windows overlooking a city street. It was a nice day, with a lot of light coming through the windows.

Laura's mother was brought from the Women's Correctional Facility for the hearing, although she had written to the social worker that she did not want to come. She had written, *I would like to place my daughter in the permanent custody of my sister, but I cannot bear the thought of being there in court. It hurts too much already to know I've had chances to fulfill my duties as a mother, but I've made the wrong choices and decisions. I really do love her.* Like Ruth, whom she resembled somewhat, Laura's mother was articulate, composed, and pretty, even in an orange prison jumpsuit, leg irons, and handcuffs. She looked small, sitting at the long table next to her attorney, a stocky middle-aged woman with black hair and vivid pink nails. In a quiet voice, Laura's mother told the judge it would be best for Laura to stay with Ruth.

Afterwards, Ruth and I ate lunch at a Mexican restaurant nearby. "You look beautiful, Ruth." The color of her short-sleeved red dress suited her. She seemed happy and relaxed, making plans—thinking of starting community college, she said, although it would be hard with her job and Laura.

"You know what? I might become a social worker. I'd be a good social worker."

Because it was true, I told her she'd be a great social worker.

Guided by some internal compass, Ruth maintained through another summer, although her life did not get easier. The hotel where she worked was bought by a prominent chain, and while she still had a minimum-wage job, under her new employer, she had a minimum-wage job that no longer provided benefits. No more vacation but, much more alarmingly for Ruth, no more health insurance. Her new supervisors pushed her to work harder and faster at a time when her doctor's main concern was that she not work any harder. Making beds became increasingly difficult as her wrists gave out to repetitive motion syndrome. Finally, in the fall, she had to file a workers' compensation claim, and when the employer fought it, she called me.

"I'm not a comp attorney, but I know a few. There's a guy down the street I like. Why don't you make an appointment to talk to him? I'll go with you if you want. If you don't like him, we'll find you someone else." I rambled on that I thought they'd hit it off, that the problem is surviving financially while waiting for the outcome because even if you win these cases take forever.

Essentially, my case with Ruth is over now, and my job is done. She and the comp attorney will have to fight this next battle together. I keep my voice calm until Ruth and I hang up. Then, I put my head down on my desk and cry but only a little because I am afraid if I don't stop myself now, I will never be able to stop. I will drown. I go into the bathroom, splash cold water on my face, and smear some makeup across it.

★ ★ ★

This essay is dedicated to my mother, Dorothy Gibbons Haegele, a woman of courage.

walking out

Bonnie Lyons

I know what you think:
weak and disobedient
vulnerable—duped
by the wily serpent.
Think again.

Our life in Eden was an idyl—
no work, no struggle,
an unbroken expanse
of pleasure,
a garden
of perpetual plenty.
We were protected children,
and I was bored.

When the serpent told me
eating the fruit of that tree
would make me wise
I hesitated
like any child
about to walk out
of her parent's domain.

Had I foreseen
that my first son
would kill his brother—
but who knows the future?

Biting into the sweet fruit
meant entering the world
of time and death

adventure, change, possibility
including the possibility
of murder.

I chose life.
I would again.
Do you wish
you were never born?
Do you wish to be
a child forever?

Then celebrate my wisdom.

Reprinted from *In Other Words* (Pecan Grove Press, 2004).

free

Valerie Bridgeman Davis

Don't go
his words
whispers of chance and change
dangle on her lobes
like heirloom earrings
from her grandmother's
jewelry box

His words
promise and chains
to the life she
has come
to long
to leave
and now,
his words are charms,
narcotic antidote
to her first attempts
at freedom—
if she does not go
this time,
she will never
leave

I must
her words
echoes of resolute and resistance
hang in the air
like perfume
from his mother's
chest of drawers

Her words
promise and release
from the life he
has come
to leave
in longing
and now,
her words are spells,
herbal remedy
to his last attempts
at repentance—
if he does not succeed
this time,
he will never
win

The risk
too great to stay
too daunting to let go

she leaves
he longs
they are both free
to try again.

SEAMS OF OUR LIVES

seams of our lives

I am a part of all that I have met.

"Ulysses," by ALFRED, LORD TENNYSON

Far greater than the tiny seams in sewing are the invisible ones that bind parts of our lives together intricately with those of others. They also appear where different aspects of one's own life are tied together to form a continuity of life's cycles. The expansiveness of these pieces forms a rich tapestry.

Gail Hosking Gilberg begins this chapter with her poem, "Traveling Words." She created from her own ache, "language / whispered in solitude." Yet, "transmitted like light / on its own journey," her words became vital in binding her to another writer.

Such threads bind not only our lives together, but can form the fragile connection between life and death. In her piece, "Jared Found," Bert Kruger Smith initially shuts down because of her tremendous ache over the loss of her son. Convinced that Jared is just missing, in her distressed state she says, "A six-year-old can't get lost forever." This is a story where life and death are woven together, where mourning and celebration are closely connected by a jagged edge. She can develop the courage to re-connect with the love of her husband and remaining children only when she finds that, through love, Jared will always be part of her being.

Nanette Yavel's "The Pinochle Game" demonstrates what happens when the connection is lost between mental illness and mental health. Sarah was twenty-four, a brilliant young psychologist, "ready to ... become the healer she always knew she was." Yet, at this point she lost touch with reality and was institutionalized, medicated to keep her quiet. Her story is about giving strength to others, about understanding and being understood. Through a deck of Pinochle cards, she skillfully provides the therapeutic relationship the patients need. Yet, because she relies on her heart, or intuition, she lacks credibility and her efforts are suppressed by traditional medical attitudes.

Agreeing with this frequent denial of intuition as binding us together, Ruth Kessler portrays the "False Prophet." Instead of believing that our heart can teach us things beyond "anything we have ever dared dream," we don't trust it. Even "when handed a sunlight— / sun and light, hope and grace," we deflect the ray, choosing "a leader who is bound to betray us." Her words underscore how denying our spiritual connectedness dooms us to failure.

We see the community of lives in Janice Brazil's poem, "Purple Passion." Smiling from within while watching children playfully tossed into a pool by their fathers, perhaps the old woman is remembering a time when she too was thrown over her father's shoulder into a pool. Or maybe she just likes being around other people. This is about the authenticity of life, the joining of the young and the old. Instead of withering away, she is "Regal in a suit of purple passion" as she "continues to sip her sweet wine, cooled / by the splashes."

Hilda Raz's "Stock" begins with illness. We watch the sons sit with their seriously ill father, tending to him "in silence, the family way." Yet Raz reflects throughout that tending is most often women's work. When she herself becomes deathly ill due to a virus, she questions who will tend her. We see how her life fits with those around her as she continues to explore the dimensions of the real self and its relationship with family, despite gender and religious differences, illness and death. In their new book, her son wants her to write only about herself, but she's not sure. She writes, "one of the four pillars of our story, rests directly in all its heavy weight on my daughter Sarah, who wasn't Aaron until s/he was thirty years old." In exploring the many facets of the self, Raz tells a stream of stories that weave their lives into a tapestry of humanity and acceptance.

In "Facing Masks," Wendy Barker also explores the hidden faces of our private selves. The mask-maker has produced hundred of masks, some with lines "like blood running through them, / some made of lace, delicate / as expensive underthings." The voice asks, "What kind of man is he/ to know so many faces?" She wonders what *she* would do if he "would loosen / all her old tight masks, / take them off." Whom would she find? She longs to reconnect with the purity of the self.

The subsequent four poems take love and attachment from its beginning, through marriage and passion, to its ending in divorce. Amy Freeman Lee begins with the need to be with the one we love without the constant knowledge of an imminent departure. Despite her loneliness, she chooses to meet and treasure her loved one, "knowing the joys of Now."

There's a continuity of life's cycles found in Barbara Lovenheim's poem, "Two Aisles." The old has become new in the eighteenth-century church "restored to its former spirituality." We know what to expect as we watch the wedding party move "in a sea of azure to the front of the church." Yet

Lovenheim reminds us that this may be the last time that life "can be so clearly orchestrated," as the complexity of marriage envelopes this innocent couple.

After seven years of "poems and birds crossing and / re-crossing the continent," lovers spend three days together in Rosemary Catacalos' "Final Touches." However, the man has another life away from hers, one to which he must return. Although something has ended, this is a poem about continuing: "the fact remains that I love you. / I love you," Catacalos writes. While she may "limp toward whatever else there is," she will continue to love him, even while "having to drag this bulging grief around." Even in pain, the woman is able to affirm "Gracias a la vida" as her love and memories sustain her.

However, love has torn apart in Demetrice Anntía Worley's "Judgment of Dissolution—Found Poem." Through newspaper clippings of judgments, she weaves the story of how two people's lives, once sewn tightly together, have unraveled at the seams. "Irreconcilable differences / between the parties have caused / the irreparable breakdown / of the marriage." Court language has made them into "parties," obliterating the human element. The woman retains only "her birth name, her current name" as her real self.

Relationships take time and also include choices. Journalist Estelle Shanley, born in Ireland but living in Boston, was a forty-year-old wife and mother of three teenage daughters when she was assigned to cover the hunger strike of Irish prisoner Bobby Sands in 1980. In her essay, "Belfast: A Woman's Story," Shanley writes of the women of Northern Ireland, "Wives, mothers, sisters, helpless in the face of political strife and danger. These women were survivors, street smart, but inept in dealing with the media who crowded the streets and all public places." While Shanley is fired with the desire to devote six months to helping the women deal with media, her family wants her home where she will be safe. It is also a story of woman's responsibility both to family and a larger group, as well as regret over missed opportunities.

From Northern Ireland we move to the West Bank, where danger is a constant presence. Yet, in "Her Way," Naomi Shihab Nye's grandmother goes about life the way she always did. The soldier "flipping ID cards, / the men who editorialized blood / till it was pale and not worth spilling, / meant nothing to her." We see the commonality with the elderly woman in Shanley's Belfast: When asked why she didn't move on after her two sons were killed, she replied, "'This is my home, where I was born, and I won't leave unless in a wooden box.'" Similar to Nye's grandmother, "Already she had seen the brothers go off / in airplanes, she did not like the sound." She was tied to her land, to the children who "had names / and a scraped place on the elbow." These relationships give her comfort and hold her world together during times of human madness.

We see scars, jagged lines, as well as perfect seams throughout this chapter. There is an understanding, a connection to other human beings, as well as a celebration of life and the mourning of its passing. But mostly, we see people coming together, touching upon one another even if for a short time, in the tapestry of a woman's life.

traveling words

Gail Hosking Gilberg

An ache put words down,
with no seismic shock, no
re-ordering of the world, only language
whispered in solitude,
drowned in desire and
later transmitted like light
on its own journey.

Then at a writer's retreat
a stranger ran from our table
and returned with her notebook.
Here, she said, look at this—
you're the writer I quote.
You're the essayist
I carry around.

jared found

Bert Kruger Smith

Now sitting in the darkened living room with the afternoon sun trying to shine through the blinds, she remembered. On the dark blue rug she saw a shaft of light, almost silver in the dusk. And she recalled that day when she was a little girl, still in pigtails, and her father had brought home the piece of quicksilver. There she had stood, her square hand sweating with excitement, holding the shimmering object. In its depths she had seen pure silver and had thought of how she would spend it on licorice and peppermint sticks. How the light had gleamed, giving promise to her heart.

And then, in an instant, it was gone. Shining warmly from her wet palm, it had disappeared. And with it the dream had gone.

The living room smelled stale from the withered carnations, and she wiped her head damply with one hand. The yellow telegrams looked withered too, like old rose petals, and she closed her eyes briefly against the reality. But the dream was worse, and she quickly opened them again.

She didn't hear Henry come in, only felt his hand tender on her shoulder. "Louise," he said gently, "Jimmy and Ellen want their dinner. Come, let's eat."

She shook her head and leaned it against the warm brocade cushion. "I'm—not hungry, Henry. I'll wait awhile."

Henry's hands on hers were cold. "Louise—darling, what are you waiting for?"

She looked up at him, quickly angry. But then the anger left, and there was only the dead weariness. "You know what I'm waiting for, Henry. He'll come home."

In the deepening darkness Henry's eyes looked very large. He ran a finger through his dark hair and licked his lips several times.

"Louise, you won't face the reality. And yet you know. Jared isn't coming home—not ever."

There was a strange confused blur of images before her eyes, and she could feel the pulse in her head begin to throb painfully. Her anger was so great that for a minute she could not get words past her throat. And when she spoke, her words were dry too, and harsh. "You're saying it, Henry. He's lost. He was sick, and he got delirious and left the hospital. He'll come back. He always has."

Henry took her shoulders now and shook her tenderly. "Louise, my darling, come out of your dream. You were too sick to go to the funeral, or you'd be sure. Jared died, darling—died five days ago. Don't you remember?"

She couldn't recall where she was or what Henry was so excited about. Jimmy and Ellen scuffled in the other room. She could hear them faintly, as through a thick wall. She opened her eyes against the darkness.

She supposed she should get their supper. They must be hungry. It was time to call Jared for dinner. He was probably riding his red tricycle up and down the driveway. He played too hard. His hair was always wet when he came in, and his eyes were big and tired. She stood up. "I'll call Jared in now, Henry, and then we'll eat."

The colors came and went again before her eyes, and she could feel her heart begin to thunder as Henry sat her back down on the couch. She heard his voice, again, faintly, and the pain that was like an ax pressed against her stomach.

"Louise, don't—please don't shut yourself up in that dream world again. We need you, we three. Don't keep waiting for the little boy who's lost forever."

She felt that sudden biting anger, but she spoke rapidly, against reality. "You don't know Henry, don't know what you're saying. I've always been the one to hold up. Remember when Jared was two, and we lost him at dusk? Remember how frantic you were? I was the one who found him. There he was, sitting in the middle of the street, with all the cars coming. I found him." She knew her voice was shrill. "A six-year-old can't get lost forever. I'll go out tonight. I'll find him again."

She could see the tears in Henry's eyes, and she was instantly sorry she had made him cry. "Don't worry so, Henry," she said softly. "I'll find him. He can't have gone too far."

"He's no further than our hearts will let him go, Louise."

Ellen was crying now. Jimmy must have knocked her down. Louise raised her head briefly, but somehow it didn't seem to matter.

"Won't you come in and eat with us, Louise?" Henry seemed so urgent over a little nothing like supper, and so she rose and said, "All right. But it doesn't seem like supper without Jared."

"No, it doesn't," Henry said softly, piloting her by the elbow.

The lights in the dining room were too bright, and Louise blinked against their glare. Jimmy and Ellen were already seated, but Jared's chair was empty.

She'd have to find him. Tonight. After Henry and the children were asleep. She'd go out, and then Jared wouldn't be lost any more.

Henry filled her plate, and she took a bit of the round steak dutifully. Henry worried so about her eating. She began to chew; then it happened again. She saw Jared lying in that hospital bed in the polio ward, saw him sipping the root beer she had fixed for him. Then she saw his brown eyes grow wide with terror as he tried to swallow and couldn't. And then she couldn't either. She pushed back her plate and fled into the living room and the darkness.

She did not hear anything else until Henry spoke again. Dinner must be over. There were no dishes clattering, and the children were quiet. Henry took both her hands and began rubbing them as though she were sick or in a faint.

"Louise, we must talk."

"I'm tired, Henry."

"Of course you are. You're worn out, not eating, not sleeping, trying to keep alive a dream that's died."

The rest of Henry's words were drowned in memory. Somehow she recalled again the quicksilver, the future promise, and the way it had disappeared.

"Jared's—just lost, Henry."

"You're losing him, darling. You're not letting the reality he was become a part of our lives."

She reached for the cigarettes in her dress pocket, but her hands shook too much. Henry held out his lighter.

She took a deep puff, and then said tiredly, "Why do you keep nagging me, Henry? Jared's been lost before. Remember the second week of school this year when we let Jared ride the bus alone? He didn't come home for hours, and you thought he was gone then. I was the one who found him, in the wrong bus. He's been lost before. I can find him!" She didn't know she had begun to scream until Henry held his hand over her mouth.

"Louise you're … you're wrong. You're harming all of us … yes, and Jared too. You don't cry, don't eat, don't sleep, don't really live any more. Darling, what is it? What are you afraid of? What will happen when the gates open?"

Louise's head ached, fiercely, but Henry seemed to be waiting for an answer. So she tried to tell him. "Henry, if, if I thought Jared was lost forever, I wouldn't want to live either. I'd—I'd be a failure for the rest of my life. It's intolerable." She shut her eyes again, and she seemed to be walking in a big forest with Jared, holding his hand with the sapphire ring, the one he had picked out for his birthday. They were walking along together, and the path was wide and very far away. It was Henry's voice that brought her back. "Don't you see you're losing him forever this way, Louise?"

She stood up. "No, I'll find him. I'll be the one."

She stayed motionless while Henry went out and came back again with a capsule and a glass of water. He had turned on the lamp by the piano, and she could see how the pill shook in his hand.

"Louise, take this."

She shook her head. "Why should I? I'm not sick."

"This once, Louise. For me. It will help you rest." He sounded as urgent as he had at dinner; and since she wanted to be alone, she took it. She started back to the couch, but Henry's hand was on her arm, taking her down the hall, just past the bulletin board with Jared's last report card and the picture he had drawn of himself and Jimmy at the beach. Her legs began to act queer, and she scarcely felt the stairs under her feet. In fact, she was hardly aware of anything, didn't know how she got into her nightgown, only remembered that she must wake up later and must find Jared again.

When she opened her eyes, the room was very black, and Henry lay beside her, sighing in his sleep. She felt as if she had been asleep for days, and her arms and legs were numb. But now, while she was awake, she must see that the children were covered. Picking up the flashlight by the bed, she crossed the hall to Ellen's room. Ellen's golden hair was tousled, and she was sleeping, uncovered as usual, with her little behind up in the air. Louise covered her and tip-toed down the stairs. Jimmy always kept the covers on, but Jared buried himself under them, like a little forest animal; and when she uncovered him, he was always wet with perspiration. Jimmy grunted as she straightened out his legs and pulled the sheet around his shoulders.

Then she turned to Jared's bed. Her heart began to beat fast, and that new pain in her stomach cut into her. Jared's bed looked—untouched. He was such a little boy, and he squirmed down so. She'd have to find him under that checked blanket.

The flat surface of the cover shocked her hand as electricity would have done, and the shock went through her again and again so that her head seemed to split wide open, and her legs gave way beneath her. Where was Jared? What day was this? What had happened? Her fingers picked at the coverlet, and she began to shiver.

Then it all came crowding down on her, the evening when he lay hot and half-sleeping, his right hand with the sapphire ring paralyzed on the cover.

The frantic call at two in the morning, and the bustle of the nurses and doctors, the low urgent voices, the sight of Jared lifeless in the big iron lung. And then blackness.

She rubbed her hands across her eyes, and the shock and numbness began to wear away. A scream started in her throat and died. Jared was gone now—gone, and she'd never find him again.

She began to cry, for the first time, deep, racking weeping, filled with hopelessness and bitterness, despairing. Now she knew that he was dead, the little boy with the big, brown eyes. The little boy with all the wiry eagerness for life. Jared who stayed in at recess for kissing blue-eyed Margaret. Jared of the serious drawings and the compassionate heart. Jared lost. Lost forever. Lost with all his promise and his hope, gone as swiftly as quicksilver.

When she finished crying, there wasn't another tear inside her. Nothing but bitterness against a fate which could take her tiny boy, the son to whom she had promised happiness and love and a life to live.

Her head hurt violently, and she could hardly stand. But she knew what to do. If Jared wouldn't come to her, she would go to him. The sleeping tablets she'd had when she was pregnant. They would do. She'd take just enough, not too many. She laughed, harshly. What was it Jared had always said at dinner when it was his turn for Grace? She could hear his warm little voice. "Thank you, God, for giving us such a fine time. Please help everyone have the same, not too much and not too little."

She felt the urge for tears, but she was dry, and so she closed her eyes against the pain. Now, while Henry was asleep, she would go up and find the pills. She thought briefly of Henry and Jimmy and Ellen, but Jared's need was greater.

The flashlight still glowed like a bright eye on Jared's shelf, the shelf he had cleaned last Sunday. She saw how he had put his little plaster animals in order. The yellow helicopter he had made was bright as sunshine. "I'm coming, Jared," she whispered.

She picked up the flashlight, and a writing tablet dropped to the bed. Automatically she picked it up, saw the little drawings of ships and planes and blue-eyed girls. She lifted the cover to put the pictures back, and the words danced out at her. The crude little words of a first-grader, written shakily and hugely across the page. "I am Jared. Love."

I am Jared. But I am not. I am no more. A memory. A little boy who died before he lived, who lies in a white coffin beneath the hot ground.

The tears sprang up again, and her eyes blurred. The words ran together, and the lines jiggled so that this time it looked, in its crooked fashion, like "I am love. Jared."

She sat back upon the bed, still holding the notebook. I am love. I am alive as long as there is love in our family, as long as all of you live with happiness and compassion and understanding. I am love.

She rose now, firmly, and laid the notebook gently on the shelf. She crossed the room to Jimmy's bed and patted his warm cheeks. She must hurry up the stairs and wake Henry. He'd be happy to know that she had found Jared, that he wasn't a lost boy any longer.

Reprinted from *Red Boots and Attitude* (Eakin Press, 2002).

the pinochle game

Nanette H. Yavel

The snow had been falling for several hours. The fine white powder covered the cars, the sidewalks, clung to the few trees in the garden below, and accumulated on the hats and coats of the people hurrying across the busy intersection. Under the streetlight it looked as if black pellets were shooting—machine gun-like in all directions. The delicate white matter slipped over the city like a silk shawl hiding the filth and the garbage, obscuring the subtleties, changing the sleazy dark alleyways and underpasses into a fantasy of swirls, little mosques where unknown animals foraged. It undercut the madness of the city, covering the fear and the loneliness.

Sarah closed her eyes and pressed her face against the window screen. Her body was hot from leaning into the old radiator but her face and ears were red from the raw wind and flakes, which transferred through the screen. She had been standing at the window, watching the snow collect, looking out across the hospital courtyard to the river in the distance, watching the snow glinting in the amber light. Her thoughts were sharp; she felt as clear as the hexagonal shapes of the snowflakes. She knew that her life would soon unfold. The pace had quickened. Soon they would see what she was all about. No more taunting voices calling her stupid or clumsy. Her mind was a finely honed tool. She had recently graduated Phi Beta Kappa with a degree in psychology. She had studied astrology, the Tarot, and the I-Ching. All her knowledge was at her fingertips, in position. She was ready to take her place on the Wheel, to become the healer she always knew she was.

At twenty-four, Sarah looked like a teen. She was very thin and her black hair hung limply to her shoulders. Pretty in a boyish way, she had large brown eyes and a firm mouth. She wore rouge in spite of her mother's admonitions: "You'll make holes in your face, Sarah." That morning Sarah stood up on the table and started shouting. "He is coming. Prepare ye the way of the Lord."

She screamed this out at the top of her lungs several times before Gwen and two other large female aides threw Sarah down on the table, stripped her buttocks naked to shoot 100 mg. of Thorazine into her trembling flesh. Now, she knew she must be careful, not move too quickly, be subtle as she took on

her life's work. She would start with the cards, she thought. Her father had
been a Pinochle player and she loved to play with the deck as a child. There was
two of each card, starting with the nine, up to the ace. Most cards were pic-
tures, two queens of hearts, two jacks of spades, two kings of diamonds. This
was the perfect medium, she believed. She had read the Tarot at Halloween
parties. She worked like a gypsy, quick to read reactions and able to adjust her
predictions in a split second. Her analytical mind could put together the clues
quickly and precisely. She delivered each reading in artful language and with a
rare empathy that touched her subjects. They believed her. The Pinochle cards
had the same potential power as the Tarot but were less complex. Anyone
would understand the analogies.

"Sarah, I think you're ready to come out of that now. Get away from that
window. You'll catch pneumonia." The large matronly black woman gripped
the edge of the jacket made of thick sailcloth wrapped tightly around Sarah;
and led her back into the main room of the ward. The night before, Sarah had
screamed out for a nurse to loosen the wrap. She thought it was cutting off her
circulation. No one helped her. She imagined getting gangrene but calmed
herself with prayer, accepting whatever would come. She finally fell asleep,
exhausted. She was thankful when she awoke that her arm still had feeling and
it was not discolored. She wanted her body to be perfect for her mission.

Gwen continued to unwrap the jacket. "You promise to be a good girl this
time? No more screaming, no tantrums. It's for your own good that we do this.
Don't want you to hurt yourself, you know."

Sarah extended her freed hand in a blessing. "Gwen, I know you cannot
help doing what you are forced to do. Your sins are forgiven, but you must
believe in me."

"I hope so. We all have to believe in each other."

"That's not what I meant. You must believe that I can save you."

"That's foolish talk. That's how you got in trouble before." Gwen's gold-
capped teeth flashed; a quick smile pushed up her West Indian cheekbones,
made her paunchy face look angular. "Let's talk about something else, O.K?
What do you want for Christmas?"

"Peace on Earth," said Sarah seriously.

"But what about you, Sarah? What do you want for yourself?"

"I just told you Gwen, I wish you'd listen to me before it's too late."

Sarah slipped into silence. She controlled a sudden urge to scream out
again. She was unsure now. For a moment it seemed so clear, but now she was
uncertain. Maybe she was wrong. Maybe she wasn't Christ's sister; maybe she
was just a messenger announcing His arrival. Of course, that was it. All her life

she had been readied for this. Her family had prepared her for it. They knew. When her eldest brother went crazy, had come down the stairs stark naked, broken every gift their parents had received for their twenty-fifth wedding anniversary, and accused her of causing his madness because she drew some pornographic pictures, it was just a contrivance. The others played along. They all knew that she had a special calling. God had chosen her. In His wisdom, He had planned that she be half- Catholic and half- Jewish. As a youngster, she had tried to baptize her father while he slept. She feared losing him, believing she'd go to Heaven while he was lost in Purgatory.

Gwen spoke gently. "Your parents are coming tonight. I know you want to be in a good mood for them."

The snow was slowing now; the drifts had peaked and the swirling had stopped on the sidewalks. Icicles hung ominously from the roofs of the shops.

Free of the jacket and still exuberant, Sarah ran into the bathroom. She startled Maria, the chubby short Italian woman who was at the sink staring into the mirror. "Sarah, please leave," Maria said in a squeaking voice, and then sang out the sound "Eeee," repeatedly.

"Why are you singing that?" asked Sarah.

"Those people on the wall, they talk to me through the radiator. I know where they are coming from—outer space. They only give me one part of the message at a time. Now they're saying E."

"What's the message? What does E stand for Maria?"

"I don't know, but it's very important."

Sarah's thoughts were racing. She would help Maria to understand the meaning of E. "Meditation," one of the patients yelled out sarcastically. Sarah joined the line to the nursing station. She swallowed her pills with a grimace, imagining them disintegrating into tiny chemicals that swam through her brain plugging up spaces that had too much air. She visualized her mania as a dry forest where sparks flew wildly from one tree to another, fires in all directions. The Thorazine dulled her brilliance but without it she became grandiose, delusional, and would argue with the staff. She would slip into a way of thinking about herself as the sister of Christ, using Biblical phrases and even parables. She loved the exhilaration when she had control, but she also knew that the sense of control was fleeting. In a few moments, she could escalate, lose her judgment.

A raw wind now drove the diminished snow against the windows, making tinkling sounds, which grew louder in the silence of the ward. Charlotte, a thin, attractive blond woman from the South sat with her legs drawn up, her nightgown pulled around her ankles, her arms embracing her knees and her head tipped to one side in deep thought. Her thoughts were spinning. She was hearing what she believed to be the Devil's voice. She remembered it from her childhood. The voice said, "Charlotte you are bad. You are going to hell." She heard this voice at night along with a second voice, that of her dead brother. "Get out of that place, Char, or they'll kill you." Charlotte could not sleep, so she hummed to herself like a little girl and kept herself warm and comfortable. Sarah liked Charlotte. She had a simple way, a sweetness that Sarah loved. She'd cure her first, she thought.

It was 6:30 in the evening. The aides sat playing cards. The dull, yellowed walls of the ward seemed to vibrate with apprehension. Visiting Hours. Soon the patient's relatives and friends would be coming through the locked doors, into the dining room bringing food, candy, and cigarettes. Mr. Harrison was the first visitor to arrive. He came with a shopping bag filled to the brim with other bags. Mrs. Harrison followed, talking at her usual incredibly fast rate of speed. She said nothing understandable, but the persistent chatter sounded very funny to the aides. Their daughter, Sylvia, was nearby; she walked in an angular way around the perimeter of the room, moving her hands stiffly as if she were sending a code to an imaginary passing ship. Sarah thought she looked like an exaggeration of an Egyptian queen. Sylvia was close to forty and had lost her husband in Vietnam. She lived with her parents now. She had been a librarian before Ed was killed. She hadn't spoken to anyone in more than a year. Sarah thought Sylvia courageous to go on at all.

Mr. and Mrs. David came into the room. Mr. David was a tall handsome man with small dark eyes and a prominent mustache. He seemed kind but looked uncomfortable. He smiled at Gwen, self-consciously watched the aide's card game, and gestured knowingly, indicating that they were playing it well.

Mrs. David aggressively scanned the room, sitting through the faces, looking for Sarah. Sarah walked towards the dining room. Her mother met her halfway, kissed her firmly on the lips and hugged her gingerly. Mrs. David was a short feisty woman whose belly protruded. She looked like a fertility doll.

She dramatized her facial expressions, and said with clear disgust to her daughter, "I hear you acted out last night! Why do you say these things?" Mrs. David yelled. "Why do you embarrass yourself and me AND your father?"

"How is my father's house?" asked Sarah calmly.

"Your father? Your father is right over there. Didn't you see him when he came in?" Mrs. David's voice had reached a pitch that could be heard across the room.

Mr. David had been beckoned and he came over to the other end of the table where his wife and daughter were standing. "Hello Sarah," he said in a quiet, slightly embarrassed tone. How's the food here? What'd they give you for dinner?"

"Wine with vinegar on a sponge, " said Sarah, in a half-mocking tone of voice.

Mr. David's eyes looked down. He remembered the day he had committed her. The Six Day Israeli war had broken out the day before. To end the war, Sarah had been writing a mathematical formula all over her room, on the mirror, the walls. The formula was that of a parabola, $x2 + 3x = y$. She intuited that if she substituted any value for x, y must always be greater. She thought that if the value she used for "x" were infinity, then "y" must be an even greater infinity. She had never taken a course in calculus and had no idea that she had discovered a mathematical principle that there are an infinite number of infinities. She believed that she had in fact found proof of the existence of God. This would change things for sure. People would have to listen.

The Davids had to leave the hospital early to attend a funeral. Mrs. David warned Sarah: "Stop playing with fire or you'll end up here for years, like your brother did." Sarah believed her brother had suffered for a reason, one her mother could never understand. Sarah knew what his life meant. She waved goodbye to her parents surreptitiously.

She turned away from the door and saw Charlotte. "Hi Char! Come sit down. Would you like some fruit?" Charlotte took a banana from the bag, peeled it, and bit into it. "You look tired," said Sarah.

" Jus' got to get some sleep. Satan won't leave me alone. He wakes me up just as I'm about to fall asleep and whispers to me that I'm going to Hell."

"Fight him off," Sarah yelled. "You know you're really strong, Charlotte."

Charlotte held the spent banana peel loosely like a flower in her hand. Sarah demanded that Charlotte sit down. She asked her to pull some cards from the Pinochle deck, one for each member of her family, and one for herself. Sarah placed the cards face down on the table as Char handed them to her, arranging them so that her card was at the center, her husband's to the right, her parents' above, and her siblings' below. Sarah began to turn the cards over, one at a time. The king of spades turned up as Charlotte's father; her mother was the nine of clubs; her oldest brother was the jack of spades; her youngest brother was the ace of hearts; her sister was the queen of diamonds. Her husband's card was the ten of spades, and Charlotte's card was the jack of hearts.

"What does it all mean?" asked Charlotte.

"It's clear that you were abused. Your father must have beaten you unmercifully when you were young. Was he an alcoholic? What about your eldest brother, Tom? Did he abuse you sexually?"

Charlotte was shocked by the revelation. It was true! She had been afraid to tell anyone about it. Her mother was weak, unable to help and her baby brother was too young. She hated her sister Lily, who was the family princess. Her father and Tom had died tragically, in a car accident when she was sixteen. She believed she had caused their deaths and was being punished by the Devil. Her husband turned out to be a coward and left her when she began to unravel.

Charlotte's blue eyes brightened, she seemed to come awake.

"Thank you, Sarah. Thank you for this. It means so much. I feel free for the first time in years. They were so unkind, all of them. Why should I suffer?"

Charlotte walked back to her room and got dressed. She put on her sparkling blue earrings. They matched her eyes exactly. She played the cassette of "Fire and Rain" and smiled broadly.

Sarah felt high, jubilant; she had used her power successfully. Before she could quiet down and put on her reserved face, Maria walked over to the table.

"What does E mean? You said you knew?"

"Sit down," said Sarah, now confident. She showed Maria the game and placed the cards she pulled face down. Maria was thirty-eight, had been in the convent and had suffered from paranoid schizophrenia since she was in her early twenties. Her mother and father were deceased. She had an older sister who never married. Maria's mother was the ace of diamonds, her father was the queen of diamonds, and her sister the ace of clubs. Maria's card was the nine of hearts.

Sarah took a deep breath and started to analyze the cards. "No wonder you hear the aliens, Maria. No one in your family ever talked to you. Your parents were ice-cold and your sister was very jealous of your saintliness. There was no joy in your family. It was intense, cold as the Star Nebula. Your father was a wimp. He gave you nothing."

Maria let out a surprised laugh. She thought about her years in the convent. She had really loved that life. Now she felt so alone. Why had she given it up? She had felt unworthy, thought the other sisters talked about her, thought she was a phony. She had the calling, once and now she saw it was real.

"What was your mother's first name?" asked Sarah.

"Emily," said Maria, she smiled knowingly. Once back in her room, she took out the photograph album from St. Agnes, where she had been a novice. Her friends were still there. Now they smiled back at her.

Sylvia came by at that moment and formed the word "Please" with her lips. She wanted Sarah to read her cards, too. Sarah encouraged her to ask. Her first words in over a year were: "Please read my cards." Sarah was exhilarated and curious.

Sylvia's mother was the nine of clubs. Her father was the nine of spades. Sylvia was the ace of hearts, and her deceased husband was also the ace of hearts. "This was a real tragedy," said Sarah. "You were not meant to live without Ed, but he had spiritual work to do and so do you!"

Sylvia's face brightened. "What sort of work?" she asked.

"You were given so little, but you made the most of it. You must give back. Help children to read," said Sarah, feeling tears well up in her. "Go back to the library!" Sylvia smiled and walked away from the table. She walked with a normal gait, arms swinging. When she got to her room, she opened the book of Greek mythology which her husband had given her last Christmas. She turned the pages slowly, and sobbed. Gwen had observed the card game, but didn't understand it. She was concerned that Sarah was getting too high. Gwen spoke to the night nurse who put in a call to Dr. Gary. He was on vacation but a young resident answered and listened to the problem. He knew right away from the nurse's description that Sarah was on the edge.

"It's really strange, Dr. Williams. The patients are all so quiet. No one is acting out. They all seem so relaxed, so normal. Even Sylvia had stopped walking in her weird way. Everyone seemed to get better after they sat at Sarah's table and played the card game. Sarah's much worse though. She's been scrubbing the floors in the bathroom."

The snow had stopped, but the wind rattled the windows. It was cold for Christmas Eve. Sarah had scrubbed the toilets and then stepped on a small ladder to reach the window. She looked out at the snow and felt like rejoicing, but was afraid. Her humility, she believed, would protect her. Then on impulse, she sang out *Oh Holy Night* in perfect pitch. She had a lovely voice, and heard it clearly for the first time. Things were changing. Her new life was unfolding. She had indeed become a healer.

"Give her another shot of Thorazine. Make it 150 mg," the resident said sharply. "That should hold her."

false prophet

Ruth Kessler

The heart
we consider a false prophet, unreliable teacher,
even when it teaches us things beyond
anything we have ever dared dream.
So we follow the Other,
swear allegiance to a flag foreign to us,
a leader who is bound to betray us,
like all the rest.

It's like that:
when handed a sunlight—
sun and light, hope and grace,
a key to promises we cannot even pronounce—
we always deflect the ray.
That story, you know:
we lock horns with Fate,
then atone for mistakes for the rest of our life.

purple passion

Janice H. Brazil

The old lady sits in a crowd
   alone
under cool shade of a green striped umbrella
near the edge of the L-shaped pool.
        She feels
her pulse rise, holds
her plastic wine glass by its stem, slowly
sips Blackberry Manischewitz over ice, and
watches amused, while children
squeal in partial fear, partial delight as fathers
throw them over their shoulders
    into the deep end of the pool.
An owl-like appearance,
blue eyes hidden behind
large round plum color sunglasses
sparkle
like the sapphire necklace wrapped
in tissue paper and buried in a drawer
   between
two worn flannel nightgowns ordered
from LL Bean. Strands of wispy honey yellow hair
are tucked under a lavender hat discovered
in an exotic beach store.
Regal in a suit of purple passion,
        not just
a used-up old woman whose veined skin
is as frail as phyllo dough.
A smile crawls its way to her ruby lips while she
continues to sip her sweet wine, cooled
by the splashes.

stock

Hilda Raz

"The universe is made of stories, not atoms."
MURIEL RUKEYSER

The phone rings.

I've just come through the door hot and tired from an eight-hour remedial driving class called STOP, an option for speeders like me. The other option is a ticket and a huge fine. This one is a fifty-dollar fine, no points deducted, no ticket, and only a full day of writing lost. (My younger son Aaron, who is trans-sexual and lives across the country, is working hard with me on a book of essays we're writing together.) Because it's rush hour, I've walked to and from class. The burning sidewalks have softened the rubber soles of my running shoes. The telephone receiver is heavy as I pick up but maybe it's Aaron.

My husband Dale says, get ready for a road trip, he's on his way home. Vernon, his father, is in the hospital. I pack jeans and T-shirts for two, fill the cooler with sandwiches and cold grapes. We throw stuff in the car and, as we turn onto the highway, the dashboard thermometer reads one hundred and two degrees. Then we drive very fast.

In three hours we're with the family in a second-floor hospital waiting room—three sons, daughters-in-law, their children, grandchildren, and a baby great-great in his papa's arms. What's wrong with Vernon? Does he have meningitis? His neck is stiff; he has fever. Or a stroke? Who knows? We go see. Vernon is sleeping, mouth open without his teeth. He shakes, his fever rises. A nurse with a name tag, Babs, jars his shoulder, asks him a question. He opens his eyes, answers her. She looks at us. Correct, she asks? Correct, we say. All three sons *are* in the room. Babs asks Vernon how he feels. Tired, he says. Then he falls asleep for three days.

Vernon's doctor arrives. He went to high school with Dale, who is the oldest son here. The doctor walks on his toes like a bird. In his polyester slacks, sport shirt, and stethoscope he seems to be decades older than Dale in his jeans. They walk straight to Vernon's bedside, no hesitation at the door. Dale

185

touches his sleeping dad's arms, forehead, sits down in the green vinyl chair for the duration. The doctor says he doesn't know anything yet.

All day and into the night Dale sits, bends over the bed, moistens his father's open, empty mouth with green sponges on a stick. He wipes away brown saliva with a tissue. These transactions take place in silence, the family way. For hours Dale takes turns with his brothers in the chair next to the bed, holding their father's hands through his growing agitation, scenarios, visions. Vernon was a jeweler in his working life. Now he spills tiny diamonds on the linoleum floor, reaches high into the air to sweep them up. Then he's in jail. The boys, grown men now, cooperate to help their father as they can. They sleep fitfully in recliners. The daughters-in-law leave at night taking along the kids. But everyone stays close. We're family. We have come far to be here. At last Vernon awakens, improves, and the family spreads out to interview nursing homes.

But in the middle of the third night of Vernon's crisis, in a motel bathroom, I fall desperately ill and am hospitalized the next day, two doors down from Vernon.

Nine entries to the body, seven matte bruises, seven iv sites, for support, seven veils of shiny mirage weaving their yellow leaves, paper pages I'm sorting, each swirl an event in the living world. The stories shift sleep to sleep, but always the dreamer is sorting pages, each a frame. Multi-tasking is a habit of mind, she figures, even as her body sleeps in its web of fluids. Pared down to the rinsed self focus is perception: tears, wax, snot, vomit, urine, shit.

"The thing that one gradually comes to find out is that one has no identity that is when one is in the act of doing anything .... I am I because my little dog knows me but, creatively speaking the little dog knowing that you are you and your recognizing that he knows, that is what destroys creation."

— GERTRUDE STEIN, *What Are Masterpieces?*

In creation, self is supposed to go. For sure I'm gone. No one knows me. Am I creating here? Sick, I am narrowed to a point of consciousness, blink on blink off. The porches of my ears pulse hot in their tunnels. Who wants to know me? Not me. Am I afraid? No. Nothing abstract is afraid. Window light. This question I've been trying to answer, why is my daughter now my son, flickers dimly, even here. A voice says, *He doesn't want to be your daughter.* To be self-conscious is to exist, not create. Here I am not conscious of a self. My son is my son. Also he is himself. Where is my daughter? Where is Vernon? Where are his sons? His eldest, my husband Dale, is sitting beside my bed. I tell him it's okay to go home. His eyes fill. Home is far away.

A loosely tethered identity has pleasures. I was a child in elementary school when Mother brushed and plaited my hair each morning. Then I sat at my desk and chewed on the ends of my braids in a kind of trace. A child chewing her braids has only the habit of working her jaws—soothing, the crisp resistance of hair. Here in the hospital, that sense of self, that tether to a body, attenuates in a hot sugar taffy called fever. I have no gender. I am not a mother, not a wife. To have gender is to be self-conscious, not creative. Here is a continuing zuzz in the head, a kind of being present. Uninterrupted doorbell, sotto voce, of the monitors. A present, being here. But I am not. Being is sick.

Are you thirsty? No. To create thirst someone says, cut the IV rate. Does it work? I don't remember. No. Intake is out. Sisters-in-law visit and watch.

Somewhere in my nighttime hospital room a woman without a name tag, maybe in her sixth decade, her waist as small as a girl's, floats and touches. When I moan she takes my head in her hands, promises in a whisper, "we all need help." I need help. She helps me. My thank you note is burned work on iced linen. I am a big mess. She cleans me, holds my shoulder against her belly. I lean.

The untethered self is poisoned. Virus or disease. Untethered. Impossible, says Janus / Aaron, my son who lived in my body. You have a virus. Look both ways before crossing.

"Photography taught me that to be able to capture transience, by being ready to click the shutter at the crucial moment, was the greatest need I had."

— EUDORA WELTY

"What I do in writing of any character is try to enter into the mind, heart, and skin of a human being who is not myself," wrote Eudora Welty in 1980. She dies while I am in the hospital.

How can a mother enter the heart and skin of a human being, a boy / girl she "grew in her center like the very air." Can she? The writer untethered is working again. Where is Aaron?

Excuse me, Aaron. What's wrong with the self? In my own voice: she must be poison. How can someone she loves fall ill? What am I? In my own voice: dangerous to yourself and to others.

Once a Polish survivor of the Holocaust told me that when she was safe at last, still a child, she believed the sound of her urine pouring into the bowl was offensive and distinctive, not like American urine falling without sound. She thought that she smelled foul to others. Now I am tethered to tubes, a lucky woman in an American hospital, who stinks. Did I pass on the sense of stink? "[W]hat is common to all transsexuals and what distinguishes them from other sexual minorities is an aversion toward or awkwardness with one's genitals and a desire for sex-assignment surgery" (Dean Kotula, *The Phallus Palace*, Alyson Publications, 2002).

Aaron calls me from across the country on the telephone each and every day. He reminds me for our book, when I am feeling better, not to write about him only about myself. This summer of my sickness I am supposed to be working on our book, *What Becomes You*. My mother said this phrase about clothes, wear only what becomes you. What in fact became my daughter Sarah was becoming my son, Aaron. His body is different from what it was. "Something extraordinary happened to me, and it happened in the body," he says. His surgery was difficult. Hospitals, hospitals. Where is Vernon now? Down the hospital hall in his own room.

Why can't I write about Sarah? Because "the politics of identity ... admonished the writer to 'tell her own story'; telling anyone else's risked eroticizing, objectifying" that story (Jan Clausen, *Apples and Oranges*). Clausen's explanation is as good as anyone's. Aaron is writing his own story. I don't want to eroticize or objectify my adult child. But my story, one of the four pillars of our story, rests directly in all its heavy weight on my daughter Sarah, who wasn't Aaron until s / he was thirty years old. Doesn't my life as her mother, and my daughter, belong to me? For his part, Aaron has absorbed Sarah. I seem to hold precious sixteen years of primary contact with Sarah before she went off to college, then fourteen additional years of holiday contact. Myself having disappeared because of the imperatives of illness and creation, what is left of the daughter story? Of course she can't use the telephone any more. It's Aaron's deep voice that says "Hello, Mom?"

"That famous precept 'the personal is political,' once interpreted as encouragement to analyze women's emotional and sexual experiences for clues to gendered power dynamics, was now [in the middle '70s] increasingly seen as an admonition to mend the world by reforming not only one's personal choices, but the very fabric of one's subjectivity. To use the telling phrase with which Adrienne Rich concludes 'Split at the Root: An Essay on Jewish Identity,' the good feminist's primary task was to 'clean up her act'" (Clausen, 149).

To clean up my act here, I say my children are half Jewish. This decision was made without apparent thought to save them from Red Cross refugee boxes after a holocaust in which I imagined I am killed, perhaps by Christian fundamentalists like my father-in-law Vernon and his family, which includes my husband Dale, or Germans like my daughter-in-law, the wife of my older son, John, and her parents and brother and his family.

In second grade, all students folded and packed Red Cross white boxes, each one smaller than my new shoes box. One toothbrush, one small tube of toothpaste, one white washcloth, two small bars of soap. We each added shampoo, band-aids, hard candies. The white boxes with the red crosses were assembled on long tables. We creased the cardboard at the arrows, folded the lids and tucked them in. Although no one spoke of holocausts, we knew. The Jewish chaplain for the armed forces knew. He lived next door. We mailed the Red Cross boxes to England, not Germany, not Poland. Of course our class was a little vague about geography. My house, my street, my neighborhood, my city, my county, my state, my country, the world. In that order. Later I found out where I grew up.

The father of my two sons was raised in the Episcopal church in Arkansas. My Catholic daughter-in-law was raised on a farm in Bavaria. My Jewish father, who learned to ride a horse before he could walk, was raised on the upstate New York farm of his uncles. The sound my urine makes in the bowl is very like the sound made by my family down the hall in this hospital. Vernon and his family are Christian fundamentalists who were raised in Nebraska, which is where we are now. A nice lady asked my religion when we checked into the hospital. I must have told her. Imagine what we would have done if she'd asked my gender. What if I'd said, male? Of course I don't look male. Aaron does.

"To his surprise, [Fernando] Nottebohm noticed that certain parts of the brains in the songbirds were as much as four times larger in males than in females. He also found that if you give testosterone to a female canary its song nuclei will double in size, and it will sing more like a male. 'That was a real shock, because we had all been taught that an adult brain was supposed to stay the same size, with the same cells, forever,' Nottebohm said. 'It was one of the few uncontested facts abut the brain. So how could it get bigger? That contradicted everything I had ever learned'" ("Rethinking the Brain," Michael Specter, The New Yorker, July 23, 2001).

At this point in time, I'm a very thin woman wearing a large white nightgown, thinking about a book manuscript growing in a computer. The computer and its printer belong to me. My son does not. Is his brain growing? His story is not my story. What is my story? It certainly includes regular news of Vernon, now in a nursing home recovering his strength. We're both out of the hospital. Vernon and I each have a room, a couch, a chair, a magazine, a pot, ice. He has coins in his pockets. In my purse, coins. Lying on the couch at home for weeks I am afraid of being unable to care for myself. Vernon has nurses if he will call them. Tending is women's work. In the hospital, Vernon's sons attended to their father by staying close. The nurses did the mopping up. In the nursing home, Vernon wants to get away. His sons and their families have gone home, back to work. No wonder. I'd like to get away too. Go back to work. No matter how loose the tether to my body, I can't shake it off. How lucky I am. We worry that Vernon will die soon.

Getting better is difficult. I tend myself with care. Talk on the telephone to Vernon. Wash out the nightgown. Walk before the high heat. Eat careful meals, peaches, melon, banana, and fresh local corn and tomatoes, a little fish. Who tends the fruit in their fields, the vegetables? Aaron on the telephone reminds me of the answers. I rest and read. Put on clean clothes dried in the sunshine on the clothesline, another exercise I do deliberately, slowly. I wash and dry only my own clothes. Stay home. Bend over the garden weeds for five minutes at a time. Avoid the poison ivy, another task for another day. Today is Friday. It is 10:21 a.m. and the temperature is ninety-two degrees in the fields. Vernon has moved to Assisted Living. Aaron calls again from across the country.

Friends help us. Inge will be eighty on her next birthday. She and her husband have returned from a long holiday in Europe. She totes my cordless telephone to the store and installs a new battery so I will have a way to call out for help. She buys me a new ribbon for the fax machine so if work comes I'll get it. Laura is sixty-eight with emphysema and other severe health problems. This morning she is having dye injected into her spine to discover the extent of deterioration in her hip. The socket is necrotic. She arrives with groceries and flowers, roses she piles on the counter and tears into shape, arranges in my largest vase. Neither of us can lift it filled with the flowers and water. She comes directly from Pilates class, from Take Off Pounds Sensibly class (she's lost sixteen pounds since May), from Rehab class at the nearby hospital. Her lycra exercise shorts flash in purple, silver, turquoise as she bends. Her dangly earrings are gold, beaded, silver. They flash too. Dorothy, with severe asthma and recovering from a broken spine lives around the corner. Her eight-year-old triplet grandchildren and their mother have come for a long visit from Paris. She joins me for a glass of sherry. In Paris, in a rented room, she waited to recover from her spinal fracture, the result of lifting a big suitcase. Every day her daughter came to visit bringing fresh fruit and vegetables. I am getting older and these close friends are older than I am. My sons call often but they will not after I am better. They are far away. Aaron can't leave work. John's wife, my daughter-in-law, is not fond of me, probably for good reasons.

Women my friends' age hunt and gather food during several daily trips to various supermarkets and health food stores. They lug paper sacks filled with flax seed oil and organic yogurt in and out of their kitchens, and mine. They ask for daily news of my progress, offer wise comments. What they don't know is, I'm raging. Why? I wonder. Is it death? Do I know that soon Vernon will die? That twelve months later his demented wife will die as well, in an institution? A healthy friend who retired early has built a new house, established a new career as a translator and writer. She calls to inquire, was I afraid of dying as my young nephew had, last winter of a mysterious virus? I tell her no, I never thought of his death. I wanted to die. In the hospital I'd decided no chemotherapy if my cancer had returned. Who would tend me? Tending is women's work. No women in my family.

My husband Dale is my primary contact with another human being. Our life together is ritual, boring and soothing at once, holy. But he is a bad cook. And a worse nurse. We seem to be afraid of having gone too far into illness and death. We do favors for each other. He leaves each morning before I rise, I retire before he thinks of putting down his magazine. We are animals in adjacent cages. This separation continues for weeks—until we are called back to Vernon's bedside. He is dying again. This time I stay home.

The peace and silence of the empty house is balm. I have nothing more to do than continue to recover. A small part of me wonders, who is responsible for our lives now that I'm busy healing and Dale is away? Will the sky fall? The news of Vernon is bad. The family gathers without me but then Vernon rallies and returns to the Assisted Care unit.

The recovering and healthy part of me (wearing my running shorts) asks in a loud voice, have the taxes been paid? I haven't paid them. Dale seems like a boy to me with no understanding of the heavy responsibilities of life. I wonder, what's the deal about being responsible? Why are you such a grown up? You have no one to take care of, no bills to pay that you can't pay. Why be a grown up now? The other part says, Because I have been and now someone else should take over. But no one answers. What does *to take over* mean? Fresh food. I think about food, feed myself with the care of a parent responsible for a child. And when Dale comes home, what does he eat? What I make. Aaron on the phone talks about the fields where fresh food grows, the nurture of the fields and of the workers in fields. He is close to these issues. Vernon walks slowly down the halls of his nursing home, leans against the oak railings as he goes. He sits down in the dining room at a table of eight, eats a little ham with gravy, sliced pineapple, mashed corn. He laughs and coughs.

Now I am strong enough to write for a few hours each day. I think that Aaron's and my story may not be interesting to others because Aaron was born Sarah, because he's queer and I'm straight, because he's a genius and I'm a professional woman, because he's a scientist and I'm a poet, because his male point of view is so often at odds with my feminist one, because we are mother and child. Maybe what's interesting is the mother's folly of grief, her willful projection of a gendered identity onto an inappropriate subject, a real person, her child. My obsession with gender identity and roles may not be interesting. In his old age, Vernon is male, handsome, and frail. His women caretakers are deferential and charming. So what? The entire world is turning into high summer, bearing. Vernon's sons begin to prepare for a new season.

Dale drives into the country to Beaver Crossing for Sunday breakfast with friends through a hot, lucent Nebraska countryside, the verges green and lush, and I'm alive breathing outside air again. Where is Sarah in this resurrection?

> Find someone like yourself. Find others.
> Agree you will never desert each other.
> Understand that any rift among you
> means power to those who want to do you in.

ADRIENNE RICH, "Yom Kippur 1984"

Sarah was born to Hilda who was born to Devorah, who was born to her mother, Hilda. Sarah was like me, someone who says in the silence over the newly lit candles, make with us celebrations of joy or of mourning, rites of passages for one another, the kneading of bread, the salving of wounds, flesh healing between stitches, the slow unlearning of silence, the slow recession of nausea, weakness, the intolerable flesh cut off by the friendly surgeon engaged with the help of the other. We will never leave you, never turn our eyes from each other, never shake off the fingers entwined with our own, never refuse presence at births or deaths, you are my child. I am your mother. Who is flesh of my flesh. Aaron.

For a while I am better and then entirely well. At Aaron's suggestion, I try to remember my childhood.

Greg Johnson, in his biography of Joyce Carol Oates, notes that "she patiently endured the ritual familiar to most students of the 1950s: 'emergency' drills in case of an atomic bomb attack." Oates said that the 1950s were "a period of extremes, of myths and false impressions. But there was this other world—dark, exciting and turbulent—that was inhabited by kids who were really tough." Oates and I are exactly the same age and grew up in the same geography, upper New York State, an important detail though I was Jewish and she Catholic, both lapsed, both regularly exposed to liturgy. We must have been tough.

My grandmother was really tough. Greg Johnson writes that car ownership in the '50s was reserved for boys. Still it was Victoria Raz, my paternal grandmother, who was the first woman in New York State to drive a car, in the 1920s. Yesterday at the shopping mall, my mother, a tiny lady nicely turned out, materialized around a corner and I felt instant fear. Because she's been dead for thirty years? Maybe not. Was she a good caretaker, a good woman, or tough, violent? Who knows. I prefer not to remember.

At Syracuse University, Oates found racism on campus "enormously disturbing," especially because in the late '50s racism "went unacknowledged, unspoken." She remembers a sorority alum explaining to the girls the "sorority's exclusion of Jews and blacks: 'You see, we have conferences at the Lake Placid Club, and wouldn't it be a shame if all our members couldn't attend.... Why, it would be embarrassing for them, wouldn't it?'" As an undergraduate student at Boston University, I don't remember racism expressed directly except at the dinner table of a famous and rich family. Why didn't I leave? My husband, the children's father, was seated next to their daughter who was his student and lover. So I did leave, but later. Vernon and his wife Kathryn have been married for sixty-four years.

Greg Johnson's contention that "few women were encouraged to pursue graduate study in the 1950s," is dead-on. How could I have done so? Marrying my Honors English teacher was the best I could have done, and I did it. (Our grandchild, two-year-old Anna shouts, "I did it, I did it," when she uses the potty. And she asserts on the telephone, her first comment each conversation, "I'm a gurrl, a very good gurrl." You bet, honey.) Vernon joined the Navy in World War II. He volunteered for exacting work grinding lenses in the optical lab of a ship anchored in the Philippines. His skills were superb but his story ends, "it was the only air conditioned space on the ship!" We find his entire Navy uniform in a trunk, as small as Frank Sinatra's. Graduate study was not for him, not with three sons and a wife. Nor for his sons.

And suddenly the resurrection lilies rise around neighborhood mailboxes, dark is dawn and evening walks in before dinner. What should we do with my life? Teach, says the self heading for the computer, building bibliography for class. The measure and purpose of the line, reading a new book about a favorite writer, the backlit text on the computer screen all lead me back to a familiar unbroken identity, myself. Aaron and I continue to talk on the telephone, sometimes about weather where he is or where I am, or what he should do with his life. Dale and I talk on the telephone to his brothers twice a week, then every night. One morning Dale gets into the car and this time I am with him. We drive. And one day, after Vernon's three sons have gathered with their wives to sit next to his bed, stroke his hair, whisper their love, after a luncheon spent all together in a sunlit room, after the praise blessing and the holding hands, just after his family has heard a good report from the Hospice nurse who sat next to the bed for us so we could have lunch together in the dining room, after we have returned to our vigil, just as we've raised our voices around his bed laughing in good friendship, in fellowship, just as Dale, his oldest son, takes his hand, at that minute, hearing us, Vernon is dead. And the gates close.

"Stock" by Hilda Raz was published in *What Becomes You*, Aaron Raz Link and Hilda Raz, University of Nebraska Press, 2007.

facing masks

Wendy Barker

Venice closes down early. By ten
the alleys have blackened, so narrow
the travellers walk single file.

Magic how they emerge
into the lighted campo, face
the mask maker's shop where they had

lingered that afternoon.
Hundreds of masks, their eyes
open to a dark wall,

silky, gleaming faces
of queens, demons, fish.
One of them, enormous:

silver and gold, a sliver of moon
kissing a full round sun
billowing flames like a halo.

One of the travellers
had opened her purse,
bellissimo, she had said.

But not like her to desire
something so big, expensive,
difficult to pack.

Face to face she stood
with the man who made the masks
and told him *no, grazie, no.*

Late that night
the moon will silver
the shutters of her window.
She will not sleep but think

back over a dozen canals, shadowed
bridges, and her desire will rise
for the mask,
                    the mask maker.

His faces, hundreds
of colors, some with lines
like blood running through them,

some made of lace, delicate
as expensive underthings.
The gold and silver one,

sun and moon, embracing.
What kind of man is he
to know so many faces?

He would live behind the front
of his shop. Halls would stretch
back into rooms opening

to a balcony, to the dark
water. Cushions on a tile floor.
Pillowy chairs, he might even have

one chair for every mask
he has ever made. If she could
let herself down

in them. Take her time.

And if he—with his long fingers—
would loosen

all her old tight masks,
take them off. What would she do,
then, with such lightness,

her own sun and moon
rising liquid to the zenith
of the sky she is breathing, he is

breathing her hair
into feathers, tendrils, flames that uncurl,
burst the lines of her face.

Reprinted from *Way of Whiteness* (Wings Press, 2000).

now where are you?

Amy Freeman Lee

I cannot grasp
The Now
Somehow.
Is it because
I always see you
Passing out the door
As you have done
So many times before?

I cannot ever stop
The ticking of the clock
Within my inner ear
While we eat and talk
And laugh,
Because its metal
Clicking freezes me
With fear.

Try as I may
To bask in golden light
Of fleeting sun
I see the gathering clouds
Though our meeting's
Just begun,
And I sense the coming pain
Of departure's chilling rain.

Is it better
Not to meet,
To be calm and bittersweet
Than to go down in defeat

Never knowing joys of Now?
I retreat!
When shall we meet;
Where and when and how?

I'm wondering
Where you are Now.

two aisles

Barbara Lovenheim

We are late: running across a grassy meadow
my Bruno Magli sandals are distinctly out of place
for a hundred-yard dash
to an eighteenth-century church
that has been brought piece by piece to the country village
and restored to its former spirituality.

Yellow walls with cracks, fine lines of aging
where now a baby cries
softening the solemn joy of celebration.

We sit conversationally in pews that have small doors
to receive guests and keep them safely
within a straight-backed embrace.

The bride is late; an accident:
She has swerved off the road to avoid a deer.
Her white dress and veil buy her an escort to the church
where fifty people delight in a sunny, summer day
wondering if perhaps she had other plans.

The wedding party, carefully rehearsed,
moves in a sea of azure to the front of the church.
There are two aisles: estuaries for the flow of blue dresses;
this is the final moment when life
can be so clearly orchestrated.

final touches

Rosemary Catacalos

The third and last day given to us
is gray. We are not surprised.
We rise separately, dress in different rooms,
avoid looking at one another
except in the safe distance of the mirror
and then only briefly.
The glint of your silver shaving brush
is quicker this morning, having
so little light to catch.
It is as if God had grown
a tin eye overnight.
It is as if the whole world
could go blind in sympathy
watching us trying to put everything
away without touching it,
watching us fail so miserably.
You tell me how you will pack your books
and I think it is the same story I've heard
since childhood, the one with the moral
about how to laugh at the end.
I leave you at the corner
searching for something to carry you away.
No tears on either side.
By the time I let myself look back
you're gone and it's too late
to be turned to stone or to salt.

I remain conventionally human,
having to drag this bulging grief around
in its same used skin,
its same divided cells.

I try to remember joy.
I try to remember seven years ago in Spain,
the sea pressing in on all sides,
the olive trees and almond-heavy air
always forcing us together,
always forcing us apart at the last minute.
I try to remember the first
and only kiss before now,
a promise in the dark stairwell
of a Paris hotel named after
a martyr who died by fire.

I try to remember all the fond waiting
since then, the certainty we shared.
The drunken phone calls at holidays
and times of crisis.
The poems and birds crossing and
re-crossing the continent between us,
now north toward stamina,
now south toward grace.
I try to remember finally rushing
into the arms of these last three days,
how at first we stood dumbfounded,
how quickly we learned abandon
and rose out of ourselves
and became one overwhelming thing
and shouted and shouted
like open country.
I try to remember how perfectly
we both rode out over the edge
of the world at long last,
past the open mouths of astonished stars
and every possible invention of beauty.

I try to remember these things
and in some ways I succeed after all.
This is what I know how to do.

This poem, this rude crutch I use
to limp toward whatever else there is.
I'm not new in this business.

I know how to carve my own heart,
lean from fat, fruit from sorrow,
flower from seed and vice versa.
I who sing so much about being woman.
I who believe in worshipping my ancestors,
in the serious game of enchantment,
in the ultimate triumph of memory.
When I feel myself beginning to stoop
too heavily, I catch my head
and throw it back on the sky.
Then the fact remains that I love you.
I love you
and sea stones in hot countries
and old produce vendors who carry
small ready change in their ears
and so much more.
Gracias a la vida.
The old-time moral about how to laugh
begins to take hold again.

Reprinted from *Again for the First Time* (Tooth of Time Books, 1984).

judgment of dissolution—found poem

Demetrice Anntía Worley

Now comes the Plaintiff, 32 years of age,
employed outside the home.
She manages other people's lives,
carefully penciled appointments.

The Defendant is 34 years of age,
employed outside the home.
He manages other people's money,
investing for their futures.

The Plaintiff and Defendant
were lawfully married
in this state, and said marriage
was dully registered in this county.

The parties lived together
after their marriage,
a total of 3,480 days,
10 hours, 28 minutes,

but have ceased to live together
as husband and wife,
or as lovers, or as friends,
and now reside in separate dwellings.

The wife of the marriage
is not now pregnant; there are
no living children of the marriage,
whether born or adopted.

One spring she dreamt babies,
playing on her lap, tugging
at her hair, sleeping in her arms.
He was not ready.

Four years later he pleaded,
she refused to respond.
Irreconcilable differences
between the parties have caused

the irreparable breakdown
of the marriage. Efforts
at reconciliation have failed,
silent dinners, empty kisses,

nothing is different from the way
it was yesterday or the day
before or the day before,
and further attempts at reconciliation

would be impracticable. Wherefore,
the Plaintiff respectively prays for
and seeks the following relief:
a judgment of Dissolution of Marriage

be awarded to the parties,
and the Plaintiff's maiden name,
her birth name, her current name,
is the name she wishes to remain.

belfast: a woman's story

Estelle Shanley

Risk and courage confront women every day in ways never experienced by men. In the rearing of children women become multi-faceted, while men generally live lives tackling one task and achieving one goal at a time. Men, not fragmented by the daily grind of bringing up children, are able to focus on their careers and are not easily distracted. In their lives, both genders take risks and display courage in different ways. For women, it is behavior largely intuitive, and for men, deliberative.

In the spring of 1980, nine young Catholic Irishmen, incarcerated in Long Kesh, a notorious British prison in Northern Ireland, made international news when, within days of each other, they displayed both courage and risk in launching a hunger strike. Their protest was simple but went unheeded by British Prime Minister Margaret Thatcher and the English Parliament. Rather than allow Irish prisoners to wear non-prison garb, identifying themselves as political and not criminal prisoners, the British government remained mute as nine men died within a period of weeks.

In May of that year, as an Irish-born journalist living in the Greater Boston area, I was dispatched to Belfast to cover the death of Bobby Sands, the first hunger striker to die. Sands was 27 years old, self-educated, intelligent, and common among Northern Ireland Catholics, he was politically radicalized by British rule in Ulster. He wrote poetry in prison, issued political statements in English and Gaelic, and in an historically unprecedented move in Ireland won election to the British Parliament, no small accomplishment from prison. As in most triumphs over the British government, it was a momentary victory.

I was born, reared and educated in the Republic border town of Dundalk, County Louth, barely three kilometers from the Ulster border. Dundalk lies halfway between Dublin and Belfast on the east coast, a fifty-mile-journey to either city. Our family grew up amidst the politics of the North and viewed the Irish Republican Army (IRA) as the voice of patriotism, the engine to remove the British out of Ireland. The occupation of the six counties by Britain was an old and bitter historic wound. Our childhood was filled with stories of political discrimination and the cruelty of the English, who among other crimes exported food from Ireland while several million Irish men, women, and children died of starvation or immigrated during the famine of 1845.

When assigned to Northern Ireland, I was forty years old, married, and the mother of three high school daughters. We lived in Burlington, a suburban town eighteen miles north of Boston. I arrived in Belfast as Bobby Sands reached his sixty-third day on hunger strike. His eyesight was gone and unofficial medical reports indicated he was in the last stages of renal failure. His parents and family members were at his prison bedside and a Catholic priest made frequent visits giving Sands communion and administering the Last Rites, the sacrament for the dying.

On my Aer Lingus flight, Boston to Dublin, I pondered the role of the Church. A young man, a political prisoner, electing hunger strike, taking his own life in a willful act of death by starvation. Clearly the Church was condoning his suicide by not withholding the sacraments, in effect blessing his decision. At the time, I saw this as a clear religious conflict since the Church placed such a high value on the sanctity of life. As a child living in Ireland I learned that the Church forbade a Catholic burial for those who committed suicide.

The North of Ireland, historically never calm, has experienced ongoing political strife for decades. Catholics were discriminated against, and bitterness escalated between Catholics favoring unity with the Republic of Ireland in the south and Protestants determined to maintain their ties with the United Kingdom. During the sixties and into the seventies, turmoil, violence, and controversy escalated as Mrs. Thatcher and her Parliament ignored pleas from the Irish to grant prisoners political status. The prime minister also rejected pleas from Amnesty International and other peace-seeking groups across the world.

I arrived in Dublin and with transportation provided by Martin Naughton, a lifelong friend and influential businessman both in the North, and Republic of Ireland, went to Belfast. His parting advice was to stay clear of risky situations, cover the story, and get the hell out of the mayhem that was sure to come as one man after another succumbed to starvation.

There is a heightened sense of responsibility and self-importance covering an international story. This was especially true for a woman in the early 1980s. The risks and looming danger render the work both heady and difficult. A journalist knows that the only concern of editors is well-written stories delivered on time. There are no sympathic conversations, no words of encouragement, and never an inquiry about personal well-being. Just keep the stories coming and on time. Such are the cold, hard requirements of the job.

Bobby Sands died after sixty-five days on hunger strike. Medical experts say no one can live without food beyond sixty-six days when the eyes, kidneys, and other vital organs are drastically affected and death is imminent. Despite this awareness, eight of Sands' colleagues kept the political momentum going and plunged ahead, refusing food in a show of determination and solidarity. In Ireland it is not uncommon for men and women to give their lives for their country. They are revered as heroes and embellished in songs and poetry, and Sands and his companions moved swiftly into the highly respected realm of martyrdom.

The night Bobby Sands died, women and children took to the streets. A light rain drizzled throughout the dark night and did not cease for several days. In a dramatic if primitive protest, women pounded garbage can lids on the pavement. They wailed. They prayed. They did not stop banging until dawn broke and the sky lightened. Little did they realize that within hours the world's press, captivated by the young hunger striker's death, would descend on Belfast, filling every hotel.

The streets were a disaster. It rained continually as pale-faced British soldiers patrolled on foot with rifles poised, their youthful faces anxious but alert. Land Rovers circulated everywhere, filled with soldiers and ammunition. Children with scabby knees jeered and flung stones in their rage knowing that older lads would join them at nightfall with milk bottles filled with rags and petrol. Throngs of foreign press and photographers positioned themselves on every corner to record the mayhem.

I filed my first story and the second, and in quick order, the third. Belfast, always a drab city, became a war zone. From my small room in the Europa Hotel in Belfast's city center, I wondered what was happening in Long Kesh, a specially designed jail shaped in H-block cells where the treatment of prisoners allegedly breached the European Convention for the protection of human rights and fundamental freedom. How did the prison guards cope, knowing that one after the other, nine political prisoners would begin a hunger strike? What was the mood of the prisoners? What were their fears? Did they believe their hunger strike would be short-lived, that Thatcher would relent and allow them to wear non-prison garments?

A notice was shoved under the door of my hotel room, its print still moist from the mimeograph machine. A bomb threat had been issued. Guests were instructed to remain dressed and be ready to evacuate. I lay down fully clothed in raincoat and shoes. I thought about my daughters, their quirks and their strengths. Mostly I thought about their quirks, because these become the dominant factors in rearing adolescent children. The dynamics of the quirks peel emotional layers from parents and determine the daily way of life. I thought about their father and how he coped in my absence.

I thought also about the women of Belfast and how different their lives were from the lives of women in America. Wives, mothers, sisters, helpless in the face of political strife and danger. These women were survivors, street smart, but inept in dealing with the media who crowded the streets and all public places. Bernadette Devlin McAliskey, a Catholic revolutionary and a for-mer member of Parliament, scheduled an impromptu press conference in a dingy room over a shop. She sat at a wooden table with a young man recently released from Long Kesh who remained quiet throughout the conference. His name was Gerry Adams, a name the world would recognize two decades later as the leader of the Sinn Fein political party, an arm of the Irish Republican Army.

Devlin McAlisky, a strong Irish woman with incredible verbal skills, issued a report on the status of the hunger strikers. When an *Irish Times* reporter posed a question, she launched into a gripping and vicious castiga-tion of the newspaper and its alleged policy of ignoring the political mayhem in Ulster and fostering political apathy in the south of Ireland. The attack stunned other journalists who, clearly filled with fear of a similar tongue-lash-ing, refrained from asking questions, and slithered into the streets. Meanwhile there was no media coordination, no central headquarters to check information or squelch rumors.

I decided not to wait at the Europa Hotel for the bomb threat to become a reality. The exterior walls of the hotel were encased in barbed wire that might deter climbers, but not a bomb. I left in the middle of the night and walked through a steady drizzle to the Falls Road hoping to find a safe haven at the Catholic Center, and perhaps collect data about the latest political develop-ments. Soldiers were everywhere, poised with arms, ready for trouble. Their rifles used plastic bullets, a large piece of hard rubber the size of a small juice can. Not considered lethal by the British Army, a plastic bullet when fired at a certain angle causes severe damage to kidneys and eyes, and possibly, death.

The shabby, run-down quarters at the Catholic Center on the Falls Road held about fifty people, most of them smoking cigarettes, the air thick, the conversation loud. I sat with an old woman, a kerchief tied carelessly around disheveled hair. As she chain-smoked, she revealed that two of her sons had been killed by the British, the most recent in a car explosion. She was unable to sleep at night thinking about their last hours. She hoped they felt nothing at the end. I asked why she did not relocate to a safer section of the country. She looked at me fiercely, lit another cigarette and said, "This is my home, where I was born, and I won't leave unless in a wooden box."

At dawn I returned to the hotel and filed another story. An hour later, exhausted and filled with emotion, I decided to devote six months of my life to helping Catholic women of Northern Ireland to deal with media and work the press to their advantage. These women were bright, resourceful, and able to rear their families on a small government income as their husbands served long sentences in prison. Largely uneducated, they were determined to get their message out to the world, but lacked the know-how to deal with foreigners. Most of them suffered from low self-esteem.

I knew I could teach them about how to schedule and conduct press conferences and how to impart information about the British Government and its laws, which required no search warrant and allowed trial without jury. The world needed to hear about the practice of "lifting" men from their homes in the middle of the night without charges or evidence. I could also educate them about the significance of speaking publicly about the practice of interrogation: keeping prisoners up for several days and nights without benefit of a lawyer or the right to make a phone call.

I could accomplish this in six months. In half a year my oldest daughter would graduate from high school. I'd be home for that. Surely my family could spare me for half a year. I worried about my job. I worried that a leave-of-absence would be denied, that I'd lose my position and have little status when I returned. I met a man, educated and refined, whose wife Miriam had been a Catholic activist and the mother of twin daughters. On a recent afternoon, the girls had arrived home from school to find their front door ajar, their mother tied to a kitchen chair, shot through the head. Before the British soldiers left, they had ransacked the kitchen, spilling canisters of sugar and coffee and smashing a picture of the Sacred Heart of Jesus off the wall. They also destroyed the toilet, probably with the butt of a rifle. The twins could not be consoled, nor could their father. I sat with him as he fidgeted uneasily and drank tea. I told him of the appalling lack of coordination among the Catholics of the North. He nodded, but said the price of leadership was high.

He listened as I outlined a six-month program to make a group of women savvy with the news media. He was not discouraging, and said I'd be safe because I was now an American citizen. I wrote and filed another story and telephoned home to discuss my idea. My husband answered, terribly distraught. A report had come that morning to a suburban newspaper near our home about a local reporter killed on the streets of Belfast. The editor, surmising it was I, contacted guidance counselors at the high school my daughters attended. Janet, my oldest, was summoned to the school office where she telephoned her father at work. Meanwhile, the suburban editor telephoned the city desk of my newspaper in Lowell, Massachusetts, and as he talked the managing editor was alerted that the teletype machine was transmitting my morning article. The difference in hours was counted backwards and forwards and it became clear that I was alive and well and writing at the time of the alleged incident. I listened to an anxious husband relate the harrowing events. I listened as each of my daughters, all of them in tears, talked on the phone. All of them begged me to come home. I was humbled, and mortified that I had even considered abandoning my family for a six-month stint in a centuries-old war zone. I wept.

Bobby Sands was buried following a funeral procession covered by the world media, and a few days later, second hunger striker Patsy O'Hare succumbed to starvation. As he lay dying, an assassination attempt was made on Pope John Paul II, and the world press packed up and left Belfast for Rome. Journalists are like prostitutes. They go where the action is and follow editorial instructions like blind sheep. Nothing matters but the story.

I was not dispatched to Rome, but summoned home in time to write a Sunday magazine piece on my Ulster experience. I did as directed, was reunited with my family and made the deadline for the Sunday article. That night Patsy O'Hare died. I wept for the O'Hare family and abandoned my dream of guiding the women of Northern Ireland through the media maze. I was a woman, wife, mother, and a working journalist. I continued on, and ironically my next international assignment was the royal wedding of Prince Charles to Lady Diana.

Years have passed. My daughters are married, their father deceased. My achievements have multiplied, but the sense of failure has never left me. I could have devoted six months to developing media management skills for the women of Ulster. I failed and allowed circumstances of my life to curb my courage. I felt powerless to take a risk, an opportunity lost. Perhaps another will present itself someday and I will have the strength and determination to follow my heart.

her way

Naomi Shihab Nye

He only listened to his own secret bell, ringing,
and saw another winter come.

MAHMOUD DARWISH

What water she poured on the floor
was more than was needed. Someone suggested
she mop in strips as they did
on the television, yet her buckets were full,
the great buckets of field and orchard,
she was dragging them room to room
in a house that already looked clean.

The tune she hummed was nobody's tongue.
Already she had seen the brothers go off
in airplanes, she did not like the sound.
Skies opened and took people in.
The tune was long and had one line.

And the soldiers flipping ID cards,
the men who editorialized blood
till it was pale and not worth spilling,
meant nothing to her.
She was a woman shopping for fabric.
She was walking with her neck straight,
her eyes placed ahead.
What oil she rubbed on the scalp was pure.
The children she spoke to were news,

were listening, had names
and a scraped place on the elbow.
She could place a child in a bucket
and bathe it, could stitch the mouth
in the red shirt closed.

Reprinted from 19 *Varieties of Gazelle: Poems of the Middle East* (Greenwillow, 2002).

THE REAL SELF

the real self

Eric Liddell, the famed Scottish missionary and runner, equated faith to running a race, reflecting that the power to see the race to its end comes from within. Indeed, our greatest potential and confidence may emerge from putting one foot forward at a time to take life's risks. In the following essays and poems, we read of the "truth-telling" self (Muskie, 2000), the real or inner self of women that allows them to be courageous one step at a time in the face of overwhelming obstacles.

In "When I am Asked," Valerie Bridgeman Davis delves into her reserves "To reclaim the stolen esteem / And broken spirit of my offspring," pouring herself into raising strong black men amidst racism and social hostility. Bridgeman Davis knows that they are society's future and wants her sons' first response "to every adversity" to "be a straight back / And a stiffened will."

Similarly, Joan Loveridge-Sanbonmatsu faces negativity in raising "warrior" sons. In her poems "Enroute From Japan" and "Two Warriors,"she writes about nurturing her sons in a world where prejudice abounds. "Prejudice, in an instant, / is perceived. / Prejudice, like the trailing jellyfish tentacle / stings like a sea wasp / injecting toxic, paralyzing threads into its victim." Loveridge-Sanbonmatsu knows, as Ralph Waldo Emerson writes, that "to be yourself in a world that is constantly trying to make you something else is the greatest accomplishment," and creates sons "strong enough to ward off blows."

Similarly looking inward for personal strength, Kim Barnes finds the river to be the source of her real self. "What the river takes, the river gives, and so it is with my life here. Each hour I spend with my feet near water, I feel more deeply rooted; the further I get away, the less sure I am of my place in the world." At the same time she resents the power it has over her. "Like all seductions, it necessitates surrender." When Barnes puts herself and her children in its dangerous path, she writes, "I felt suddenly and awfully alone, not because of the isolation, but because I was a woman where I should not be, having risked too much for the river." It is then that she must find the power within herself to move them to safety.

Kenneth Patton writes that "by the choices and acts of our lives, we create the person that we are and the faces that we wear." We see this reflected in the women in Pat Mora's poem, "Doña Feliciana," and Janice Brazil's "Faces." Doña Feliciana is an old Mexican migrant woman without land or family. Yet, she brings a little cilantro with her because "even a little green helps in all this dust." Faced with nothing, she finds a way to make a home; "My arms hurt from dragging / boards. My head ached from banging, / but I lifted my house up, made myself a roof." The old woman in "Faces" hides "behind no mask / to shut out pain or darkened / streams of unrestrained emotion." After a life-time of living, she knows that "Your face is your power." Like those in Mora's and Brazil's poems, the woman in Rosemary Catacalos's poem "Swallow Wings" is also a survivor. But she too pulls herself up because "It ain't nothin' / 'bout lettin' go a this life." It is not some external force that sustains these women, but instead accepting who they are at the core of their being.

In "A Heart to Run," Valerie Bridgeman Davis learns that she has "too much firepower in the heart." She is a novice marathon runner who has just finished running eight miles with friends when she has a heart attack. In "My Heart Beats for You," she writes, "My heart saved my life / Its strength, its will turning back / An attack / Beat, beat / The power of life." Within the week she has a procedure to repair her heart defect. Determined, Bridgeman Davis returns to training and races just two months later. In "Marathon," she writes: "Mile 15 and the wall and dreams of / Finishing scare you / But you keep run-ning, churning / To complete what you started." As Liddell proclaimed, the power to finish the race comes from within.

Next, we see the real selves appear in a Biblical trilogy. In "Eve," Nanette Yavel paints a portrait of "Everywoman." She is created "from a twisted root that lay broken on the ground," shaped, fashioned, and set free by her creator. She is captured within Emerson's reflection, "Everything in nature contains all the power of nature." But Bonnie Lyons tells us that according to Jewish leg-end, the first woman created by God was Lilith, not Eve. In "Lilith Whispers," she refused to let Adam rule, and while "Adam named the animals / and plants," she loved them. Because Lilith was too independent, "Eve was created out of Adam's rib, / second sex, second forever." In "Judith Mourns," Lyons depicts another powerful woman who assassinates the enemy. But while her countrymen exulted her, afterwards, "no man ever invited me / under the wed-ding canopy / or even the bed canopy." If she had known "that my heroism / would unsex me," she wonders if she would have acted: "You are ruled through your desire."

The stories span across time. "No one ever said that risk-taking was easy," begins Ginger Purdy in her essay "Dancing on the Edge of the Ledge." After her marriage of sixteen years ends, she is left alone to raise three little girls. Although she has two university degrees and has worked as a fashion artist, at times the total responsibility for her daughters is overwhelming. Yet, she initiates a path that creates support and networking opportunities not only for herself but for great numbers of professional women, enriching all their lives. She writes, "You take the risk because you know that in doing so you are accomplishing what is necessary to complete the job, whether it is in raising children by yourself or daring to do a new thing for your community."

Demetrice Anntía Worley also risks finding her real voice. "Silence comes easily," she writes in "No Position Is a Position." She reflects that girls hold their breath and their tongues when told "you can't." In "Unlearning Not to Speak," Worley says that she "was a good girl, smiled a lot, / kept clean, a model member / of polite society." But in graduate school, she "died / with my mouth shut." Now less polite, she writes about reclaiming power through finding her voice.

"Giving up doesn't always mean you are weak; sometimes it means that you are strong enough to let go," is a lesson Nan Cuba has to learn. In her essay, "Confessions of a Compulsive Overachiever," she writes how she "pulled together twelve creative writing classes," to earn some money to help her son who had been diagnosed as manic-depressive. She named her creation "Gemini Ink," and as it grew it became an obsession, with initial workshops expanding into community programs for school children, senior citizens, and other groups. Gemini Ink gradually expanded to a staff of seven and over 3,000 students and audience members. Yet, despite her vast inner resources, running it began to exhaust Cuba. An overachiever, she struggled to discover a new self—putting her own needs first to find a balance in her life.

The women in this chapter have reached inside themselves for reserves to finish the race, through finding their real voice, following a dream, and learning how to let go. Perhaps Hacker summarizes it best in her sonnet sequence *Love, Death, and the Changing of the Seasons:*

> What does a girl do
> but walk across the world, her kid in tow,
> stopping at stations on the way, with friends
> to tie her to the mast when she gets too
> close to the edge? And when the voyage ends,
> What does a girl do? Girl, that's up to you.

when i am asked

Valerie Bridgeman Davis

For my sons

When I am asked, "What did you do for the revolution?"
I will answer that I was suckling the seeds
Of the next rebellion at my breast,
Raising black men whose first response
To every request will be "Why?"

I will answer that I was instructing the saplings
Of the next revolution in the school of my experiences,
Raising black men whose first response
To every adversity will be a straight back
And a stiffened will.

I will say that I used my time wisely,
Making forays into enemy territory
To reclaim the stolen esteem
And broken spirit of my offspring,
That I rocked them back to health
Time and again in the lap of my resolve.

When I am asked, "What did you do for the revolution?"
I will introduce to the world
My sons.

Reprinted from *Austin International Poetry Festival Anthology* (AIPF) 2002.
Winner: Second Place.

enroute from japan

Joan Loveridge-Sanbonmatsu

Touching down in the U.S.
my husband sighed, "Now it's back
to being a minority again."

two warriors

Joan Loveridge-Sanbonmatsu

(Central New York 1974–1983)

"Jamie's a Chink. Jamie's a Chink,"
taunted the school bus children.
The focus narrows
like the lens of a camera
on what is to come.
He was only seven then.
His memory did not numb.
To this day he remembers.

At first, we taught our warriors
not to fight—
fist fights were out
that was the rule.
When our first son appeared
nose bloodied, face bruised
then what? Parry their words.
"I'm rubber and you're glue.
Whatever you say
Bounces off me
And sticks to you."
"Don't give the fight fuel.
Issue a warning—
once, twice, then fight back
or leave," we cautioned.

Raising two warriors
to stand undiminished
hearts full
with *gambaru**

to meet this world
giving them a shield
to deflect racism,
a shield with tensile strength.
This has not been easy.

How should a note be explained?
A note left in our mailbox
that first week we moved here
asking—
"Why don't you go back
to the grass shacks
where you came from?"

What should the response be
when white families
in a small southern town
ride in a van up a steep hill
while our family was told
"You folks must walk."
And we trudged up the hill in 90-degree heat.

What should be done
when a play is typecast
"whites only" roles
yet there is no such sign posted
at the tryouts?
How should a child be
prepared for rejection, exclusion?

Prejudice, in an instant,
is perceived.
Prejudice, like the trailing jellyfish tentacle,
stings like a sea wasp
injecting toxic, paralyzing threads into its victim.

Our warrior is little no more.
I asked him, "Have you heard of any discriminatory
        remarks these days?"

"Not in a while."
I breathed in quietly, struggled, and risked—revealing
  "I never told you about a note
   in the mailbox out front
   when we first moved here."
Standing at the stove, barely fifteen years old
stirring a sauce,
he shook his head from side to side—
              "tch—prejudice," barely audible.
He understood.
Our warrior was little no more.
Older, taller, and wiser, he knew
his life would be touched by prejudice.

In the lateness of the night
I shared with a friend
who noted—"I guess
you were never used to it."
Silently, I nodded.
As a child, I never
heard racist chants
saw racist notes.
Whiteness surfaced.

Will the shields of our warriors ever be strong,
strong enough to ward off blows?
Will they take up the battles for change?

We have taught them to defend each other,
be a supportive family.
Bonding occurred.
We have shown them
to take a stand again injustice.
We showed them
to sift out important issues
like winnowed rice.

There still needs to be laughter.
There still needs to be a stronger strength.

Raising warriors with *gambaru, gambaru*—
it is not easy.

For Jamie and Kevin
Reprinted from *Winged Odyssey* (Hale Mary Press, 2002).

*Japanese for courage and energy.

the clearwater

Kim Barnes

I take the river a step at a time. My feet slide from the shoulders of rock; my toes wedge between boulders. I am timid about this, moving out toward the center, where the water is deepest, where the big fish might lie.

Here, at Lenore, Idaho, the Clearwater is not easy. Too wide to cast from shore, too swift, too pocked with hidden currents and sudden holes. I go at it anyway, still without waders, determined to find my place of stability, the water at my belly, my thighs numbing with cold.

My husband fishes below me. On shore, our daughter and son dig pools in the sand, and I feel a rush of gratitude, the joy of living only minutes from water, the same water my brother and I played in as children. It is as though I am reliving my own young life, there on the banks of the Clearwater, as though I exist in two dimensions and know the pleasure of each—the child's pure delight in the moment; the woman's recognition of continuance, of nostalgia, of the water around her and the sun on her face.

I choose a fly I think the fish might favor, its color the color of the day's light and leaves and wings. I praise its tufts and feathers, its hackle and tail. I load the line, thinking not of the S I must make through air but of the place above sand where the water eddies, the V above whitecaps, the purl below stone.

I do not think of the line or the fly or the fish as much as I think about the water moving against me, how the sky fills my eyes and the noise-that-isn't-noise fills my ears—the movement of everything around me like the hum of just-waking or sleep, blood-rush, dream-rush, the darkness coming on, the air.

I forget to watch for the fish to strike, forget to note the catch, the spin, the sinking. I pull the line in, let it loop at my waist, sing it out again, and again. The trout will rise, or they won't. The nubbin of fur and thread will turn to caddis, black ant, stone fly, bee, or it will simply settle on the water and remain a human's fancy. Either way, it's magic to me, and so I stay until my feet are no longer my own but part of the river's bed. How can I move them?

How can I feel my way back to shore, where my family is calling that it's time to go home? They are hungry, and the shadows have taken the canyon. They are cold.

From my place in the water, they appear distant to me. I must seem like a fool, numb to my ribcage, no fish to show. But I am here in the river, half-in, half-out, a wader of two worlds. I smile. I wave. I am where nothing can reach me.

North Fork, Middle Fork, South Fork, Main: see how the flow of the sounds is smooth, so lovely. The rivers themselves flow together this way, spilling down from the mountains. They drain the north Idaho land my father and others like him logged and loved so easily in the years before their doing so seemed to matter.

Now, as sales are staked and trees are spiked, the land slumps from beneath its covering of burned slash and razored stumps, slides off the hills and down the draws, sloughs off its dying skin like an animal readying itself for another season. Always, the run-off of rain, the soil it carries, the ash and cinder, the dry bones of trees.

Here, where I live with my husband and children above the Main Clearwater at Lenore, twelve miles from where the forks have all come together, we see the movement of land in the water's flow. Spring thaw, and the trees come fully rooted, ungrounded by the wash of high current. Old log jams from previous floods break loose; new ones pile against the bridge footings and small islands. Each becomes a nest of lost things: fishing lures, loops of rope, men's undershirts, women's shoes.

I wonder, sometimes, if my own life's mementos are contained in those tangles, perhaps a barrette I lost while fishing Reeds Creek, or one of my mother's pie tins with which my brother and I panned for gold. Or the trees themselves fallen from the riverbank I sat on as a child, searching for the mussel shells we called angel's wings, though they were mahogany brown and often broken.

What the river takes, the river gives, and so it is with my life here. Each hour I spend with my feet near water, I feel more deeply rooted; the further I get away, the less sure I am of my place in the world. For each of us, there must be this one thing, and for me it is the river. Not just the river, but the composition that begins as the North Fork and flows into the Main. I have known this river from its feeding waters to its mouth where it meets and becomes one with the Snake. I have known it before the dams, and after. I have known it as a child knows water, have known it as a lover knows water, and now as a mother knows and recognizes water as she watches her own children who are bent at the waist, leaning forward to bring up the sandy wings.

I am closest to the Clearwater when I am closest to its origins, and to my own. Reeds Creek, Orofino Creek, Weitas Creek, Deer Creek, the Musselshell—they feed the river as the river feeds me. It has taken me longer to feel intimate with the stretch of river that curves into *omega* below our house. I watch it each day, uneasy with its width and deep holes. I realize, too, that I distrust this length of the river because it no longer moves of its own volition: Dworshak Dam controls a great part of it. The North Fork, the river I once knew as a tree-lined stream the color of turquoise, now ends in a man-made reservoir covering over 50 miles of land that was first logged for its timber before being flooded. The river bulges at its base, its narrower neck seemingly unaffected by the distant, concrete obstruction. People drive northeast for hours to reach the Bungalow, Aquarius—places where the water remains swift and the fish are often native.

But I know better. The river's betrayal sometimes shames me, the way it carries on as though what it travels toward is not a state of near stasis, depositing sludge along miles of rip-rap dikes, piling its dross against the pylons and locks and turbines. It cannot rid itself of what it is given, cannot carry its silt and timber and ash to the mouth of the ocean where it can be broken down, taken to great depths, washed and sifted into sand and dirt. Instead, the silt falls from the slow current, depositing itself in great layers, narrowing the river's channel. The river becomes murky, the flat color of pewter. The trout are replaced by bottom-feeders, lovers of warm water. Every year, the Corps of Engineers sponsors a trash-fish derby, paying the fishermen to catch and kill what their dams have spawned.

Like so many others who love this land, it has taken me some time to understand that this place—its rivers and streams, forests, mountains and high meadows—does not absorb but reflects what we bring to it. Perhaps, then, what I see in the river is some mirror of the contradictions that make up my own life—the calm surface, the seeming freedom. Certainly, the river is a metaphor for memory. "I am everything I ever was," Stegner wrote, and so it is with the river—water and rock, metal and mineral, stick and bone, trout-flash and deer-lick. Perpetual, even in the face of destruction, I think, even as I read the sad stories of pollution and poisoning, fish-kill and disease. Perpetual because the rain must fall and the mountains must accept and the water must run toward ocean. A comfort, knowing that the amount of water in our world never changes, that there is never any more nor any less, only the same and in various forms: ice, liquid, steam. I trust that water will withstand, given its basic demands—to fall, to move, to rise, to fall again.

This, then, may be my final recognition: the inevitability of movement. We slow, we go forward. We age. We rise to greet each morning. We fall into sleep each night. Constant as rain, perpetuated in death and birth and rebirth.

It has taken me time to understand the need I feel to be consumed by the river. Raised a stoic, I am seldom given to need. Need is a weakness, a loss of control, the Achilles' heel of human existence. My connection to the river is complicated by its pull; I resent the power it possesses to draw me. Yet I want its sound in my ears, its smell, its taste. I want to be immersed—my hands, my feet, my hips. Like all seductions, it necessitates surrender.

I am learning to let go.

I bring to the river my love and those that I choose to love. I bring to it my child's memories and my woman's life. I bring to it hunger but always joy, for whatever it is that weighs on me dissipates in those few miles between our house in the canyon and the water's edge.

I understand how water can become something grim, how it can rise and take and swirl and drown. How it can become something to fight against, something to resist. The dam on the North Fork, the largest of its kind, was built not for electricity or simple recreation, they say, but for flood control in Portland, 400 miles west.

There's less flooding now, although, in 1996, not even the dams could keep pace when the temperatures rose and the snowmelt came down with rain. We watched from our house above the river, stranded between washed-out roads, watched the roots and porches, the dead cows and refrigerators and lawn chairs, the still-intact trailer house that slammed against the Lenore Bridge.

How can I cheer such destruction? For that is what I felt, an overwhelming sense of boosterism. I wanted the river to win in some essential way, wanted to see it rise up and lash out, pull down the dams and drain the reservoirs, ferry away the docks and cleanse itself of silt. I wanted it to show a god's righteous anger, a larger reflection of my own frustration and resentment.

I didn't mind, then, that we couldn't get out. My husband had made a last, grand effort to snatch our children from their school in Orofino 20 miles east, hauling them back over bench roads not yet torn away by the massive run-off, roads that crumbled and disappeared behind them. Other rural parents with children in school were not so lucky: it would be a week before any travel was allowed in or out, except by helicopter. Our family was together, protected by our place high on the canyon wall. We had food, water, firewood. We had days ahead of us without school or teaching, weeks before the roads would be cleared, and now the sun that had started the ruin was back out and warming the air into spring.

We packed sandwiches and cookies, cheese and crackers and a bottle of fine red wine. We hiked to where we could watch Big Eddy, the place where the river curled against itself and created an enormous back current that caught and held the debris. While the river ran thick with trees and fence posts, goat huts and wallpapered sheeting, we ate and drank and gathered ladybugs for our garden. Certain logs were red with their hatching, their coming out of hibernation. We scooped them up in handfuls and carried them in bundles made of paper towels and candy wrappers. Their odor was strong, dry, astringent—a promise of summer.

We watched a jetboat make its way down the river. Foolish, we thought, to risk such danger. The river was running at a near-record high; the water was choked with flotsam, some larger than the boat itself. The two men inside were not wearing lifejackets, and I shook my head. What were they thinking?

The boat pulled in at a smaller eddy downstream, and there we saw what they followed: a large raft of finished lumber, floated loose from the mill at Orofino. Scavengers' rights. If they were willing to risk it, the lumber was theirs.

One man kept the helm while the other bent over the gunnels to grab the wood. They pulled it onto the boat's bow one plank at a time until the craft sat low in the already threatening water. We held our breath, knowing that if they were to fall overboard or if the boat capsized, we could do nothing but watch.

They loaded the wood. They let the current swing them about, turn them upstream. They made their way slowly, navigating through tangles of barbed wire still stapled to barn doors, past trees three times the length of their boat. They had their booty. They were gone.

I couldn't imagine such nonsense, such greed. What desperation could bring on the willingness to risk so much for so little? I felt content, driven by nothing other than the warmth on my shoulders and the love I felt for this land and my husband and daughter and son, who gathered around me to show what they had found: a mantid's egg case, triangular and strangely textured, like meringue hardened and fired to a ceramic glaze. We would take it home as well and put it in the garden, where it would hatch its eaters of grasshoppers and aphids.

I must have believed, then, that it was love that would see me through the long hours of darkness, that would keep me grounded during the wild summer heat. I must have believed that, like the river, what we love may surge and wane but remains nonetheless constant, giving, taking, carrying on.

And doesn't it? Perhaps it is we who fail love, refusing to allow its seduction, its pull and sway. Love is a river we step into, like the waters of baptismal rebirth. We close our eyes. We bow our heads. We allow ourselves to be taken as the water closes over us. For that moment, we must believe.

"I don't think we can make it." I looked at what was left of the road, stretching down before me into a dusk of low trees. August, and I needed the river's cool.

My daughter and son moaned. After a day of writing, I had picked them up from the sitter's in Orofino, promising a late afternoon along the water. My husband was in the mountains near McCall, hiking the upper lakes, safe with the friends he'd known since high school. There was a place I'd heard of, just down some side road, where Ford's Creek met the river, a place with sand and eddies, where Jordan and Jace could swim and I could spread my blanket and think. The stretch of river we were after mattered to me: it was a section of the last few miles of the Main Clearwater, the last free-flowing water between the headwaters and the ocean.

I needed the river in a way I had not only hours before. It wasn't fishing I was after. I was sour with bad news, begrudging even the rod, line, and fly their pacification. That afternoon, I'd gotten a phone call from across the country and learned that our close friends' marriage was in sudden and serious peril, rocked by confession of a particularly insidious spate of infidelity. The levels of betrayal had shocked me, and the narrative of contentment and ongoing friendship that I had trusted was suddenly gone.

The anger that I felt surprised me. I am not comfortable with anger, having been taught from the cradle that anger, like need, is best kept under lock and key, somewhere in the heart's deepest chamber. The river would sweep away the confusion of emotions with its own ordered chaos. The river would help me find my footing, my point of rest.

But now this: I'd chosen the wrong road. Even after having made the decision to put the car into reverse and back our way out of the ravine, we were going nowhere. The tires of the front-wheel drive Toyota spun and chattered in the gravel, unable to push the weight of the car up such a steep incline. The dirt and basalt-studded bank rose close on my left; the road crumbled away on my right, slumping into a gully of black locust, poison ivy, and blackberry brambles thick with thorns.

"Now what." I said it in the way my mother always had. Fatalism. Tired resignation.

I eased the clutch, tried again. Nothing but smoke and the bitter smell of burning rubber.

"I think we'd better get out of the car," Jace said. At seven, he was the cautious one, always sensing the adult's boundless capacity for error.

"No," I said. "It's okay. Let's just go on down. We can turn around at the bottom." I had no idea if this were true, but my choice was to keep going or for us all to begin the long walk back to town for a tow-truck. I also felt a kind of apathy: what was the worst that could happen? The river was only 500 yards away. We'd find our way out.

What we found instead was an increasingly narrow once-road. I saw that, for years, the rain had washed down the path scraped from the hillside, taking what dirt remained with it to the river. What was left was a deep schism that forked and meandered its way around rocks too large to be moved. I concentrated on riding the ruts' shoulders until there was no rut to straddle but only a series of woven ditches. I kept thinking it would get better, that the road would even out, that *someone* had made it down here because the vegetation was scraped from the center. I kept wishing for the old Suburban with its high clearance and granny-gear, but I doubted that the path we traveled would have allowed its girth.

We bounced over boulders the size of basketballs. The skidplate caught and dragged. Jordan and Jace whimpered in the backseat. I tried to act as though this were nearly normal, to be expected. If I stayed calm, in control, they would feel safe.

"Mom, please." Jordan had her hand on the doorhandle, as though she meant to jump.

"We're almost there," I said. "We'll get to the river and be glad." We were far into the darkness of trees now, the yellow pine and locust, the dense undergrowth of vine maple. I jostled the car around a corner, then stopped. I could see ahead to where the road leveled off, where sunlight broke through. Between us and that point of flat ground was a final pitch downward, where the road hooked a 90-degree right angle. The bigger problem was that the trail became narrower still, hedged in by the bank on the left and, on the right, an old tanker truck settled into a bog of brambles.

I examined my passage. A boulder twice the size of our car protruded like a tumor from the eight-foot dirt bank. The abandoned tanker, its red paint faded to rust, was just as intractable: steel and stone, and only the space of a small car between them.

If I stop here, I thought, the tow-truck might still be able to reach us. But I had begun to doubt the plausibility of such a rescue, given the tight turns and narrow corridor down which we had traveled. I thought cable, winch, but could not imagine the logistics of being dragged backward from the ravine without damaging the car beyond repair.

"Mom?" My son's voice quavered.

"What?" I was snappish, weighing our chances, calculating the risk.

"Can't we just walk from here?"

I thought of the brambles, the probability of rattlesnakes, what unseen dangers might wait around the corner.

"Just hang on." I inched the car toward the passage, like Odysseus steering his ship through the straits. I sucked in and held my breath, giving the air what room I could. One scrape and we were through and bumping into the clearing.

Whoops and hollers from the backseat. "We made it!" Jace shouted. Jordan crowed. I stopped the car, got out and circled it twice, looking for damage. Nothing but a few shallow scratches. No dripping oil. The muffler remained miraculously intact.

"Watch for snakes. Wait for me." I gathered our water bottles and bag of sandwiches, taking in the lay of the land. Between us and the river was the railroad track, built high on its ridge of rock. To the left, I saw the remnants of a gold mine, its entryway framed in old timbers. To my right was a settling pond, green with algae. As we began our short walk, two blue herons rose from the still water, awkward on their wings.

There was a game trail, which we followed to the tracks and over. What we found was a long beach of rocks and a smaller one of sand. The children had all but forgotten the trauma of our trip and stripped themselves of shoes and socks before wading in. I felt the heat, then, the sweat gone sticky at my collar and waist.

I walked a few yards upstream, found a rock close to water, where I could dangle my feet and keep an eye on my son and daughter. I tried not to think of the sun's low slant, the hard way out. I tried not to hear what I was thinking: there is no way out of here except to leave the car and walk. No way I could make that first climb and twist between the rock and truck.

I closed my eyes. The river filled my ears, and I began to float with the sound. I needed to find something to dislodge the fear—not only of the trek ahead of us, but the fear that had come while listening to my friend's grieving. It could happen, any time, any place, to anyone. One minute, you're on solid ground, the next moment the earth has cracked open beneath you. You get up in the morning and look in the mirror and tell yourself what the day will consist of, and then the light jerks sideways and you are left falling through the dark.

Behind me, a dog barked. I turned to see a large yellow Lab, and then an older man walking the tracks. He stopped and raised his hand in acknowledgement of our presence. I hesitated, suddenly aware of another danger: a woman, two children, alone.

He could help us, I thought. He might live close by, have a tractor or winch. I thought, I can't let him know we're stuck here, can't let him see how vulnerable we are.

"How's it going?" he yelled.

I nodded and gave him a thumb's up. He stood for a long time, and I thought he might decide to walk toward us. And then what? For all I knew he was one of my father's old logging friends. For all I knew, he was a transient bent on some evil.

He stayed on the track, and I watched him disappear around the bend. There was too much to be afraid of, too much to fear. I rose and waded the rocks toward my children, suddenly distrusting even the river, its currents here strange and unpredictable.

They were making a catch basin for the small minnows they caught in the net of their hands. They hardly noticed my presence. I should have them gather their things, I thought, hustle them toward the car, or herd them in front of me up the rag of road, where we could walk the asphalt into town. It would take hours, I knew, hours into dusk, a woman and two children on a rural road where few cars traveled after dinner. I could hear my mother's scolding voice, the one I have known all my life, consistent through all my unwomanly adventures and forays: "What in the world were you thinking? What could have made you take such a risk?"

Risk. I looked across the river, where Highway 12 tied east to west. Cars flicked through the trees, distant and quick. I knew the benefits of being where I was: the water comforted me, the sand and rock and cottonwood leaves turning golden in the last rays of sun. I needed this, often and sometimes desperately. I believed, too, that my children were made better by such a landscape, that every handful of water they dipped from the river was an hour they would later remember as good.

But why here? Why hadn't I been content to take the easy way, pull off the road and find the familiar beaches and banks, Pink House Hole or Big Eddy, Myrtle or Home Beach?

I looked up, then down the far bank. This part of the Clearwater was different than farther downriver. Not so big. The rocks on the other side seemed still part of the canyon wall, huge and jagged from the blasts of road-making. Maybe it was good to be in a place I had not memorized, to be surprised by stone and current. I ran my hand through the water, patted the back of my neck. I needed to remember what I believed in, remember that things might just as easily go good as bad.

I called my children in. They refused to be hurried, reluctant as I to face the trip out, though it would be much easier, I had cozily assured them, going up than down.

Mosquitoes clouded around us as we walked from the river toward the pond. My daughter swatted frantically: they are drawn to her especially, and their bites leave her swollen and miserable.

"Hurry," I said. "It's getting dark. We need to get out while there's still light."

We crowded in, full of sand and river smells. I made a last check of the ground beneath the car: no oil or other inappropriate leakage. We made a tight turn, and I sighed as we faced the hill. What was it worth to attempt the ascent, lose the muffler, bash in the doors? We wouldn't be killed. What were my choices? It seemed an impossible decision.

I thought of the mosquitoes, the long walk out with two tired children, our feet rubbed raw by wet shoes and sand. I said, "Buckle your seatbelts and lock your doors." I gave the engine more gas than usual.

The first pitch was not dirt and rock but a slick of muddy clay beneath a thick layer of pine needles. We spun, then began sliding backwards, back into the long thorns of locust, over boulders and humps because the car could not be steered in such muck.

When we came to a stop, I leaned forward, rested my forehead against the wheel. I thought I might cry.

"Mom?" My son's voice was high, nearly shrill.

"Yes, Jace."

"I'm out of here."

He opened his door before I could stop him, slammed it shut and ran for the railroad tracks. Jordan was fast behind.

I rolled down my window. "Okay," I said. "You stay right there, this side of the tracks. Don't you move. If I can get past this first pitch, we'll make it. When you hear me honk, come running." They nodded, miserable among the mosquitoes, shaking in the suddenly cool air.

I backed up as far as I could, put the car in first, gunned the engine and popped the clutch. I hit the hill with my tires screaming, went up, careened sideways, bounced off the boulder, lost traction and stalled, then slid all the way back down, cringing with the screech of metal against rock, wood against metal.

I need to focus on the initial few yards instead of the dog-leg corner at its summit, I thought—the boulder bulging from the hillside, the tanker truck with its sharp edges. If things went well, we could get out with minimal damage. If things went badly, I might slide down into the gully with the truck, be swallowed by blackberries, have to fight my way out of thorns and lord knew what else.

I got out of the car, tried to pull some of the larger rocks off the road, broke off what branches I could. I scuffed at the pine needles, realizing the uselessness of it: the ground underneath was saturated with moisture. I backed up, got a stronger run. Black smoke clouded around me. I gained a foot before sliding back down.

I went at it hard then, again and again, as the sun settled lower in the west and the sky darkened. I was still afraid, still fearing too much power, too much speed. It was best to keep control, stay steady. But I got no farther. Always, almost to the top, and then the sudden spin and slide.

How many times? Twenty? Thirty? I didn't care about the car anymore, hardly heard the worried cries of my children. I was feeling something building inside of me, something I hadn't felt for a long time. It was hard and headlong, heedless in a way that might be brave. I'd felt it often before, when I was younger and wildly free. No husband. No children. Only my own life in my hands. I'd felt little fear of anything then, and it was a comfort. Now, with so much to love and lose, I'd come to cherish the expected, the easy ways. Risk came in larger increments: sickness, infidelity, divorce, death. I'd begun to live my life as though, by giving up the smaller risks, I could somehow balance out the larger, keep the big ones at bay with a juju bargain—the sacrifice of whatever independence and strength such risks brought me.

Sitting there, the car smelling of rubber and smoke, the heat and the mosquitoes and darkness coming on, I felt something else, and it was anger. Anger at what I feared and must fear, anger that I was where I was and in possible danger.

I felt suddenly and awfully alone, not because of the isolation, but because I was a woman where I should not be, having risked too much for the river.

The car idled. I hit the dash with the heel of my hand. I let all of it come into me, then—the anger I felt at love and death, at men who might hurt me and men who never would, at the car and the land in its obstinacy. I felt the quiver in my belly and the rush of heat that filled my ears. I needed speed, momentum to carry me through.

I revved the engine, popped the clutch. I made the turn and didn't slow down. I kept it floored. I hit the boulder, jerked the wheel hard to the left, hit the truck. The tires spun. I didn't know what was behind me now, what I might slide into. I turned the wheel this way, then that, seeking purchase. I yelled at the top of my lungs, "You son-of-a-bitch, go!" And then I was up that first pitch and breathing.

The kids came running, screaming, shouting. They piled gleefully into the car. We were going to make it. Everything was okay.

But it wasn't, because now there was another pitch, and then another. We spun. We stalled.

They got out. They ran all the way back to the railroad tracks.

I rocked the car back against the tanker. Bounce, spin, back. Bounce, spin, back. Each time a little farther, and when I found my ground and started careening up, I didn't stop. I bounced the car out of the canyon, figuring the exhaust system was already gone, figuring it had all been decided hours ago and this was the final scene.

When I got to the highway, I set the emergency brake and jogged back down. Jace and Jordan were coming to meet me, exhausted and still frightened. I batted at the mosquitoes and hurried us all up the hill. I was laughing, giddy with adrenaline. They were weepy, a little confused by my gaiety. They never wanted to do it again.

"It was an adventure," I told them. "And see? We're fine."

As we drove the highway home, I felt vibrant, exhilarated. The moon rising was the most beautiful thing, the wind through the windows a gift. I'd check the car for damage tomorrow, but for now nothing could touch us.

My children would sleep well, and I knew that in years to come, they would tell this story and the story would change and remain the same. Always, there would be the road we traveled, the rocks, the ruts, the mine to the east, the tanker to the west. There would be the night and mosquitoes, the smoke as they watched the car beat its way out of the canyon. There would be their mother's foolishness or her bravery, her stubborn refusals. The words might change, and maybe their fear. But always, there would be the river. It would run cold and loud beside them, the water they cupped in their hands and held above the sand to be sieved and drained and cupped again.

It will keep them near me. It will carry them away.

This essay first appeared in *River Teeth: A Journal of Non-Fiction Narrative* (Fall, 1999). It was reprinted in *Written on Water: Essays on Idaho Rivers* (University of Idaho Press, 2001).

doña feliciana

Pat Mora

Ven. Come inside. Es mi casa,
two rooms I built from wood scraps.
Look at the nails, bent como mis dedos.
They spilled us like garbage,
the landowners with the big trucks, spilled us
in this bare field with our pots, sheets,
shoes stiff and old as tree bark.

At first, niños raced across the land,
gulping in all the new wide air.
They ran laughing into the emptiness,
no trees, no mangoes and avocados lying in the shade,
no houses, no plastic water buckets,
no tomato plants, no small fires, no gallinas,
nothing, no thing in their way.

I brought just one plant, a little cilantro,
placed it in this blue tin pot. Smell it,
even a little green helps in all this dust.
Es mi casa. I am my family, widow
without children. Mis compañeros and I have no land,
not even a stream of water thin as a thread.

The first nights in this bare place, mosquitoes
sucked and sucked until I had to build a house.
Alone, at sixty-three. My arms hurt from dragging
boards. My head ached from banging,
but I lifted my house up, made myself a roof.
See? Two rooms: here I sleep, here I cook arroz.

Nights I lie in the dark and listen to the wind,
whisper to my viejo, "I did it.
I built myself a house.
I hung my blue tin pot outside my door."

faces

Janice H. Brazil

"We make our faces as we go along."
The ancient woman spoke in a dream—
like trance, staring out from sightless
eyes, her vision 20/20. Old age
burned in her eyes, wrinkling

once smooth skin. Yet her words
danced upon the ear in rhythms
the very young could feel.
Power and perception
from a lifetime of living,

were channeled in features
chiseled by nature's sculptor.
Her face, creased and engraved
with rivulets of time, harbored
memories of an earlier spring.

She hid behind no mask
to shut out pain or darkened
streams of unrestrained emotion.
"Your face is your power." She continued
to sing, chanting her song of life.

swallow wings

Rosemary Catacalos

for Maya Angelou, with profound
respect and gratitude

I been to church, folks,
I'm an East Side Meskin Greek and
I been to church. I'm here to say
I grew up hearin' folks sing over hard
times in the key of, *Uh, uh, girl. It ain't nothin'*
'bout lettin' go a this life.
I grew up in a 'hood where every day at noon
black girls at Ralph Waldo Emerson Junior High School
made a sacred drum of the corner mailbox, beatin'
on it to raise the dead. And make them dance.
I grew up readin' in the George Washington Carver
Library, and marvelin' at the white
lightnin' gloves that Top Ladies of Distinction
use for church. I grew up where grits is *indeed*
groceries, and a huge mountain of a woman passed
my house daily, always sayin' the same thing:
Your name Rosemary? My name Rosemary, too.
I grew up, folks, and I been down 'til I couldn't
get no more down in me. And now a preacher lady
come to town and caused me to paint my face and
put on some good clothes and go to church.
And I'm here to say I have a right
to take this tone, 'cause it ain't nothin'
'bout lettin' go a this life.
Swallows keep makin' their wings
out to be commas on the sky.
World keep sayin' and, and, and, and
and.

Reprinted from *Again for the First Time* (Tooth of Time Books, 1984).

my heart beats for you

Valerie Bridgeman Davis

One beat, two, three beats of the heart
This is the part that matters,

The gift of life

One beat, two beats away from the truth
No ruthless undertaking
As we unfold a divine plan,
A holy order taking over
The universe

The heart tells a tale of strength—
Makes sense of nothing,
Sense of everything
Power surging,
Urging the Powers That Be
To sing a lullaby
To each of you

My heart saved my life
Its strength, its will turning back
An attack
Beat, beat
The power of life

Here's what I remember: running, breathe
Rhythm, breathe
Wind in my face,
The grace of sure-footed power,
The knowing: you're in it for the long haul

And then, the rest, and restlessness,
Feeling light-headed, heart racing,
Tracing every memory of a heart open
To new and rare experiences,
The love of many people
Every memory a prayer,
Daring my heart to stop

Here's what I remember: breathe, beat, rhythm, beat

I am fading to black; a one-ton man is on my chest,
My arms, my heart hurt; I can't feel my legs
Panic in the face of companions, stricken
With fear of death

I close my eyes, hold my breath,
A prayer: O God, my heart beats for you
O God, my heart beats for you
My heart beats for you

One beat, two, three beats of the heart
This is the part that matters,

The gift of life

One beat, two beats away from the truth
Death is no friend of mine
I offer my life to a saving,
Creating divine

Here's what I remember: Breathe, beat, rhythm, beat

One tech, two, three techs reporting
Distorting facts: I can't get a pulse,
I can't find a pressure—can you?

No fear of death
I close my eyes, hold my breath
A prayer: O God, my heart beats for you

O God, my heart beats for you
My heart beats for you

My heart saved my life
Holding on to all that matters:
LIFE IS PRECIOUS/LOVE IS RARE
There are those, like me, who dare to live
With a wide-open heart
Full of power, unafraid
Of inescapable pain

With a heart open
Without reserve, without borders
To pull people in, near
Give each of you a separate room,
To groom you for your own power
My heart beats

Here's what I remember:
Fading to black
Coming to life
Holding my place on the planet:

For my God, my kin, my loves, my friends
My heart beats for you.

Reprinted from *My Heart Beats for You*
(Friendship Ring Publications, 1999).

a heart to run

Valerie Bridgeman Davis

We had just finished an 8-mile run along the Town Lake Hike and Bike trail in Austin. All of us, novice marathoners, were tired, but exhilarated. I decided on my fortieth birthday, January 15, 1999, that I would train for a marathon as a challenge to myself. I joined the Leukemia Society's challenge, sure that running for a good cause would keep me interested, and running with a group would keep me motivated. The day of the first 8-miler was March 13. When we started training just over eight weeks before, none of us imagined that we would get to 8 or 10 miles and not keel over from exhaustion. We high-fived each other congratulations around the water cooler, then headed for our cars. We were proud of our selves and of each other.

By the time I reached my car, I began to feel light-headed. My heart was racing. I thought, "it'll calm down in a minute; I'm just excited." But by the time I reached my car, I was afraid that I would pass out. I got into the car and pressed the horn. My running mates thought I was saying goodbye. To get them to come over, I leaned my seat all the way back and put my foot on the horn. Several people ran to the car. I was reaching for my cell phone; people were screaming. "I'm having an asthma attack," I reasoned, trying to calm myself down. I tried to take deep breaths, and then use my inhalant. But my arms and legs were getting heavy, and my chest felt as if someone was sitting on me. I called 911. So did three other people.

Within two minutes, a police car was on the scene; right behind them was the fire truck. A minute or so later, EMS was giving me oxygen and an aspirin. I thanked God for cell phones, and closed my eyes trying to calm myself.

When I arrived at the South Austin Hospital, my husband and a friend met the ambulance. Hooked to monitors and prayers, I just kept telling myself to calm down. I nodded to my husband, trying to let him know I believed I would be okay. I watched the team of medical personnel work around me and told myself that they were doing all they could.

When the emergency room doctor came in, he said my EKG indicated that I had a rarely seen congenital defect. "Did anyone ever tell you that you had a heart defect as a child?" he asked. No one had. "I'm bringing in a cardiologist," he said. "He'll be here within the hour. In the meantime, try to relax."

Relax. I consciously had been trying to relax all along. Now I was curious about a congenital heart defect. Hospital personnel walked in and out of the room, looked at the monitor, and made grunts and nodded at each other. Whatever was in my IV made me relaxed and sleepy, so though I noticed them, I tried not to be concerned. Finally, the first doctor came in and said that people were coming in because it was a teaching hospital, and I was probably the only person they would see with WPW in their practice. "What's WPW?" I wanted to know. Wolff Parkinson's White Syndrome, the doctor explained: too much firepower in the heart.

By the time the cardiologist Dr. Tucker arrived, I was just anxious to go home. Dr. Tucker came in dressed in a leather jacket and Texas boots. A biker doc, I laughed to myself. "Well, now. I see your heart decided to attack you," he said. So, I'd had a heart attack. No one had used that phrase.

"You had a heart attack because of the congenital defect," Dr. Tucker explained gently. "But your heart saved your life. There's no damage to the walls of the heart. Good thing you were training for a marathon. And, if you're going to have a heart problem, better an electrical problem than a plumbing problem," he said.

The look on my face said I didn't understand. "You have an extra electrical path in your heart," he said. "We need to go in and repair it. I'd like to do it tomorrow." Tomorrow!!! I was not ready for heart surgery. "Do I have to do it this soon?" I asked. "I need time to get ready for a major surgery."

Dr. Tucker said that if I promised not to do anything strenuous, including walking fast, and promised to get the surgery within the week, he would send me home. "Oh, and thank your heart," he said. "It saved your life." Twelve days later, on March 25, I lay in the outpatient surgery unit, waiting to have a procedure that would not open my chest, but would repair my heart.

"I have a party hat and the happy juice," the technician said.

"As long as I'm the only one drinking it, we have a party," I joked.

Four hours later—two hours earlier than expected—the doctor who'd actually performed the procedure, Dr. Randall, stood by my bed. "You came out very well," he said. "If you'd have had the same heart attack ten years later, you most likely would have died on the spot. But your heart's strong. It probably saved your life." I smiled—thankful for the idea to start training for a marathon, thankful for a heart attack that uncovered a congenital defect. Thankful for modern medicine. Thankful to God.

"You can still run the marathon, you know," Dr. Tucker said when he saw me a week later. "Just slower than you expected, but your heart's good to go." I had thought I wouldn't be able to give myself my fortieth birthday present. But I started back training. On May 23, 1999, I completed the Suzuki Rock n' Roll Marathon in San Diego, California, in just less than six hours. I didn't set any course records. But two months after a heart attack and surgery, I danced my way across the finish line.

marathon

Valerie Bridgeman Davis

"Oh, hell, you've come this far, you
might as well finish"
> —a sign along the Suzuki
> Rock-n-Roll Marathon route at
> mile 25, May 23, 1999.

The first 14 miles are pure adrenalin,
Running in the press of the crowd,
The thump of your heart
In your chest, frantic,
And you know you can make it,
Destination secure, pace sure—
No doubt—the crowd amens
Your resolution with each pound
Of sneaker to pavement

The first 14 miles are pure adrenalin,
The pacesetters run to keep up
With the throng, several among many,
Many and the one together

When the wall arises, sizes you up,
Trying to determine how determined
You are—but your destination is blurred
By the whirr of racers outpacing you,
By the sound of your heart in your ears,
By the strength of your own panting,
The ranting in your brain: "what have I gotten myself into?"

And you're afraid to stop for water,
For air, for relief, afraid you'll never start
Running again. It's your will
Against the wall, and stopping is not
An option. You will not allow
The overwhelming distance
Between beginning and ending to co-opt you,
Change a decision you made to finish
When finishing seemed possible

The tears well up, fall down
Your cheeks and stopping
Is not an option, even with the burn
In your thighs, the sting in your eyes,
Mile 15 and the wall and dreams of
Finishing scare you
But you keep running, churning
To complete what you started

At mile 25, a sign of sagedom greets you,
Arises to meet your tired and dropping resolve,
And new decision forms at its reading:
"Oh, hell, you've come this far"—
A man, the age of your father, waves
This wisdom from the crowd, and loud
Echoes sound in your feet—
"Oh, hell, you've come this far, you might as well
Finish"—and you do

eve

Nanette Helena Yavel

This carving of Eve, emerged like David.
He from an abandoned marble slab,
She from a twisted root that lay broken on the ground.
With clear intent, I peeled the bark,
And found her shapely waist,
The bulbs of knees,
A single breast.

One arm spiraled, its hand a serpent's mouth.
The other, large and like a wing, lay welded to her back.
She was burdened by this weight,
So I whetted down the knife and shaped her gently,
Not to break her crucial parts.

I took her shoulders in my hands,
And scraped the dust,
Until the Devil's horned embedded head
Peered up at me. The tie was strong.

So I took her long eccentric limbs and fashioned swans,
Cut elephants and apes into her graceful frame,
And on her slender neck,
I placed a silver ring, one that I had never worn.

I had bought it years ago,
Not knowing that it held,
Diana's handsome features,
With turtle doves entwined.

Eve's stately form,
Unbalanced, could not stand.

The Tempter's weight
Was far too heavy on her wings.

I wound a wire above her ribs,
Where he and she were joined,
And set her free.

Now she sails above my bed
At her own deliberate speed.
A huntress smile on her face
The Devil hoisted on her back.

lilith whispers

Bonnie Lyons

Don't turn around.
Even though I'm clothed
in dark disguise
you do not dare
look me in the face
even in your sleep.

I'm Lilith, the original woman,
the one you call the first witch.
Let men scare you and control you
by telling you I kill babies
and you, docile daughters of Eve—
believe them.

I'm not mentioned
in their magic book,
but you can find me
in the traces
of the true version they
forgot to erase.
I am the woman
God created when God created
humans—female and male in God's image.
Made of the earth like Adam
and at the same moment;
from the beginning
I refused
to let him rule.

Adam named the animals

and plants
but I loved them.
Adam divorced himself with his words;
I embraced them
with my body.

So in the second version
Eve was created out of Adam's rib,
second sex, second forever.
And look at the punishment
for curiosity and independence.
Don't you see?
You are ruled through your desire.
But my boundless ecstatic
desire to mate
with the world itself
is the source of my power.

My existence
between the lines
is necessary.
This alone explains
those scorched bodies
of free women.
How else explain
men's dreadful fear
of you?

Wake up now, and forget.

In Genesis 1:26–28, there are two versions of the creation of the first woman. According to Jewish legend, the first woman, who was created at the same time as Adam and out of the same earth, is Lilith.

Reprinted from *In Other Words* (Pecan Grove Press, 2004).

judith mourns

Bonnie Lyons

Devout, comely, wise
even rich,
I was all
these things
but the defining word,
the only one that matters

is widow.

As a virgin or a wife
how could I have gone?
What husband or father
or leader
would have permitted me?
It was only because I belonged
to no man
no father, no husband.

Did I kill Holofernes
or did he kill himself
when he threatened to have me
in the morning
and then collapsed
into a drunken stupor,
head thrown back
beckoning my knife?

I returned
carrying his head carefully
wrapped in the canopy of his bed
and they exulted:

the enemy killed
and by a *woman*.

But later, no man ever invited me
under the wedding canopy
or even the bed canopy.
If I had known
that my heroism
would unsex me,
would cost me
the swooning ecstasy
of the piercing thrust
would I have taken on
my saving plan?

In Judith 1–16, Holofernes, the chief captain of the enemy Assyrian army, threatened to annihilate
all the children of Israel. After piously praying for God's help, Judith determined to deceive Holofernes
into thinking she was a traitor to her own people and to murder him instead.

Reprinted from In Other Words (Pecan Grove Press, 2004).

dancing on the edge of the ledge
Ginger Purdy

No one ever said that risk-taking was easy. I discovered that for myself when my marriage of sixteen years came to an end. I was left alone to raise three little girls, one of whom was just three weeks old. Knowing that I was responsible for their future well-being sometimes overwhelmed me, even though I had two degrees and freelanced as a fashion artist.

I had inherited a good work ethic from my mother and since my husband contributed only a small amount toward child support, I swallowed my fear when I was asked to lead the San Antonio Professional Chapter of Women in Communications, Inc., now called "The Association of Women in Communications." During my tenure with them, I learned that I could lead, and that in turn prepared me for one of the greatest risks I would take in my professional career.

At a conference in San Diego in the fall of 1979, I attended a seminar called "Network Power." This was a new term for women coming together for mutual help. At the conference I met my networking mentor, Alina Novak. Alina was one of the early networking "mothers" in New York who had started a corporate networking group in one of the largest businesses in the city. Her influence helped change my life.

I came home convinced that this "networking" would not only bring awareness and prestige to my chapter, but would help many other women outside communications as well. Alina promised to come to San Antonio to teach us how to network with power. But instead of embracing the idea, the program chair and the special events chair of my group believed the concept was too risky. They said that women were sick of seminars and that it wouldn't work.

Because I believed fervently that networking would empower women, I was devastated. Seeing my disappointment, my new husband suggested that I just organize the first Network Power Conference in San Antonio myself.

The next morning, after assuring my organization that I would be solely responsible for the outcome of the conference, I called the presidents of seven other women's organizations and held my breath after introducing myself and telling them about my plans. Unlike the women in my organization, however, they were as excited about the idea as I was, and a steering committee was born.

The results of that first Network Power seminar were truly historic. Ten days before the event, we were sold out. Five hundred professional women attended and word spread like wildfire about the conference. Six months later, the second Network Power Conference was held at the Convention Center with a thousand women. Alina Novak came to San Antonio four times in eighteen months for these record-breaking conferences. By 1997, there had been seven Network Power Conferences with nationally known leaders as keynote speakers, such as Abigail Van Buren and Maureen Reagan. All were very successful.

I learned that being a good, well-rounded risk-taker calls for a deep sense of compassion and caring for others. You take the risk because you know that in doing so you are accomplishing what is necessary to complete the job, whether it is in raising children by yourself or daring to do a new thing for your community.

About this time another opportunity came up. The Board of Network Power/Texas, a non-profit support group for women, which had grown out of the original steering committee, became aware of a trend across the country. Many women were leaving corporations because they could not break through the "glass ceiling," that invisible barrier which kept them out of the boardrooms and leadership positions commanding higher wages. Instead of becoming leaders of corporations, they were becoming that new catchword: *entrepreneurs.*

Over spring and summer, the board considered how it could help women start their own businesses. There was a group in Austin called The Women's Chamber of Commerce of Texas. While San Antonio had five chambers of commerce, not one of them had specific leadership training for women to teach them how to be successful businesswomen. The board of Network Power/Texas decided to provide funds to start a women's chamber in San Antonio. For six months, we were associated with the Austin group. Unfortunately, although the two cities are only seventy-two miles apart, we were many miles apart in what our members wanted. We had to break those ties and go out on our own.

Many men in our community thought we were crazy to start a women's chamber. One lawyer said it was the most asinine thing he had ever heard. From his point of view it probably was, but from ours it made good sense. How were entrepreneurial women going to learn to grow successful businesses unless they had the proper training to do so? But in 1988 few gave the San Antonio Women's Chamber of Commerce a chance. Yet, in 2003, with an elegant gala, we celebrated our fifteenth year of helping women make our city a better place. Even though it is a women's chamber, it has always welcomed men into membership and into service on our Board. Members have earned a place at the civic table and a reputation for producing first-class events.

While in 1988 we were the sixth chamber of commerce, we are now part of some fourteen chambers. San Antonio is a city rich in diversity, and different chambers meet the needs of different groups. We feel that we helped lead the way, stepping out early to start a Women's Chamber of Commerce.

With every risk I took, my life has been enriched beyond my wildest dreams. I have been privileged to travel to many parts of the world to lecture about the benefits of networking, from West Germany to Xalapa, Vera Cruz, where professional women came together to start "Mujeres en Enlace" (women being "woven" together).

If truth were known, on my return to San Antonio from the Women in Communication's National Conference in 1994, I have no idea what made me blurt out, "Next year I'm going to Beijing for the United Nations 4th World Conference on Women." Three days later, my middle daughter, who was then a reporter for the *Houston Chronicle*, called to say that she had been given an assignment to cover the China event. Was this coincidence, fate, or serendipity? All I know is that both of us were supposed to be there. What fun to have a daughter with me in China!

During the conference, an opportunity presented itself to do an unexpected seminar on empowering women. At the conclusion of my talk, a Japanese woman approached me, took both of my hands in hers and said, "You have changed my life!" I was filled with surprise and happiness. When I returned home, I told my mom that I knew that my friend upstairs had sent me to China to reach that one Japanese woman. And only SHE knows what that woman might do with her life to help other women, since she had apparently empowered herself.

Those three weeks in China were life-changing for me. The opportunity to meet and share with thousands of women from all over the world was a joy beyond belief. Whether we could speak each other's language or not, we communicated through love and caring. I have never been so filled with hope for the future. It was then that I knew that upon my return, I would give up my public relations business and become a full-time advocate for women. While there, I also determined to publish a book that I had been working on for several years, since an appearance on *Good Morning, America*, where the interviewer tapped me on the knee and said, "Lady, you need to write that book." And, in 1996, I did. It's called, *Come on In, There's Room for Us All!*

Sure, it's scary to get out of one's comfort zone. Certainly, we cannot know the outcome of the risk. But in these last twenty-five years, I have learned that one must walk through the fear. I was the woman who could not give her "fish pond booth" report to her PTA group because the frog of fear had almost struck her dumb. But I discovered that with practice I overcame my fear of speaking in public. Today, I am a motivational speaker and I get paid for my efforts. Not too long ago, as I walked into a convention center to speak to an audience of some fifteen hundred, I had a moment of reflection. I thought, "Can this be the woman who froze up in front of her PTA?" Miracles do happen, but sometimes they are the results of daring to take a risk.

One of my most requested presentations is entitled, "If We Can Dream It, We Can Do It." I believe that with all my heart. My most fervent desire is to get this message out to as many women as I can. With the state of the world today, we desperately need more women leaders. I came home from China convinced that if this sick world is ever to be healed, it is women who will heal it.

Many of my presentations end on a light note about Cinderella's networking and risk-taking expertise. She trusted in a fairy godmother (read "mentor"), she knew what she wanted (a first-class life), and she had the skills she needed (knowing how to dance). In those days she didn't have business cards, but she knew to leave something behind.

no position is a position

Demetrice Anntía Worley

As girls we catch our breaths
when family, friends, teachers,
stranger say *no*; we hear
you can't, ugly, skinny/fat,
nasty, bitch; slide into a vacuum,
silence comes easily, comforting.

As women we long for love,
partners to fill spaces we've
purposely have left open:
hearts waiting for completeness;
intellects waiting for challenges.
When partners, lovers,
and those others we sex
just for the fun of it, say *no*,
we silence our tongues, swallow
whole words until we feel full,
then we starve/gorge ourselves
with food/clothes/relationship drama
until we are in comas,
eyes open wide shut.

We women want change,
new spheres, power.
We silence our tongues,
fear political labels,
the F word, *feminism*,
hyphens do no better,
radical-, black-, eco-;
we search for more inclusion
without losing what separates

us—perhaps *womanist*.
In the end, we might as well
speak for ourselves,
hold the positions
we want,
love ourselves
with wicked glee.
All our words/silences
demonstrate our politics—
our power is in choice.

This position is my position;
I name it with my voice.

unlearning not to speak

Demetrice Anntía Worley

To survive they passed on
what had saved their lives:
Don't let your mouth
overload your ass.
So, I learned to keep quiet.
In school I avoided the five *W*s.
I was a good girl, smiled a lot,
kept clean, a model member
of polite society. Wrote
nice, nice poems. Won
nice, nice prizes. Went
to a Midwestern "Ivy League"
graduate school, died
with my mouth shut.

Eyes opened years later,
not by a kiss from a prince,
but by *Who, What, When,*
Where, Why? Questions
I couldn't answer. Found myself
in a world I had helped create
with silence. Started asking
anyone who would listen
the five *W*s and *How.*

My poems aren't so nice
anymore. I'm trying on answers,
turning them over, exposing
their undersides, discarding ones
that don't fit. These poems make
readers uneasy, they are afraid

my words are autobiographical;
these poems make editors write
polite rejection letters, *the tone
of writing doesn't fit the needs
of our journal.* These poems
my gifts, allow my mouth
to overload my ass,
make me ready to survive.

confessions of a compulsive overachiever
Nan Cuba

I'm such a compulsive overachiever that I tell my family and friends to make sure I'm pointed in a safe direction. Earnest and well intentioned, I can rally a crowd or whip up a controversy in a heartbeat—disasters when I'm even slightly off target. You know the type: high school student council secretary, college class officer, and later an entry in *Who's Who of American Women*. I'm used to pushing Sisyphus' boulder, but the last eleven years almost killed me.

I recently confided to my 35-year-old son Don, who is a bearded, six-foot seven-inch tall neuroscientist, that I thought I was too stable to be a serious writer. We had been discussing a published excerpt of a book by Alice Weaver Flaherty,[i] in which she analyzed a connection between the brain and the act of creative writing. Dostoyevsky and Flaubert, Flaherty noted, had temporal lobe epilepsy, and citing Kay Redfield Jamison, Flaherty said, "[P]oets are up to forty times more likely than the general population to have had manic episodes."

"What do I say?" my son chuckled, sounding like his favorite jazz solo of synchronized tones. He smiled and shifted his magnificent body in his chair, waving one hand, surprisingly animated. "I don't think you have anything to worry about."

Halfway through his fourth year in medical school, Don was diagnosed as manic-depressive. He needed medications and therapy, and I wanted to help him and his wife pay the expenses. My list of options included clerking at the kitchenware shop on the corner or teaching, a profession I had practiced during most of my adult life. But I needed immediate cash, so I postponed my work on a novel and pulled together twelve creative writing classes, the series to last four months, taught by me and a few friends, all held at my husband's small law office. I cranked out fliers on the Xerox machine and mailed them to former students and those who had signed up at reader's theater shows I co-produced with another writer. Thirty minutes before each weeknight class, I rushed into the office and shouted to my husband and his secretary that they had to leave. Papers were shuffled and computers shut down as I made coffee and arranged chairs around a second-hand conference table. I taught three of the classes and played hostess during the rest, introducing students to one another, announcing upcoming classes, and afterward collecting rumpled napkins, forgotten pens, half-full Styrofoam cups. The poetry workshop had only two students, a teenager dressed in black and an Irish college professor; an all-day Saturday seminar on Camus had a waiting list of high school English teachers hoping for insights to use in their classrooms. During the fourth month, two board members from a nonprofit women's resource center offered the use of their space for my classes as part of their organization's outreach. I could have the downstairs of their gabled 1930s house, including the kitchen and living room, for the next five-month semester at a cost of $300. A benefit reader's theater show was held at a neighborhood restaurant, producing the needed rent. Presto: from the workshops I led, I had teaching fees to pay for my son's therapy; a home for my creation, now called Gemini Ink; and a place to vent my anxiety and expend my energy. Except for the anti-depressant I was now taking, life, I thought, was working out. As usual, I was hopeful, upbeat, driven. My husband wondered what had hit him.

Although I rebelled years ago against my Southern Baptist upbringing, I am a spiritual person. During the beginning of Don's treatment, I suggested that he go to the Quaker or Unitarian church, that he incorporate ritual into his life. I gave him a St. Luke's charm, which he still wears around his neck. At certain times each day, I chanted a mantra: *patience, health*. Don, who has always been an avid reader, studied textbooks, lay books, self-help books— anything he could find about mood disorders. When he read Jamison's description of her own experience with manic depression in *An Unquiet Mind: A Memoir of Moodness and Madness*, she became his role model. If she could succeed as a scientist while living with mental illness, so could he. After leaving medical school without a degree but with staggering medical bills and school loans, he worked as a manager at a pet shop and read books on meditation and spiritual healing. He quoted William James and Jung. He learned self-hypnosis, and his father and I gave him a light machine, its rhythmic flashes used to induce sleep. Don's wife became his gauge. She measured limits that regulated the building of their family's emotional house, and together, they began that hard work. Their marriage made him determined to get well.

Meanwhile, my creation had become an obsession, a welcome distraction that kept me from panicking about my son. Gemini Ink's first staff consisted of ten volunteers, along with my daughter who'd recently moved from Chicago where she'd worked for three years as a nonprofit special-events coordinator, and an assistant who traded her graphic design services for permission to take as many classes as she wanted. My husband incorporated the organization and acquired its nonprofit status from the Internal Revenue Service. I worked in seasonal loops, booking semesters, cranking out course catalogues, monitoring classes, hosting out-of-town faculty, updating an expanding mailing list, creating dramatic reader's theater shows, producing a faculty reading series, holding special event fund-raisers, managing financials, generating a board of directors, and marketing, marketing, marketing. I did everything but wear a sandwich sign. In fact, I kept a laminated nametag in my purse and slapped it on whenever I found myself surrounded. I knew most students by name and the short stories of those who took my classes. I followed each person's development, recommending courses while courting potentially useful alliances. Wanting to serve the local community more directly, I sent writers to work with schoolchildren in the city's district, senior citizens at community centers and branch libraries, women with AIDS, and inner-city residents at a public housing facility. Periodically, my husband would say, "Tell me again why you're doing this?"

"Literary art opens minds," I'd say, "forcing people to think, to be more tolerant, to face difficult truths. It tells us," I'd add dramatically, "who we are." Then I'd march back to the phone.

Soon after reading Jung, Don became fascinated with Eastern religion. He quoted Chuang Tzu: "A true man of Tao does not distinguish himself." Since I squeezed in work on my novel from 4:00 until 9:00 each morning, I'd been researching Gnosticism and the history of Christianity. During Don's periodic visits to San Antonio from Houston with his wife and baby daughter, he and I talked before anyone woke, him listening politely as I lectured about Alfred North Whitehead's process theology.

"In order to be motivated to create the world, God needs to be enriched by it," I explained. "We are co-creators. God is permanently changing in response to our actions."

Don sighed, leaning forward, organizing his words in space before speaking. Opening a book, pointing, he softly shared that he'd become interested in Goethe's ideas about process, as opposed to Kant's moral absolute.

In October 2000, I mechanically whizzed through each day, my compulsive gears whirring. Single-handedly, I spearheaded the renovation of a dilapidated warehouse in the downtown arts district, wrangling contributions as well as donated labor and supplies. I painted the concrete walls exuberant colors, hung Latin American art from a benefactor's estate, then moved in Gemini Ink. The mayor attended our open house, where a founding board member cut a huge cake and described our first board meeting—three of us over a Thai lunch. "Keep doing whatever you're doing," had been his official advice. Little had he known that his encouragement had wound my excessiveness even tighter. Now, while supervising a paid staff of seven, I reported to a fifteen-member board, annually served over 3,000 students and audience members who came from across the country, had an impressive list of public and private funders, and built a fund-raising support group of almost 200 paid members. I didn't stop there, calling the heads of other literary organizations together to launch a statewide literary partnership. I had plans. Time was ticking, and I didn't understand why I couldn't move faster. My staff became extended family; we celebrated birthdays, the occasional published freelance article, lost loves. Visiting luminaries like Annie Proulx, W.H. Merwin, and Terry McMillan became my acquaintances, if only temporarily. I was given the Mind Science Imagineer Award and the Women in Communications Headliner in Education Award. Articles about me appeared in the local paper. One of my husband's business friends introduced me to her husband. "She's really famous," the woman absurdly announced.

Meanwhile, my writer friends marveled at the way I could work nonstop for days, even weeks on my novel during the rare occasions that I could get away. Two or three times a year, I rented a cheap room at a B&B, stayed in a nearby monastery, or escaped to a house in Colorado that was jointly owned with my three brothers.

One Mother's Day over lunch at a Cuban restaurant, gifts unwrapped, the paper folded underneath my dessert plate of fried plantains, I pressed my husband and Garbo-like daughter to name my faults, an unfair request that my husband wisely avoided. Feeling obligated, my daughter tentatively confided, "You always seem busy, like you care more about Gemini Ink than anything else," meaning, I recognized guiltily, more than her. For two years, she'd driven from Austin to San Antonio twice a week to help in the office so she and I could be together.

"Be careful," I snapped defensively. "You'd never accuse your dad, or any man, of doing that."

About every two weeks, I had a migraine, continuing to work until the weekend when I went to bed with a wet washrag over my forehead. My husband served meals on a tray, a habit that soon lapped into the workweek. I carried a large bottle of Extra Strength Excedrin in my purse and sometimes rewarded myself by marking three days off the next month's calendar, hoping an escape to the monastery would allow me to write. I didn't tell my husband, Don, or his sister that I wished I could quit Gemini Ink. How do you explain that your good intentions were a booby trap? Even though Don no longer needed my financial help, 3,000 others depended on me instead.

A few months after Don began a PHD program in neuroscience, two faculty members invited him to work on projects in their labs. He chose to study Circadian rhythms, not surprising since he didn't sleep well and became agitated during hot, humid seasons. He and his psychiatrist adjusted his medications, trying newer ones in hopes of improvement, sometimes causing stomach irritation, anxiety, weight gain, and, in two instances, chronic depression. During those months, my husband and I started each day with a phone call to help Don tackle the hours that loomed ahead. Afterward, as parents, we wept and then consoled each other, noting our boy's steadier voice or clearer focus. Besides depression, Don often seemed stricken with a cold or flu. In spite of these scares, however, Don's health steadily improved, the manifestations of his mental illness better controlled. He relaxed, spending afternoons in the park with his daughter and participating in family board games at our house, cooking marinated steaks on the grill, teasing and hoping for an intellectual spar. At work, he repaired complicated lab equipment and performed intricate microscopic cellular testing, garnering encouragement from his faculty supervisor. Together, they began planning his thesis.

By 2002, I had to get out of my job. I increased staff salaries, including mine even though it was still lower than anyone else's. Since I needed to entice someone to take my place, that amount would somehow have to be doubled. In tears, I announced to the board that I had to leave in order to concentrate on my writing, a vocation I had honored by dedicating myself to Gemini Ink in the first place. A national search was launched while I supervised the creation of staff performance manuals, designed an evaluation process, and scheduled staff training sessions on budgeting. When the organization cleared its second professional audit, I acquired a sizeable two-year operational grant from the city's Cultural Affairs Department, padding the coffers as much as possible. My committee meetings and paperwork mounted, and although I rarely had time to write, I told myself I would soon devote my life to nothing else. Relieved, my family hoped our lives would return to what we had come to think of as normal—a balanced interdependence.

Six months after I left Gemini Ink, I finished my novel and began work on a second. Since then, I've completed short projects like this essay. At a national neuroscience conference, Don gave a presentation about the effects of nitric oxide on Circadian rhythms. A scientist from Harvard offered him a job, which he said he'd think about. During the following semester, he taught an undergraduate biology course and developed a theory about the biological clock found in each human cell. "Wouldn't it be great," he says, "if I could prove that people with mood disorders have clocks that need synchronizing? Imagine if I could fix that."

Three years later, Don had to leave the PHD program. His supervisors said his mental illness interfered with his ability to complete a degree. In spite of that, he was asked to teach another lab; so in between classes, he's now working with a job hunter to find where he'll go next. His wife admits being anxious yet remains his stalwart emotional gauge.

My days are purposely slower as I try to appreciate life's process and avoid distinguishing myself. For my birthday, Don wrote a poem: "Words are the ultimate paradox. / We would not know what words were without words. / How can the subject be the object of itself? / That's magic." He says his gift is a "tribute to the medium," but it also reminds me of Flaherty's book excerpt on the brain / writing connection. In it, she notes that the limbic system controls our drives, like mine to communicate, and that emotional or limbic aspects of speech are noticed before a speaker's actual words are deciphered, as when someone is frightened. Therefore, she says, "a major reason for creative writing is an abstracted version of the same biological urge that causes you to cry out in sorrow or anger." Reading that, I suddenly understood the source of my compulsive creation of a place devoted to writing, of my own need for literary expression.

My remarkable son is learning to live with his mental illness, and I must keep writing. Patience, health.

---

i Flaherty, Alice Weaver. "Writing Like Crazy: a Word on the Brain." *The Chronicle of Higher Education: The Chronicle Review* 50.13. Nov. 21 (2003): B6.

CROSSING BORDERS

crossing borders

to be nobody but yourself—in a world which is doing its best, night and day,
to make you everybody else—means to fight the hardest battle which any
human being can fight, and never stop fighting.

—e. e. cummings

Despite Robert Frost's admonition concerning unthinking acceptance of
"Good fences make good neighbors," as humans we have continued to create
countless borders, often assuming their necessity. Some are political, others
physical or religious. This chapter deals with obliterating the personal bound-
aries that restrict the development of our real selves as well as those that keep
us from reaching out and being part of the total community of humanity.
Camus reflected, "To know oneself, one should assert oneself." In this chap-
ter, the "real self" of these authors forced them to step over social boundaries
as well as those formed by a lack of understanding or empathy from others and
set by the limits of their own mortality.

The initial selections deal with parents' impact on their children and
grandchildren, forging a direction for future generations. In "Ruth Marantz
Cohen: Une Vie Exceptionelle," her daughter, Rosetta, recalls her mother's
crossing the conventions of time, being different from most women of her day.
She kept her maiden name, spoke French to her children, and chose a career
over being a "housewife." Cohen writes, "I grew into adulthood watching my
mother forge her own unique identity as intellectual and existentialist, a phi-
losophy which celebrated free will, 'choice,' and the preeminence of acting on
one's convictions." She adds, "My mother had taught me that the self is some-
thing you construct out of your own imagination and creativity, and that the act
of self-creation is the most important work of a life."

Joan Loveridge-Sanbonmatsu's grandmother would find a good friend in
Cohen's mother. In "The Telling of It," she is "a woman, independent and
strong," who wasn't afraid of her granddaughter crossing cultural borders to
marry a Japanese-American husband. Yet, Loveridge-Sanbonmatsu must
answer questions about her own parents' refusal to attend her wedding or even

to acknowledge her children. "How do you tell your sons / you stepped beyond the pale?" By leaving the bounds of her limited "white world," she found a better life. Yet, she understands that there will be more tests for her sons when they choose their own future paths.

Gail Hosking Gilberg's choices have impacted not only her own life, but her sons' as well. She grew up on an army base where "one was either Catholic or Protestant," so until college she didn't know any Jews. When she met her future husband on campus and he told her he was Jewish, she insisted that he meant "Irish." In "Conversion," Gilberg has to redefine her religious truths when she changes faiths. "I wanted a common language in my home; I needed to pull together the disconnection of husband and wife like one might pull together community to the earth." She explores "how to live with threads of two separate histories" and how to deal with society's often negative response to her decision.

"We Who Believe in Freedom," by Connie Curry, and "Turbulent Odyssey for Justice," by Joan Loveridge-Sanbonmatsu both also involve responses to discrimination. Curry writes about two courageous women who risked intimidation and harassment to break down boundaries imposed upon them by segregation. Loveridge-Sanbonmatsu takes SUNY Brockport to court for sex discrimination. All these women become empowered by their own willingness to fight injustice. They model activism at the most moral level. As Shirley Chisholm, the first African American to win a seat in Congress proclaimed, "In the end, anti-black, anti-female, and all forms of discrimination are equivalent to the same thing—anti-humanism."

Demetrice Anntía Worley reminds us that there is still a long way to go. In her poem "Dancing in the Dark," she straddles two worlds: One is white academia where she presents a paper "in a herringbone tweed suit," and the other, where "Soul slow dances back into my body." Balancing dual identities is also paramount when feeling forced to learn another language. Pat Mora relates the overwhelming frustration and humiliation of crossing language barriers. In "Elena" and "Learning English: Chorus in Many Voices," we feel the embarrassment of not speaking English well, but being driven to learn it. At age forty, Elena pushes herself to learn English knowing that she must keep trying in spite of her difficulties: "for if I stop trying, I will be deaf / when my children need my help."

"I am very fortunate to have known strong women as well as weak ones," Jean Flynn acknowledges in her essay, "Sharecropper's Daughter." Flynn was born during the Depression when women had no voice, but she knew in her heart that there was more to life than poverty and silence. She looked up from the cotton fields to become a respected educator and author, speaking out against racial barriers and oppression. When she was paid less than half the salary of a man she replaced on her job, she argued with the owner "that it wasn't about a person's status or gender but about the quality of work." Her own work has given many others the courage to overcome personal obstacles.

But inevitably, discrimination and oppression cause bitterness to occur. Rachel Naomi Remen writes that "often anger is a sign of engagement with life." The woman in Janice Brazil's poem "Questioning" is on the verge of changing, of allowing her voice to carry the depth of her anger. Owning her own emotions is another border she crosses.

Perhaps the greatest boundary is between life and death. Karen Waldron relates her mother's passage from an awareness of "life's weighty fears in a fully-stocked purse," to her entry into a universe of doubt as she attempts to cross over to a spiritual world, "Her Place." Ruth Kessler voices wonder and dismay at the move "past all things that had ceased to matter," in "No Traveler." And it is the unknown, things we "refused to learn," that haunts Naomi Shihab Nye as well. Her grandmother dead, Nye wonders about the secrets hidden in her green trunk and the woman who chose to remain on her land when all others left. She laments, "we never stayed." Times lost.

Elizabeth Kubler-Ross contends that we are solely responsible for our choices and as such must accept the consequences "of every deed, word and thought throughout our lifetime." Ruth Kessler senses this truth in "Elegy for an Angel," as she depicts how humanity turns away from love. Our choices continue to affect our lives. Kessler seems to ponder the question, "When will the human race learn?"

We see this bitterness and lack of understanding between cultures in Karen Waldron's story, "Next Year in Jerusalem." In 1989, Waldron agreed to speak about issues pertaining to the quality of care for children worldwide at the Conference of the General Federation of Iraqi Women. However, instead of being welcomed, she writes, "I have never been so hated and terrified in all my life." She is vilified because she is from the United States, and "anti-American sentiment had poured over into a tidal wave." But as Waldron listens to the other women dedicated to saving children's lives, she realizes that the issues of daycare reform that she was going to speak about "would seem trivial, even laughable, when so many children lacked a home, a parent, even a daily meal or hospital bed." She searches for ways to bridge cultural barriers, to find a way where all people can connect and come together to support the children. She reflects, "When a child dies, a mother cries. The child's nationality and race don't matter."

This sense of humanity is extolled by Maya Angelou in the final poem, "On the Pulse of Morning." She pleas for humanity to "Lift up your faces. You have a piercing need / For this bright morning dawning for you." She advises us to move beyond our past differences, to put war aside and begin anew. Her final words, "Good Morning," awaken us to the possibilities of our own risk and courage as we begin a new day.

As we find in Waldron's essay and Angelou's plea, sometimes initiating growth takes a profound awakening to the needs of others. Crossing borders of understanding allows each of us to heal and develop as an authentic person. It is in the crossing that women reclaim their freedom.

ruth marantz cohen: une vie exceptionelle

Rosetta Marantz Cohen

This is an essay about my mother, Ruth Marantz Cohen, who risked being different during an era of enormous conformity. Her risks made the risks I've taken in my own life easier. She was my role model and inspiration.

My mother was born in 1926 in Brooklyn, New York. Her parents, Gertrude and Sam, were Russian immigrants, Jews who came to New York during the time of the Soviet pogroms. Like many only children, Ruth was brought up to adore her parents, and to perceive their world together as a kind of closed system. My mother used to tell stories about how she turned down dates and rejected the invitations of friends because she genuinely preferred the company of her parents. And her parents devoted themselves to their only child with a passion and singularity that is characteristic of certain immigrant families: She was their past, present and future. Her slightest need would become their central preoccupation. I always delighted in my mother's descriptions of her parents' devotion: how they would spend their evenings discussing Ruth's homework assignments, or her thoughts on various neighbors, or what she wanted to eat for dinner. The three of them would do errands together on weekends—the neat trio moving from the fish market to the library to the tailor shop, enmeshed in secret conversation. My mother claimed that she passed her entire childhood like this—speaking softly, venturing only blocks from home, conforming to the loving strictures of her parents.

In high school, however, something odd took hold of my mother. For reasons she has never been able to adequately explain, she fell passionately in love with the French—French language, French culture, French fashion, French food, French literature. As she tells it, one day a guidance counselor informed my mother that she would be taking French in the fall, and (according to her testimony) the word rang like a church bell in her soul: French! Therein lay her destiny. From that point on, my mother threw herself into a blind devotion for all things French. She won high school French awards and city competitions; she ventured away from her fretful parents to study first in Quebec, and then—alone and already engaged to my father at 20—in Paris, absorbing all the while that powerfully evocative post-war Parisian culture, a culture in which high and low, the intellectual and the aesthetic, merged in a delectable froth: Givenchy and Dior, Jean-Paul Sartre and Andre Gide. My mother loved all of it, as she loved the make-up counters at Au Printemps and the articles on celebrity love affairs in *Marie Claire* and *Elle.*

When she returned home, my mother carried Parisian culture with her as a permanent mark of difference. She had met my father in her first year at Brooklyn College, but instead of following him to graduate school in Missouri, she chose to pursue her own PHD in Wisconsin—tucking his love letters in her copies of *Huis Clos* and *La Poesie d'Appollinaire*. She taught traditional undergraduates, but also returning GI's, men older than she was, in classes on Existentialism and Modernist Poetry. Once she married my father, Ruth insisted on keeping her maiden name and then persuaded her husband to take on her own name as his middle name. She resumed her teaching at the University of Missouri, and stayed there, happily oblivious to the conventions of the era, living a life of art and literature—albeit in a dusty, midwestern college town.

Pregnancy, however, ended her university career and closed the door on her work at Missouri. My father, newly graduated with his own degree in chemistry, moved the family to suburban New Jersey, a place characterized by a kind of middle-class conformity that seemed calculated to blunt my mother's style. We lived in a split-level tract house, in a large development of the sort that was then burgeoning in suburbs throughout the United States. Around us everywhere was the sprawling, post-war American culture—a world of steak house restaurants and giant automobiles, block party cook-outs, Elvis and *Leave it to Beaver*. The women in our neighborhood, and those we knew from our synagogue or through other organizations that educated women joined in those days, all seemed to be creatures of their decade: They were stay-at-home mothers and dutiful wives. Their homes—at least the ones I saw among my friends—had a pristine homogeneity that impressed me. They seemed like the homes that appeared in *Life Magazine* and on television shows, with their wall-to-wall carpeted rooms redolent with the scent of fresh-baked cookies. Though our house looked on the outside like one of dozens in the neighborhood, on the inside it was wholly different. We had large abstract canvasses on the walls, and an imposing bust of Voltaire in the living room. The house was filled with French *objets* —Guimper vases, provençal linens, Limoges china. French magazines were everywhere, in the den, the bathrooms. Baskets of magazines sat in the corners of bedrooms, filled with pictures of Brigitte Bardot and Leslie Caron—the figures who influenced my sense of womanhood more than any of the American icons of the day. My mother prided herself on never baking from scratch; "working women," she said, "don't bake." But we did eat Camenbert cheese and Salade Niçoise, foods that were quite uncommon in the late fifties and early sixties, and which conjured up the Paris for which my mother constantly yearned. Inside the house, she spoke in French to my sister and me—an exotic practice that confused our childhood friends and surely evoked suspicion among the neighbors. Even in her look, my mother was different from everyone else: Cultivating a kind of French "chic," she wore scarves tied in interesting ways, and cut her hair very short—like Jean Seaberg—and wore very high heels. Even as a young child, I sensed that it took a kind of courage to make such choices in our little suburban community. Dressing differently, eating differently, raising her children to perceive the world with a caustic eye that was decidedly French—all this set us apart.

But the greatest risk of all, for my mother and for her family, was her insistence on pursuing a career. As soon as she could, several years after I was born, she went back to work fulltime—the only mother we knew who did so. Indeed, work was so crucial to her that she took the first job she found that would allow her to speak French—a junior high school French position in which she was required to teach eight classes a day at a salary that was less than the wage of a supermarket clerk. She didn't care. Nor did she budge from her resolve when I began to loudly protest our separations each day. I had been put into daycare at a time when none but the poorest children were placed in such facilities, and though I cried and threw up and acted in other ways that were quite alarming, she continued to work—cheerfully kissing me goodbye each morning as the childcare van drove me off to a day of (what I perceived to be) unremitting misery.

As she grew older, my mother's work and career became increasingly central to her stubbornly original conception of herself. After several years at the junior high, she moved on to high school teaching where she embraced the persona of French teacher with a passion and adamancy that was truly groundbreaking. I grew into adulthood watching my mother forge her own unique identity as intellectual and existentialist, a philosophy which celebrated free will, "choice," and the preeminence of acting on one's convictions. At home, she was constantly surrounded by the French novels she taught in her A.P. literature classes—by the existentialists Camus and Sartre, and also by Balzac, Hugo, and Stendhal. She was also continuously mired in student papers, endless folders of them that she graded with fierce precision. At one point, after my mother had been teaching perhaps ten years, my father proposed that we move to the West Coast; he had been offered a good research position at a large aeronautics firm near Los Angeles. My mother, risking both her marriage and her children's happiness, refused to go. Her identity, she claimed, had been painstakingly forged in the local high school, and she would not give it up. She believed, I think, that her carefully crafted life in New Jersey had been wrought against all odds, that it was fragile, and that she was unlikely to be able to replicate it again. She had capitulated to her husband's desires once, in leaving her position at Missouri; if she did it twice, she might lose herself in the process. Ultimately, my father backed down—resentful ever after—but reconciled to the odd logic of her arguments. In time, I believe my father came to admire my mother's staunch non-conformity, and her idiosyncratic love of all things French. By the mid-1960s, he had bought her a small, green Peugeot, a kind of mobile emblem of her individuality. Later, he added a license plate for her car that read "Mme C."

When I was a girl and then a teenager, my mother's difference became not a source of unhappiness for me, but a badge of pride, and a model for liberation. I remember feeling none of the embarrassment or self-consciousness that pre-teens feel in their parents' presence. Her non-conformity seemed to mitigate against any kind of generation gap; and her natural candor—refined by decades of decidedly non-puritanical French magazine articles—made me able to speak to her, without fear, about any subject at all. By the time I was old enough to suffer the conformist pressures of adolescence, I was better defended than most. My mother had taught me that the self is something you construct out of your own imagination and creativity, and that the act of self-creation is the most important work of a life. She knew from first-hand experience how difficult that work could be, but also how crucial it was to become an authentic person—to resist what she called the "gaze" of the outside world. Throughout her life, my mother's favorite book was *The Stranger*, by Albert Camus. She must have taught it thirty or more times, and a dog-eared copy sat on her bed-table as a kind of habitual reference. My mother must have seen in the protagonist, Meursault—an enigmatic misfit who is ultimately condemned to death for not showing "appropriate" emotion at his mother's funeral—some essential truth about herself. Like Meursault, she was a person profoundly out of sync with the norms and values of those around her. My mother was a person who could not conform, even if her life (or marriage) was at stake, a person who ultimately defined herself by her own actions in the world. "Choose who you want to be, live that choice, and ignore the gaze of other people." This was my mother's mantra. Such an attitude represented a true risk for a woman who came of age in the 1940s. For a daughter who came of age in the 1970s, I couldn't have received a better gift.

the telling of it

Joan Loveridge-Sanbonmatsu

I had to run the tape
a thousand times over
in my mind
knowing that today would come.
The moment of truth was upon me,
the telling of it.

Was I ready to tell this story?
How did we get to this moment?
At dinner, my two sons and I
were chatting.
An easygoing question about our wedding
set the story in motion.

"It was a simple wedding," I began,
"celebrated at a small university chapel,
by close friends and relatives."

> "Did your sister come?" asked my son.
> "Yes, and many from far away," I offered.
> "Did my father's brother come?" my
> fifteen-year-old son asked.
> "Yes," I nodded.

> "Did your father come to the wedding?"
> "No."
> "Did your mother come?"
> "No," I responded.
> Carefully, like holding a fragile crystal
> that might shatter if dropped,
> I replied, "No. They couldn't,
> they didn't ...," groping for a word.

"Find it acceptable," my older son filled in.
How do you tell your sons
you stepped beyond the pale?
Perhaps, the questions would stop.
Perhaps, a reprieve ...
And the questions never stopped.

> "Did your parents approve of your
> sister's marriage? Did they
> attend her wedding?"
> "No," I acknowledged.
> "So it was your mother who ...?"
> I clarified in as much of an even tone
> as I could muster.

"Actually, it was my father
who couldn't accept things."
In a different country, he was born.
In a different country, he lived.
Vancouver was home to my father.
It had North America's
largest Chinese settlement.
Then the Japanese Canadians were interned
in camps in Canada's interior.

Continuing my story, I explained,
"After my father, U.S. bound,
married my mother,
the hysteria on the West Coast
broke, with a mass removal of
Japanese Americans who were
interned in concentration camps.
Asian Americans were forced
to discard all *Made in Japan* china,
kimonos, scrolls, paintings;
thrown out treasures wrapped in memories."

The telling
of my decision to marry
a Japanese American
brought total rejection from my father.
"From the time you marry, you
will be dead, in my eyes. Forget
about me," my father asserted.

My mother heard from my father,
"Choose between your daughter or me."
Mother, a woman shaped
by traditional values, never
having lived on her own,
a woman who promised
at her wedding to never
work for money,
a woman who arranged
schedule, household, meals
around my father,
a woman who voted Father's views,
stood
by my father.

"Did you ever see your father again?"
"No," I whispered.
"So you mean your mother only visited
us when your father died?"
I nodded, "yes."
"But there's my grandmother,"
I added, to diffuse the situation,
to be fair.

Grandmother, a woman unlike my mother,
a woman who drove and owned a car,
a woman who had worked
during the depression
during the war, wearing pants
a woman, independent and strong.
"She met your father

visited us
visited my sister
cared for you
cared for us."

"Were you glad your father died?"
probed my younger son.
"No. You see, my father and I
had two similar threads.
He fought in court for a principle of justice
in science and invention seven years and won.
I fought in court for a principle of justice
in women's rights for twelve years and won."

"What if we marry someone with
different values?" questioned my older son.
"Like a Moonie?" demanded my younger son.
The test again—
another test, this time, theirs.

"We would never disown you.
We love you too much.
It's sad that my parents disowned me;
they missed a great deal.
In fact, that rejection
bonded us more closely.
We are family.
Trials, difficult times, we
confronted together
found strength together.
We've developed family relationships
with my sister and your father's family,
a family extended."

"An international family
is what we are.
Remember your great uncle's memorial
service and supper?
Around the table sat my sister's husband from China,

my cousin from France, your father-
Japanese American.
You know your great uncle was Swedish.
Your grandfather was Canadian, your great grandmother-
Polish. Your father's relatives draw from
Jewish, Spanish, and Mexican cultures.
They enrich our family."

Dinner finished.
As I drove Jamie to soccer
I fumbled with my sunglasses
so he would not see
hot tears forming
sinking, heavy,
heavy into my eyelids
lodging there.
He could not sense the lump in my throat.
    "Even if I marry someone
    with really different values like racist values?"
    Jamie advanced this one last question.
    Stunned, I reassured him, "Yes,
    we will stand by you."

    An epiphany came to my son,
    "Now I know why you insist
    on particular restaurant seats,
    never in the back,
    with the dishes clattering.
    I've never experienced prejudice before,
    except on the bus, a long time ago.
    But there is prejudice."
"Yes," I agreed. "that's why
your father and I may
move after you're in college.
It's very isolated here."

Driving home alone
Two or three tears trickled.
"Why?" I wondered.

Public ignorance or stupidity
or sadness or
painful memories resurfacing?
Did I meet my test?
Did I meet their test?

Reprinted from *Winged Odyssey* (Hale Mary Press, 2002).

conversion: the trail of a resident alien

Gail Hosking Gilberg

"I am descended from a people who knew there is a God with the same certainty that they know walking into a river will get them wet."

RICK BRAGG

I'm afraid my ancestors would roll over in their graves at the thought of my conversion. My great-great-great grandmother, Mary Sophia Ramsey, who never played cards on Sunday and donated a stained glass window for the Dutch Reformed Church in Wyckoff, New Jersey, would think my children heathens. So would my ancestor, Guilamme Bertholf, who came here in 1694 as the first pastor of the Dutch Reformed Church, though I imagine he knew about crossing borders because he made momentous shifts in his own life with a new language, a new land, and a new people. In the end, he reflected more a mosaic shape than the steadfast Flanders man he was when he first arrived on these shores. He who tried to convert others should understand.

Though my mother attended a Pentecostal Church at the end of her life— a church that could not fathom someone not accepting the Trinity—I think she understood my conversion. She wouldn't have been able to explain it to Brother Tommy the minister, or the others who fell on the floor weekly in frenzied ecstasy and sang songs like "What a Friend We Have in Jesus." She never said so, but I imagine she based her acceptance on her understanding of people, the spirit, and her own concessions within a marriage. She never asked me why my children weren't being baptized or how it was I could change after so many years of Sunday School. If she prayed about my conversion, she never told me so.

I've been Jewish now long enough to have memories when I sip the ceremonial Passover wine, long enough to let Yiddish phrases roll off my tongue naturally as if my great-grandfather came from Russia instead of Cornwall, England. I've been Jewish long enough to argue the value of a briss, to respect kosher laws, and to dance the hora at Bar Mitzvahs as if God himself were my partner. Sometimes I forget that I once sang in the Presbyterian Church choir or took communion every Sunday. So when people ask me questions about my conversion, they surprise me; though they shouldn't after so many years—twenty to be exact.

For the sake of the question, I try to return to the moment I decided to convert, but I don't find it easily. No *I saw the light* murmurs from my memory. What I remember instead is not having ever met a Jew before my husband—at least not one I recognized as a Jew. Growing up on an American army base an hour from Dachau, I thought all Jews had been killed. My father drove me to the concentration camp several times after the war. As I stared at those gruesome photographs and thought about the graves of millions, I couldn't imagine that anyone had survived such terror. There were no Jews on the base—one was either Catholic or Protestant. I knew of no other choices. So when my husband-to-be first told me at college that he was Jewish, I insisted he was Irish. No, he kept saying. I am Jewish. The history between that moment and the day we decided to get married was fraught with my own spiritual crises. How to love and still hold fast to the person I am? How to balance two different worlds? How to live with the threads of two separate histories?

My decision to become a Jew came nearly six years after my wedding. We lived on an Israeli kibbutz that first year of marriage, just off the road to Damascus and above the Sea of Galilee—places I had studied in Sunday School: Paul of Tarsus, the fishes and the loaves, the Sermon on the Mount. It was my husband's idea to take a break from his graduate studies and travel to Israel, not mine. I had no idea what to expect, but I followed him anyway to a country where people on a bus headed for Jerusalem fondled my long blond hair, where children who had never met a Christian before quizzed me on my family history, where strangers continually asked me if I were a Jew. I learned to read the Hebrew my husband had studied in childhood, to write down those crazy shapes that looked as foreign as Chinese symbols to me, and I learned what it felt like to be a minority. I practiced my new language with the four infants I helped take care of in one of the kibbutz baby houses. I learned about apples and honey on Rosh Hashana, the quiet of a Yom Kippur, the eight nights of Hanukah lights, and the frivolity of a Purim. But on Christmas Eve when a car of volunteers drove to Bethlehem, I did not go for fear of calling attention to the differences between husband and wife.

I didn't come home with plans to convert; though upon my return I did teach my few Hebrew skills to children at a synagogue in Pocatello, Idaho. My husband bought me a Christmas tree that year after friends said it would be a good thing to do. We hung gold Hanukah coins and chocolate Maccabee soldiers on the limbs, and a Star of David on top. I was touched by his gesture, his simple acknowledgement of my past and my longings, but it was not an easy Christmas, and it wasn't the last time our religious differences caused tension in our home. We didn't talk about it much, but nonetheless our basic upbringings rose to the surface on these occasions, and an air of something we couldn't will away lingered like smoke from cigarettes. Finally, the thought of having a child brought up my own question of converting. I wanted a common language in my home; I needed to pull together the disconnection of husband and wife like one might pull together community to the earth. My need for a family overrode my need to stay a Christian.

Then suddenly as if I had been working towards this moment my whole life, I sat in a synagogue conversion class learning ethics, ritual, and words like *fleishig* and *milchig*. I learned about a people who had no Hebrew word for religion. I made a rabbi promise me that converting did not mean that all I had been before, all that I believed before had not been real too. When the classes were over, I immersed myself in the mikvah, a five-foot-deep pool filled with rainwater, and I chanted a prayer as my head went under and a woman with a number tattooed across her forearm helped me remember the exact words. In that moment of immersion, I understood baptism and the universal notion of beginning anew. *Baruch atah Adonai, Eloheinu, melekha-olam, shekeanu, v'key'-manyu, v'heegeeanu lazman hazeah.* Praised are you, Lord God, King of the Universe, who has kept us alive, preserved us and enabled us to reach this day.

We weren't sure how to celebrate such a momentous occasion except to go out and eat Jewish food. There was a moment somewhere between matza ball soup and a knish, that I felt suddenly as if I belonged to a larger family—an international family with members represented in all countries. I took solace in that, as I did feeling I had brought a divided household together. I lit Sabbath candles that Friday night on my husband's grandmother's brass candlesticks, and I imagined Jews all over the world doing the same thing at the same time.

How can the act of entering a mikvah not alter one? How does one invent a new life from what's at hand? What makes us change from our origins? It was practical on one hand: I, who had come to feel comfortable in Jewish homes, was the obvious one to create a sense of continuity for the two sons I would soon bring into the world. On the other hand, I can't deny the mystical side of my conversion. I awoke slowly to a life that would one day feel as comfortable as trimming a Christmas tree or closing my eyes to say the Lord's Prayer.

Any big change in our life demands what Kierkegaard called "a leap of faith." One can't know completely what will be on the other side until one arrives there. You must close your eyes, hold your nose, and plunge into unknown waters. You can see all the elements of change until you come to the almost-there, and then you must leap to complete the line. In calculus, mathematicians call it "approaching the limit." I don't think my husband ever understood what a large leap it was after a history of Protestants that went all the way back to Martin Luther himself. One can study to convert, one can read piles of books on Judaism, but in the end one merely jumps and trusts.

My sister feared my change from the beginning, and she was right—growth creates a departure. Our convictions come with consequences. My children do not enjoy my sister's pork chops; they don't sing our familiar childhood songs. They can't join some of the country clubs my sister can, and neither does she understand the Yiddish my children and I sprinkle into conversations. I can't lie: One never goes home again the same—though any adult might tell you that. With my conversion I entered a new place with gefillte fish, kugels, and matza balls. Sometimes that feels like living on a separate island from my sister.

I put myself into this conversion tale, but the story begins with other people's intrigue. It starts with the interest in identity. I look out to a nation of converts. Most of our ancestors once immigrated here and left a past behind. In this melting pot we call the United States, it is increasingly difficult to find someone exactly like our family of origin unless we live in a ghetto. Ghettos still exist—Hassidic in Brooklyn, African Americans in Harlem, Cambodians in Los Angeles, and Hispanics in San Antonio. We move these days for economic and psychological reasons, rarely ever for familiar or spiritual ones. We've been breaking molds in this country since the beginning in order to create new shapes. With each generation we invent our truths again like a continual revision.

Maybe it's because this nation grew from a people who dismantled their worlds, who arrived disoriented from the start, and who lost childhood homes, countries, and languages, that the thought of conversion intrigues us so. We carry within us that which our ancestors brought to this country—both a need to start again and a need to transport the past. It is a difficult way to live sometimes. We welcome the new, but hold our muscles metaphorically tight as if we fear losing what we once had. We fear crossing borders again.

Human beings want fixed points of reference in order not to fall into vertigo. A conversion sets that dizziness into motion. People contend vigorously with contradiction: Where should they place my blond, blue-eyed face that speaks Hebrew? They ask me how can I ignore the teachings of my youth? If my parents did it right by sending me to church, if they were good enough people, then why do I need to change? Conversion forces people to enter a gray area of life and challenges our pasts. It engages our struggle to live within paradox.

At the bottom of this story, and most importantly, I think conversion brings up the question of home itself. Ruth, the Moabite and convert, said to Naomi: "For whither thou goest, I will go; and where thou lodgest, I will lodge. Thy people shall be my people and thy God, my God; where thou diest, I will die, and there will I be buried." But now in this century of banishment, where exactly should what Beckett called *the cell of the self* reside? We live in a multicultural country, and still we struggle with more than one truth—truth with a capital T. As a convert, one must redefine home and thus, truth. That thought ripples through any group that asks me about my conversion. It stirs up the dust of an already existing conflict, and this crisis of wisdom hangs in the air.

What I have never told anyone is that the past, like some quiet shadow, never leaves us completely. In that way, no true conversion according to the books exists; there is, as the saying goes, no one and only Buddha on the road. Though the Talmud refers to a convert as "a child newly born," I'm more inclined like the ancient Hebrews to think of conversion as a turning, with each rotation slightly different from the one who's come before you. History spirals through time that way, picking up pieces of by-gone moments, lifting them into the present, swirling back for some other segment of our past.

Sure, some converts stand on the bimah and chant the Torah like traditional Jews born of Jewish mothers, though I can't. Many converts only eat kosher food, though I don't. The longer I am Jewish, the more I see we are all—Jews, Gentiles, and converts—a hybrid of sorts. Our individual histories make their way to the surface in one way or another. This isn't to say that we fall back into the religion we once had, or that a power struggle exists between two equal forces. For me, it's appreciating what I pulled together to create a new shape. I might know Rosh Hashana tunes better than some of my Jewish-from-birth friends, yet I still pray in that one-to-one way I first learned in a Protestant Sunday School on the second floor of an American military base in Bad Tolz, Germany. I know what foods are kosher and what aren't, and I light Sabbath candles every Friday night; but still I know all the words to "Amazing Grace" and the Lord's Prayer. Spirituality, like passion, can not be put into a box. Some things never leave us. Still, being a Presbyterian abates in my memory with each passing year.

My Dutch Reform/Presbyterian grandmother used to say that love doesn't butter your bread. I laughed at her when I was young. Love conquers a great deal, but because our pasts can't be erased completely and because children force our pasts to the foreground, it is not the entire truth to say that religious differences in a marriage don't matter. One can't sweep the contrasts under the rug. This isn't to say that we should go back to the days when only Catholics married Catholics and Jews married Jews, but only to say we can't enter relationships blindly. I am proof that one can change along the way, and I suppose that's why Jewish mothers love to hear my conversion story when their sons date Christian girls. But I am quick to tell them it isn't as simple as that.

My son David says he will never convert. Fresh off the Inquisition in his Western Civilization college course, he can't bear the thought of becoming a Christian. The problem is that he loves an Episcopalian girl whom he says he wants to marry someday. My Episcopalian grandfather, who became a Presbyterian as a compromise when he married my grandmother, might smile at that thought if he were alive. Neither my son nor his girlfriend wants to give up a religion. I am old enough to know that I can't tell them anything, for religion, like love, is something for each of us to decide. I only say that one doesn't know the path one might choose as life unfolds. Experience can alter our aims, and if love can butter your bread, that love must be very strong to tolerate differences. History, destiny, and the soul have their own needs.

My Buddhist convert friend tells me that she thinks maybe my dead soldier-father has come back to this world as a Buddhist. My father who spent his entire adulthood in one war or another, who visited Buddhist monks in their temples during his Vietnam R&R time, who wore a Buddha around his neck because he swore those without the Buddha never returned from battle, is perhaps a Buddhist himself now. If my friend is right, that we learn lessons in this life and bring that wisdom into a next life, then surely my father who saw towns destroyed and friends killed, decided to live now the antithesis of a warrior's life. He shifted the risk of battle and conflict into the risk of suffering and peace. Perhaps he learned from this life how to live daily in the tension of opposites.

Sometimes I picture my mother watching my life from some cloud, trying to tell me that all this Buddha, Jesus, Mohammad, Jerusalem stuff doesn't matter in the end. I imagine her saying that what her brother Ishmael once said about Jews not getting to Heaven, isn't the truth. From her big view of the spirit world, I imagine she wants me to know the value of the human heart.

To change religions shocks many people, but it also frees. A person who converts exercises that freedom. One who changes moves toward something, not necessarily away, and the elements of our past can provide the basis for moving on. A rabbi once told me that the strong change and open their life to what is in front of them. I like to think he is right. I like to believe that the God of us all understands our need to find ourselves, to find love, and to find that thread which connects us to something larger than our few years on this earth. I'd like to say that God knows about crossing borders, about rearranging our lives and about creating new stories. I believe it isn't the form that he or she is concerned with, but rather the spirit itself.

She'ma yisrael, Adonai Elohainu, Adonai echad. Hear, O Israel: the Lord our God, the Lord is One.

Reprinted from *The Cream City Review*, Fall 1999, Volume 24, Number 1.

we who believe in freedom

Connie Curry

On a winter day in 1990, Mae Bertha Carter and Winson Hudson, both from Mississippi, were visiting me in Charlottesville, Virginia. They were to speak that morning at the University of Virginia in Julian Bond's class on the civil rights movement. I was there with a year's post-doctoral fellowship at the Carter Woodson Institute, working, in fact, to document the story of Mae Bertha Carter. Earlier in the year, I had met Maxwell Kennedy, the youngest son of Robert Kennedy, who was in law school at the university, and I had invited him to meet Mrs. Carter and Mrs. Hudson. They were so excited.

As with many black people in rural Mississippi, they saw in the 1960s, in both John and Robert Kennedy, the beginnings of recognition of and caring about the blatant racism they faced on a daily basis. Just before Max Kennedy came, the two women disappeared in the back of the house. Max arrived and was sitting on the couch, and the two women came in. Embraces and introductions were exchanged, and then Mae Bertha and Winson sat down side by side on straight-back chairs—tiny, light-skinned, blue-eyed, 68-year-old Mae Bertha, and 74-year old tall, erect, strong-featured Winson Hudson—both from the back roads of Mississippi. They took out small pieces of paper and began to sing in clear, sure voices, the 1960s song, "Abraham, Martin and John." They changed the last verse to:

> Has anyone here seen my old friend Bobby?
> Can you tell me where he's gone?
> I thought I saw him walkin' up over the hill
> With Abraham, Martin and John.

Well, Max cried, I cried—we all cried, and I met Julian at his car, and told him what was happening inside, and he cried.

I never dreamed that 12 years later, I would have completed books telling the stories of the lives of those two incredible women.

* * *

In 1964, I went to work for the American Friends Service Committee, as their Southern Field Representative. Beginning in 1960, I had been on the executive committee of the Student Nonviolent Coordinating Committee (SNCC)—the first white woman in those early years of SNCC—and AFCC wanted someone who knew the South and had worked with movement people. They were anxious to help implement Title VI of the 1964 Civil Rights Act, mandating local school districts to come up with a school desegregation plan or risk losing federal funding for their schools. This would have been devastating for most rural schools, and the plan that many of them drafted was called "freedom of choice." It entailed informing all parents that they could select whatever school they wanted their child to attend in the district. A good plan on the surface, it was a snare and a delusion for the black families caught in the peonage of the sharecropping system.

Nonetheless, in Sunflower County, on a cotton plantation in the middle of the Mississippi Delta, Matthew and Mae Bertha made the decision in 1965 to send seven of their school-age children to the previously all-white schools in Drew, a small town nearby. The Carters had thirteen children in all, and the first five who attended the shamefully inadequate "colored" schools had left the Delta as soon as they graduated. Matthew and Mae Bertha never hesitated in the choice to get their remaining children a better education. The AFCC office was alerted to the ensuing intimidation and harassment that followed this choice, and I first went to visit the family in January of 1966. The previous fall, their house had been shot into, credit had been cut off, their crops were plowed under, they were being evicted, and their children were suffering terrible treatment from both teachers and students.

On that first visit, when I asked why they had made this choice, in light of the consequences for the whole family, Mae Bertha in her eloquence told how she was tired of the worn-out school books coming from the white schools and the raggedy school buses also handed down and black teachers who had no degrees.

And when I asked Matthew the question about the "freedom" of choice, hands gently folded in his lap, he looked me right in the eye and said, "We thought they meant it." Certainly a tragic revelation of U.S. history that, in spite of a hundred years of broken promises, a black family in rural Mississippi would still believe.

Mae Bertha then told me about the overseer coming and trying to talk Matthew out of sending the children to the white schools and how she had sent the message back to him that she was a grown woman who had "birthed those children and bore the pain" and nobody could tell her where to send her children to school. She spoke of the embarrassments and persecution the seven children faced in the schools. First grader Deborah and third-grader Beverly were taunted and called names, including "walking tootsie roll." Pearl's fifth grade teacher had her sit in a desk isolated from the other children and had the white children rotate their seating so they would only have to sit by her one week at a time. And for high-schoolers Ruth, Larry, Stanley, and Gloria, it was a constant barrage of name-calling, whites jumping aside from them when they passed in the hall, moving away from tables in the cafeteria as the Carters approached, to the point where the Carter children wouldn't even eat lunch. "We would just go outside and stand by the wall of the school." Joined by Carl when he became of school age in 1967, they remained the only black children in the schools for five years until Marian Wright Edelman filed suit in 1970. The suit asked for relief against a discriminatory system that placed a "cruel and intolerable burden on black parents and pupils."

I lost track of the Carters when I left the AFCC in 1975 and began to work for the city government in Atlanta. Then in 1988, I saw Mae Bertha across the room at a conference on Women in the Civil Rights Movement. We rushed to hug each other, and I asked about the family. She told me that Matthew had passed away earlier that year and that all of the children had graduated from the white schools, had gone on to college and that seven of them had graduated from the University of Mississippi. I was inspired to write and spent many hours with Mae Bertha in her living room in Drew, interviewing her and all of the children. The result was *Silver Rights*, published in 1995 by Algonquin Books of Chapel Hill. Mae Bertha Carter died in 1999, and there is a red leaf maple tree planted for her in the "circle" at Ole Miss—with a plaque in her memory and to her seven children who graduated.

Winson Hudson was from a much different area and background from Mae Bertha Carter. She was born and raised in the all-black community of Harmony, Mississippi, in Leake County, in the hill country northwest of Jackson. Harmony was comprised of some 5,000 acres owned and farmed by independent black families who had bought the land after the Civil War and passed it down to succeeding generation with great care. Winson and her siblings were raised by a strong and outspoken "Grandma Ange" and a father who taught them to stand up for themselves at all times. I was working in Mississippi the summer of 1964, and Jean Fairfax, another AFCC staff person who was working in the Harmony community, had invited me to visit and meet the Hudson family. They were preparing for the first year of school desegregation under a court order. I did not work directly with Winson Hudson later in the 1960s, but I would see her at meetings from time to time, then in Virginia, and we had stayed in touch over the years.

In 2000, I got a call from Winson asking me to please help her finish her book—that she was going blind, couldn't walk and wanted to hold it in her hands before she died. She had had several people trying to help her, but there had been various delays, and she had been waiting so long. I had great admiration for this woman and her sister Dovie, who were legendary in their long struggles in and around Harmony—often in the face of violence and reprisals from a very strong Ku Klux Klan in the area. We spent many hours going through the materials and clarifying her stories to finish our collaborative work *Mississippi Harmony*, published by Palgave/McMillan, in the fall of 2002.

One of my favorite stories recorded about Winson is how she was finally able to register to vote. She was turned away, time after time, on one or another pretext—usually her "inability" to interpret a long passage from the Mississippi Constitution. In 1962, under the watchful eyes of a Justice Department representative whom she had contacted, the registrar again asked her about the meaning of certain paragraphs. She told him, "it said what it meant and it meant what it said." She passed the test and helped to head a voter registration in the county that registered over 500 black voters in a year.

She details in story after story her work in the county, including the freedom schools established during the summer of 1964 with the help of young volunteers. She had been elected president of the local NAACP in 1962, served for thirty-eight years and used the organization and her position to bring many programs to the county. She became recognized for her leadership and courage and lobbied in Washington and Chicago for local health care for blacks, and ever active in the Democratic Party, she was a delegate to several national conventions. As she says, however, the children were her "main love," and she worked throughout the state to establish Head Start programs. Right up to her death in 2004, she worried about the young people not understanding about holding on to the land or continuing to fight to preserve the gains made in the freedom movement, and waging new battles against the massive incarceration of youth of color. She wrote for the young people:

> Oh come my dear children and sit by my knee,
> And let me tell you the cost to be free.
> If I don't tell you, you never will know,
> Where you came from and where you should go.
> You contributed more than any race in this nation,
> Coming through hard trials and tribulation,

Fought in every war in America's name,
You never have dragged her flag to shame.
You can't afford to wait another day.
If I don't tell you, you never will know,
Where you came from and where you should go.

I believe that one of the blessings at this stage of my own life is to be able to tell about these two women whom I knew and loved over such a long period of time. They are a constant inspiration to me. For all of us, they serve as shining witnesses to the challenge from Ella Baker, another amazing leader in the movement, "We who believe in freedom cannot rest until it comes."

turbulent odyssey for justice*

Joan Loveridge-Sanbonmatsu

"And do you declare yourself a pauper?" asked the judge in Rochester, New York. I nodded. My lawyer directed, "You must answer verbally for the record." "Yes," I whispered in a faltering voice filled with shame, my cheeks flushed with embarrassment. We had no money to pay for the printing of court briefs. And so my sex discrimination court trial began with those words in 1972. Growing up in Vermont, I had been raised to be self-reliant, to have a job, to not be a burden to society.

In the Beginning

I was hired in 1963 as an assistant professor in Communication Studies after having worked two years in the Far East with the National American Red Cross, and having completed my master's degree at Ohio University. It was my first full-time teaching job with a tenure-track appointment. Brockport, New York, was a small town and I lived in an apartment on College Street and walked one block to Hartwell Hall where I taught.

The new-faculty orientation at State University of New York at Brockport was held in the Campus School Library. It was a crisp fall day in September with the maple trees turning golden when I walked into the library wearing my red coat. Everyone was sitting in little children's chairs at low tables. There were several empty chairs at one table where a handsome young man in a dark suit was sitting. *Destino!* To my surprise, this man was going to teach in the Communication Studies Department, and even more surprising was that his assignment was to share an office with another colleague and me. Akira Sanbonmatsu and I fell in love and married. I felt so excited and challenged to be teaching at Brockport. I had begun my doctoral work at Penn State in the summers, studying with Dr. Carroll Arnold in Rhetorical Studies. At Brockport, the students were responsive and highly motivated in my Oral Interpretation classes. We traveled to many festivals and their culmination project was to present a reader's theatre program at the Crypt, the local coffeehouse. A definite glow emanated from those early years of teaching.

Just moments after my wedding, though, without my knowledge, my line appointment had been changed to a temporary appointment due to the nepo-tism policies, antiquated policies established during the Depression in the early 1930s based on the idea of one salary from the same company for each family. In the radiance of new love, what did it matter?

Slowly and painfully, I learned year by year how it mattered. "You can't serve on the Personnel Committee. You're only a temporary," I was told. "But you can be on the Textbook Selection for the Basic Course Committee and on special committees to develop the undergraduate majors, and graduate pro-grams and courses."

"Search Committees?" I wondered. "No, only tenure track folks can be on those, but you can be on the committee to write departmental basic course exams."

And then during the departmental election for chairperson: "You can't vote on any personnel decision. You're only a temporary."

Now, the Faculty Senate was another avenue for university service, but again, rejection. I could, however, be a member of an ad hoc committee on the quality of student life, which I did. I felt like a third-class citizen.

Denial of Rights and Benefits

Denial of benefits, merit, and promotion opportunities followed. When it came time to do my residency requirement for my PHD at Penn State, I was forced to resign and be rehired on a temporary appointment. As far as merit pay increases went, I was told that I wouldn't get a salary raise because hus-bands should earn more than their wives. Again, with the birth of my first son, Jamie, I had to resign and be rehired in January. With the advent of the birth of my second son, Kevin, I requested a maternity leave which was met with the single statement that my request was moot since I was a temporary appointee. Due to the nepotism policies, I would not be reappointed.

The academic environment at Brockport was ill with a malignancy which devoured professional opportunity. The president, in addressing the Faculty Women's Association, told us that women belong in the home, raising chil-dren and cooking. Can you believe this? I was utterly shocked to hear him say this to a group of professional women with PHD, MFA, and MLS degrees.

Stand Up and Be Counted

There comes a time in one's life when one must stand up and be counted. I could have moved away, but I didn't. I stayed and challenged the nepotism policies in local and state grievance proceedings, the Human Rights Commission and finally in court, suing the SUNY Brockport and the SUNY system for sex discrimination. At first, I thought the subject of my court case would be only SUNY Brockport, but inequity was a pervasive policy in all the SUNY units. On this long, arduous road trip, tolls were taken.

One day when I was walking down Main Street in Brockport, passing the Strand Theatre and Liftbridge Bookstore, some "friends" crossed the street when they saw me approach. Yes, I felt shunned, not just once but time and time again. My toes were tender and they were being stepped on.

When I finally got up the courage to ask a "friend" of mine to testify, I knocked on her front door, only to be greeted and then cross-examined. "How could my testimony help your case when you already have my name on a list?" The list was comprised of twenty-seven pairs of relatives who taught at the college—wives and husbands, father-daughter, sisters and cousins. These twenty-seven cases favored the man, placing the woman in a temporary position. In any event, she refused to testify.

When it was my turn to testify, I felt as nervous as a deer treading in our backyard to eat apples. I remember waiting in the outer corridor of the Rochester Court House and walking down to the water fountain with my good friend, Harriet Sisson, and gulping down two Excedrins as a tension headache attacked me. Migraines and headaches came more frequently now. I couldn't even keep my weight up.

The press, television news, and radio call-in shows drained me of any joy in radio work, an area in which I had worked for nine years. A lack of privacy prevailed. I learned first-hand that anything said to the press "off the record" would be sure to show up in the next day's newspapers.

There were the endless credential evaluations, cross-examinations, and harassing phone calls. Reluctantly, we made the change to an unlisted phone number.

The Long Haul

At first, I told myself: I'm young, I'm strong, I can do this. I can outlive and outlast this administration. My lawyer, Tom Fink, explained, "This suit might take some time." To me, "some time" meant six months or so. To him, it probably meant more than that. As my younger son was born and both boys grew older, year after year, so did the court case with its illegal and frustrating disruption of life and my academic career. The courts were slower than cold molasses running uphill in the wintertime.

With the state's battery of attorneys appealing at every level of the court system, I began to lose confidence and self-esteem. I felt myself grow smaller. Transcribing hours upon hours of grievance hearings on tape got me down.

We couldn't afford to pay a professional to do it. I felt as if I wore a backpack filled with rocks strapped over my shoulders.

What lifted me up, though, was a ground swell of support from the Brockport United University Professions, Faculty Senate, loyal friends who stood by me, and many professional organizations.[†] The National Organization for Women launched the Rochester Legal Defense Fund for my case. Several other women involved in court cases on nepotism policies in the United States connected with me, in particular, Barbara Eakins from Ohio. We supported each other's cases and shared information. I learned it takes more than one purple finch to make summer.

Little by little, I regained some of my self-esteem by teaching as an adjunct at Monroe Community College, joining NOW, helping to found a Brockport NOW chapter, and working on the Women's Studies Committee to develop a major at SUNY Brockport.

Stunning News

On July 10, 1974, our family returned home from a visit to my brother-in-law in Spain. At the Kennedy Airport gate, Rosabel, my sister, and her family greeted us by waving a copy of *The New York Times* and wearing a huge smile. "You won your case!" she exclaimed, pointing to the headline: "State U. Nepotism Rule Voided." Rosabel read to us, "The Appellate Division of the State Supreme Court in Rochester has struck down the so-called nepotism rule of the State University of New York system. It called the prohibition against relatives working at the same institution illegal and arbitrary. The court's unanimous ruling came...."[†] Justice Simon wrote that the college's nepotism ruling constituted sex discrimination.[§] What a homecoming that was!

The *ACA Bulletin* concluded, "Thus Joan Loveridge-Sanbonmatsu's victory established a precedent in higher education: For the first time, an appellate court had ruled that a nepotism rule enforced in a university is a discriminatory practice. Her case will have the most impact on future decisions and challenges to nepotism restrictions." [‡] Tom Fink, our attorney, looked "forward to other cases being brought with the same result in other states."[‡]

Still, SUNY appealed. At the Court of Appeals in Albany, Tom Fink argued the case brilliantly while we bore witness in the courtroom and our two little boys stood outside the partially open door and listened to the arguments.

Victory

Elated! That's what we were when we heard that the Court of Appeals had unanimously concurred with the Appellate Court's unanimous decision that nepotism laws were, in fact, discriminatory and should be struck down. Our victory party celebrated six years in court. Many, many well wishers crowded into our home to share our joy.

By court order, I was reinstated at SUNY Brockport in 1976. A year later, I moved to a more hospitable environment in the Communication Studies Department at SUNY Oswego and became involved in the Women's Studies Program. It was a breath of fresh air! Six years later, the case was finally closed including the award of damages. Oswego was a new beginning for me, a rebirth. Tenure, merit, and promotions to associate and full professor followed with the support of many good women and men. I had moved on.

Surprises

At Oswego, my case preceded me in 1977. Two very active faculty members of the Women's Caucus were taking a law course and had just studied my case within the first few days of my arrival on campus. I was in the library when they were coming out of class. "Are you the Sanbonmatsu in the *Sanbonmatsu v. Boyer* case?" "In person," I smiled. With that, they welcomed me with open arms.

In 1987, I received a phone call. To my great surprise, I had been honored with the Trailblazer in Higher Education Award by the Central New York NOW Chapter to be presented at the Unsung Heroines Awards Dinner. It was an emotional and memorable night with my family, my sister, and friends there for me.

Life-Changing Event

This case was definitely a life-changing and life-measuring event. In 1969, I was preparing for my doctoral comprehensives and expecting our second baby when I put forth the first grievance proceedings. At that time, I had to make a decision whether to go forward with a court case. I decided at that time to complete my doctoral exams. In 1970, another crossroads emerged. The case was a path I did not ask to go down, but life handed me an opportunity. I had an unwavering belief that women should be hired on merit, not marital status nor relationship status. And as they say in Vermont, I stretched my arm longer than my sleeve would reach.

In the beginning, it was my own situation which motivated me to challenge nepotism policies. What kept me going was a growing knowledge that those policies affected more than myself, more than the Brockport campus, and more than the SUNY system with its 47 colleges. These academic policies affected such states as Pennsylvania, Ohio, Arizona, Massachusetts, Indiana,

Connecticut, and many other states. I learned this first hand by the requests made for copies of the Appellate Decision and Opinion or the briefs.

This turning point in my life developed my political awareness, a strong resiliency, and a revealing insight into the importance of a support network. Indeed, I learned to give back to the community by creating social change. This verse, adapted by me from a 1977 speech by Jill Ruchelshaus, says it all:

> For though it had been a long trek,
> we never gave up.
> We may have lost our capacity to lighten up,
> our youth, our tolerance, and our sleep.
>
> In return
> we have our self-worth in womanhood
> and dreams for us
> and our children.
>
> At Oswego when related professionals
> were hired on a tenure line and
> received tenure due to nepotism laws
> struck down, a sense of
> accomplishment washed over me.
>
> In Ohio, when my niece was hired on
> merit and tenured at the same university
> in the same department as her spouse,
> a thrill rippled through my heart.
>
> There is a certain knowledge
> that in the end
> we will be able to recall and
> say that
>
> once in our lives
> we gave all that
> we had for
> justice.

* This story is dedicated with special thanks to Akira Loveridge-Sanbonmatsu, my sons Jamie and Kevin, Tom Fink, Harriet and Ralph Sisson, Paula Morris and Barbara Eakins and all folks who supported the court case over the years. Further, grateful appreciation is given to Nancy Seale Osborne for her insightful suggestions and comments.

†National Communication Association Action Caucus on Anti-Nepotism Practices; Eastern States Communication Association Voices of Diversity; New York State Speech Communication Association; Rochester Women's Career Center; Genesee Valley NOW Chapter; Brockport NOW Chapter; Brockport Professional Women's Association.

‡The New York Times, July 7, 1974, 36.

§NY Supplement, Court Appeals, Sanbonmatsu v. Boyer, 357 N.Y.S. 2d 245, 45 A.D. 2nd 249, 245–250.

** Barbara Eakins, R. Gene Eakins, and L.J. Harris, "Anti-Nepotism Policies and Changes," Association for Communication Administration Bulletin. Issue #13, August 1975, 35.

†† Joan Loveridge-Sanbonmatsu, Speech Presented to the Action Caucus on Anti-Nepotism Practices at the National Communication Association Conference, Chicago, 1974, 5.

dancing in the dark

Demetrice Anntía Worley

At an English conference presentation,
77 people and I breathe molecules

from Julius Caesar's last dying breath.
This is the only connection between us.

I am in a herringbone tweed suit.
Gray and black crosshatch pattern confines

my hips, chest, back. Hair twisted,
tight coil, no loose ends escaping.

Small pearl earrings, one in each ear,
match the thin strand around my neck.

I present papers in white academia.
I match their foreign movements.

My jerky fox trot is invisible to them.
They see a waltz of standard diction.

"She speaks so well for a black woman."
One or two others like me,

dancing to a rhythm, they can't hear,
smile, nod, exchange partners.

I return home, shed herringbone layer,
run hands over warm caramel skin,

wide hips, small breasts, ashy knees.
Put my hair in thick braids.

Muddy Waters on the box.
Soul slow dances back into my body.

Reprinted from Spirit and Fame: An Anthology of Contemporary African American Poetry
(Syracuse University Press, 1997).

elena

Pat Mora

My Spanish isn't enough.
I remember how I'd smile
listening to my little ones,
understanding every word they'd say,
their jokes, their songs, their plots.
      Vamos a pedirle dulces a mamá. Vamos.
But that was in Mexico.
Now my children go to American high schools.
They speak English. At night they sit around
the kitchen table, laugh with one another.
I stand by the stove and feel dumb, alone.
I bought a book to learn English
My husband frowned, drank more beer.
My oldest said, "Mamá, he doesn't want you
to be smarter than he is." I'm forty,
embarrassed at mispronouncing words,
embarrassed at the laughter of my children,
the grocer, the mailman. Sometimes I take
my English book and lock myself in the bathroom,
say the thick words softly,
for if I stop trying, I will be deaf
when my children need my help.

Reprinted from *Chants* (Arte Público Press-University of Houston, 1984).

learning english:
chorus in many voices
Pat Mora

i feel like a small child
only able to speak very simple
all the time i feel incomplete

when i have children they laugh maybe

       i am trying to get out of ignorance
       a hole so deep

there my mother a professional
here no job   no friends but still i see
strong woman goes to school does not care
that people laugh when she speaks

       i am not shy just do not know
       english my big problem i believe
       i talk choppy
       but want opportunity

my husband helps me

       at my pronounce   mine sneers

mine an obstacle but
i never listen to him inside
i want my degree

       i cannot understand
       my tongue tied and nervous
       ashamed i feel

i am old so sometimes disappointed
pessimistic of my english   i study
                              i sometimes weep

my baby son three months   an american
will he tease his mother
who can not speak english so perfectly

     i am embarrassed
     almost every day
     why people so mean

I feel stupid
when i watch TV

     people still laugh at me
     when words stumble out
     i want to disappear

my child learns faster
how can i   what if we
use different languages some day
fat fear

     i feel a little burdensome
     much homework   teaching more fast here

it is not easy
in our new dream country
our language may not help our family

broken my english
but doing my best
to express
me

for the brave students who write me after reading "Elena"

Reprinted from *My Own True Name*
(Arte Público Press-University of Houston, 2000).

sharecropper's daughter

Jean Flynn

There were worse things than being a white sharecropper's daughter in the 1930s and '40s. But at the time I didn't think so. I didn't compare myself to people in the same economic class as I was. I compared myself to landowners' daughters who seemed to have everything: new, store-bought dresses; more than one pair of shoes at a time; their own rooms at home; white, manicured hands; and popularity among the classmates. My dresses were hand-sewn from flour sacks or hand-me-downs from my sisters, cousins, aunts, and friends, altered to fit me. My mother had no sewing machine and sat by lamplight in the evenings hand-stitching clothes. We had one pair of shoes at a time and wore them until we outgrew them or they wore out, which generally happened about the same time. My hands were callused by the time I was a teenager, but there are advantages to having older sisters. I wouldn't let them polish my nails because I didn't want to spend that much time keeping them looking fresh, but I let them trim and file them as long as they didn't take up too much time.

I had never thought a great deal about my childhood until I was in my forties. There is nothing like researching other women's lives to bring your own life into perspective. My life span ran parallel to many of the women I was researching for my book *Texas Women Who Dared to be First*. I began to look at my own background and the experiences I had as a female in the twentieth century.

I was born near Fitzhugh, Oklahoma, in 1934, during the Depression when women, especially poor women, had no voice but had as many children as possible to help support the family. In 1941, my family—mother and father, six siblings and two cousins—moved to northwest Texas and settled in the Lockett community nine miles southwest of Vernon, Texas, the nearest town. Two of my father's sisters lived in nearby communities and had encouraged my mother and father to join them. My father had always done odd jobs including working for the Works Progress Administration (WPA). The government established WPA in 1935 to relieve the jobless situation in the United States after the Great Depression. My mother and my older siblings had worked in the cotton fields and picked up pecans for extra money. Although my father knew nothing about farming, it was an opportunity to find work that provided a house for his family.

Northwest Texas was cotton country. The cotton rows were long and straight in flat, sun- baked fields. We looped around at the end of the rows to begin another long row only to loop around at its end. Chop out the weeds and grass around the short, new cotton. Thin the rows with a rhythmic chop, skip, chop. Never look up hour after hour. Stop only to drink cool water from a burlap-wrapped, tin milk can buried in the sand and to sharpen hoes when they became dull from chopping.

The same concentration went into pulling bolls from the cotton we had chopped during the summer. Some people in the South "picked cotton" from the hull and left the shell on the stalk. We pulled bolls including the hull which was later separated from the cotton, ground and used as feed for animals. We bent over row after row, not looking up until it was time to weigh a full cotton sack.

Except, I did look up.

Often when I reached the end of a row that bordered a road, I paused and looked both directions up and down the straight, unpaved, hazy, red road that disappeared into the horizon. I don't know how old I was when I thought *There must be more beyond this road.* My experience with a world outside my own limited life was in the pages of *Heidi* and western movies at the Pictorium Theater in Vernon on Saturday afternoons.

My father was a sharecropper and when we finished the fields owned by our landlord, we hired out to other farmers. I was considered a full hand by the age of ten. As most children began a new school year after Labor Day, we began pulling bolls and went to school only when it was too wet to work in the cotton fields. When I was in the fields, I prayed it would never rain. I was embarrassed to go to school because my classmates were so far ahead of me. Once I was there, I prayed that it would rain forever so I could stay in school.

We often worked in the fields with other families during peak boll-pulling seasons. I was just as obsessive/compulsive as I am now. I competed with the teenage males against my sisters' advice. "You are not as big or as strong as boys," they told me. "Once you pull as many bolls as the boys, you'll have to do it every day." And it was true. I was the shortest in my family of six children, but what I lacked in strength, I made up in stubbornness. I hated when we worked near the school bus route and hid between the cotton rows until the bus passed with my classmates in it. With the exception of the landowners' children, most of my classmates were as poor as I was, but they went to school and worked after school and on Saturdays.

My father was never meant to farm. He was generally hired because he had a wife and children who were hard workers. As I grew older, I realized that landowners took advantage of my father's weaknesses. They made their profits on the backs of women and children. It ingrained in me a strong sense of responsibility to fight for women and children's rights. My experiences on the farm also taught me to accept people, regardless of race, as human beings. We worked in the cotton fields with African Americans and Hispanics. We all struggled to survive.

My father accepted a job with the Vernon City Water Board in the summer of 1949 before I began my freshman year in high school. My mother became the cook at the Busy Bee Cafe where I was a waitress on Saturdays. The cafe had a back entrance off the alley into a room with one long counter and stools for "Coloreds Only." It was separated from the "white" area by the kitchen and dishwashing space. My mother and I were the only workers who would serve African Americans. Most of the time I divided my time between my customers in the "front" and the "back." When I saw black customers on the street, they wouldn't speak to me until I spoke to them and wouldn't look me in the eye for fear of being accused of insolence. Even though I served them in the cafe, they didn't know if they could trust a "white" girl. My father didn't like my being friendly to African Americans and Hispanics and we had many arguments over the treatment of minorities. It just didn't make sense to me that people could use them to make money and then treat them as if they didn't exist. It was not a popular opinion during the late '40s and early '50s.

I am the fourth child of six children, two sisters and one brother older than I and two brothers younger. My mother used to say that had I not been born at home, she would have sworn somebody mixed up the babies. By the time we moved from the country into town, my two sisters had quit school and married, and as soon as he was old enough, my older brother quit school to enlist in the military. I was determined to finish high school, although I received little encouragement from anyone.

The spring of my sophomore year, Mr. Benson, the Distributive Education teacher, approached me about entering his program my junior and senior years. (There were no school counselors those days.) He said, "Since you won't be going to college, this gives you the opportunity to go to school and work so you can graduate." I committed for my junior and senior years. The program required three core courses in the mornings to meet state minimum requirements for graduation and a work program in the afternoon.

The first year, I was secretary to T.G. McCord, an elementary school principal. Mr. McCord was ahead of his time. He was the first person to encourage me to go beyond high school and to tell me that I had rights as a woman. He also told me that I would have to fight for those rights. He inspired me to take risks that I otherwise would not have taken. I was also fortunate to have two remarkable women teachers in areas that have served me well over the years. Mrs. Abbott taught English and was the most beautiful woman I had ever seen. She had dark, curly hair and skin so white and smooth it was almost translucent. Her black eyes sparkled when she read poetry, and her love of words was contagious. Mrs. Pennington, a petite, blonde-haired woman with a leg and foot prosthesis, taught American history. While many students watched her, hoping her leg would fall off, I watched the expressions on her face. She was excited about American history and made it come alive for me. I know nothing about their personal lives, but I can still see their faces in my memory.

In the summer of 1952, just before my senior year in high school, I met Robert Flynn, whose parents had moved from their Chillicothe farm into Vernon. Bob was just discharged from the Marines and was re-entering Baylor University at Waco, where he was a sophomore. We began dating and saw each other only on the weekends that he hitchhiked home and on holidays. Those were the days when if hormones were stronger than common sense, you got married. I graduated on Friday night, May 29, 1953, and we were married on Monday night, June 1. I had worked as a shoe salesperson my senior year, so we had no doubts that I could get a job. At the age of eighteen I joined my life with a partner that I scarcely knew and moved to Waco, a town that I had only heard about.

In a friend's Studebaker, we blissfully moved everything we owned to Waco and rented a furnished house across the street from Baylor. Actually, it was a little "shotgun" house that had once housed black servants behind a stately home. We could stand in the front door and look through the kitchen window. But we didn't have much and no plans to increase our holdings anytime soon, so it was ideal for us. Bob enrolled for the summer while I applied for a job at the Texas Employment Commission. I was so recently married that they had to call my new name three times before I responded. It was probably the only laugh some of the people waiting had had all day.

While I was waiting for a job interview, Bob and I went to Baylor to register me at the university. The registrar said I would have to have the Academic Dean's permission because I had no high school transcript. We went to the dean and explained that I had not applied to Baylor, but that Bob was a student in good standing and I desperately wanted to be a Baylor student. Things were a lot looser in those days. The dean asked what my standing was in my graduating class and signed the enrollment form. I have never kidded myself that I am an intellectual, and I was petrified. I enrolled in Religion 101 which was a requirement for all students, and if you weren't a Baptist, you didn't admit it. I was a Baptist and still hated to admit it because I couldn't stand the superior attitude and piety of some of my classmates.

Most of the students in evening classes were married and either ministerial students or wives of ministerial students. Southern Baptists did not believe as Fredrick Nietzsche did that "Woman was God's second mistake." They believed she was his only mistake. They believed that since God had created such sinful species, that women were put on earth to serve men, and used Bible verses to prove their point: "Wives, submit yourselves unto your own husbands, as unto the Lord / For the husband is the head of the wife..." (Ephesians 5: 22–23). I pointed out that their interpretation of the Bible was hypocritical since most of their wives were working to put them through school. If she were smart enough to support the household, she should have a say in her own life. Their favorite rebuttal was to quote Paul "Let your women keep silence in the churches: for it is not permitted unto them to speak .... / And if they will learn any thing, let them ask their husbands at home ... " (I Corinthians 14:34–35). I reminded them that Paul contradicted himself because he also wrote, "I commend unto you Phoebe our sister, which is a servant of the church which is at Cenchrea" and other women "Who have for my life laid down their own necks: unto whom not only I give thanks, but also all the churches of the Gentiles" (Romans 16:1–4). I also reminded them that there would be no Sunday schools, Wednesday night suppers, nor choirs in any church without women. (No, I am no longer a Southern Baptist, but I am still an active member in a Baptist church that has women deacons and an associate female pastor.)

While Bob was working on his master's degree, I worked for Seven-Up Bottling Company in Waco. One of the questions E.E. Holt, the owner, always asked when interviewing was "Have you ever pulled bolls or chopped cotton?" I later learned that he hired anyone who answered "Yes" regardless of his or her qualifications and found a job in his company for them. I replaced a man as office manager but I earned less than one-half of his salary. He was paid $95 per week and I was hired at $45, which was considered a very good salary for someone my age and lack of experience. Nevertheless, I complained to Mr. Holt that I was doing the same work and should make more money. He disagreed with my reasoning with the statement "He was head of a household and you are not." I argued that it wasn't about a person's status or gender but about the quality of work and I was helping to support a household. He said he liked my spunk and raised my salary to $50 per week. We were great friends, but I never reached $95 per week although we frequently argued about it. He did allow me to take an early morning class and work later in the day because I had taken all of the evening classes available to me, and he encouraged me to finish my degree.

Our daughters, Deirdre Siobhan (1958) and Brigid Erin (1959) were born in Shelby, North Carolina, where Bob taught two years at Gardner Webb College. (We were so poor that we couldn't afford other entertainment!) When Bob joined the Drama Department faculty at Baylor in the fall of 1959, I returned to school to finish my degree. I wish I could say that I eventually graduated magna cum laude, but I didn't; however, nine years after enrolling in 1953, I graduated from Baylor with a BA degree in Secondary Education, English and Spanish. The fall of 1962, I began a teaching career that lasted thirty-two years.

My husband and the entire Drama Department resigned from Baylor in the spring of 1963 over a censorship issue with Baylor president, Abner McCall. My high school principal, a deacon in one of the leading Baptist churches in Waco, asked me to resign because of my association with the Baylor Drama Department. He said, "If you will resign, I will give you a letter of recommendation to another job." I refused and finished the school year. The entire drama faculty was hired by Trinity University in San Antonio, which meant a change of school districts for me. I was hired immediately for the fall semester, but my new principal told me later that my former principal had not recommended me.

In the spring of 1971, our younger daughter, Brigid, died suddenly of encephalitis. We didn't know who we were anymore. One-fourth of our lives was missing. It was an unfathomable abyss in our family structure. We each reached out for something to fill the void and anesthetize the pain.

I decided to get my Master's degree in Library Science at Our Lady of the Lake University, in San Antonio, while I continued to teach English. One Wednesday, I went to see an advisor at Our Lady of the Lake. He told me that they had just approved a program where a student could enter a class at midterm and receive full credit if all class requirements were met by the end of the semester. They needed a student to test the program. Midterm began the next Monday. I would have to take the entrance exam when it was administered on the following Saturday. He allowed me to enroll with the understanding that I had to pass the exam or be dropped from the class and lose my money. I enrolled believing that I would fail the test. I barely passed, but it was enough to keep me in graduate school. I completed my MLS in eighteen months.

As I struggled during those months of emotional upheaval and insecurity about who I was and what I was doing, I could not have done it without strong women in my life: friends who laughed and cried with me, who gave me the courage to wake up each morning and the wisdom to live only one day at a time, who promised me that eventually the pain would lessen, and who listened to my angry tirades without passing judgment while I questioned every aspect of my life.

After thirteen years of teaching English to high school students, I became an elementary school librarian. I often wrote materials for students and teachers, but a search for printed materials on Texas heroes and patriots led me to Ed Eakin of Eakin Press. Eakin was familiar with my husband's writing and asked me if I would consider writing children's biographies for his press. I was incensed at first. Did he think I knew how to write by osmosis because I slept with a writer? Ultimately it became a challenge I couldn't resist. I had taught research skills to students for many years, and now was the time to see if they really worked. I never believed that my first book, *Jim Bowie: A Texas Legend*, would be published, but it was the first of a series of biographies on men and women that I have written in the past twenty years.

Research for my books brought new understanding about how long women have fought for survival. Reading about the struggles and risks of other women gave me insight into my own identity and brought my own life into perspective. All of my life I have made unpredictable choices that are contrary to the expectations of others. My family expected me to marry young. I did, but I viewed marriage as a partnership in which my opinion carried equal weight to that of my husband. My parents, siblings, aunts, uncles, even cousins my own age never understood my desire for my own identity. It was sheer luck that I married someone who supports women's rights. (At the age of eighteen, no one is smart enough to recognize that or even understand the importance of it in a relationship.)

Women in my family always deferred to the men. My maternal grandmother was married three times and widowed three times. She always married older men and although she birthed only six children, she raised twenty-three. Each widowed husband brought children into the marriage, plus she raised two orphans on her own. All of the children loved and respected her. I knew only the last husband, my mother's stepfather, who counted his chickens before the families could leave after a reunion to be sure no one had stolen one to take home. After all the children married and moved to various places, my grandmother used illness as an excuse to gather all her wayward children around her. When everyone had been there long enough for her to tire of them she saw Jesus at the foot of her bed and recovered rapidly. I didn't know the word "manipulation" at the time, but I knew she was doing it. Even as a child I disliked it. I can remember no occasion in which she discussed politics or social issues. For her, that was a man's world.

My paternal grandmother was under five feet tall in comparison to my grandfather's six-foot, four inches. She was emotionally stronger than he and better able to deal with the tragedies in their lives over seventy-two years of marriage. She was always her own person and exuded an inner strength and peace that neither her husband or children had. She never voted in an election, but she had her own opinions and expressed them about politics and social injustices. She was lively and alert until her death at ninety-two. My grandfather, an outwardly gruff man, lived only a short time after her death. She had been his strength.

Most of my aunts, maternal and paternal, worked outside the home, many in farm fields beside their husbands. But the men were still considered the "head of the household." The men never helped with everyday chores around the house. My brothers disliked it, but they had to help wash and dry dishes after we had all worked in the field all day. They were the only males I saw doing any domestic work while I was growing up. I remember waking up early in the mornings and hearing my mother in the kitchen preparing lunch to carry to the fields while she was cooking breakfast. I remember thinking, "Why do mamas have to do everything? It's not fair." And yet, when I married, I tried to do it all.

My mother was a hard worker and cooked in cafes until she retired because of ill-health. Her legs could no longer stand the eight-hour shifts in a hot kitchen on concrete floors. She prided herself on a reputation of being the best cook in several counties, but never understood my desire for an identity based on my own merits. She thought that I should be happy as "Rosie's baby girl" or "Robert's wife." I was fortunate to be able to spend long weekends over the last months of her life telling her all the things she had taught me that were the foundation of my life. From her, I learned a work ethic that sustained me in all my jobs; I learned to feed a multitude of people at one time and enjoy doing it; I learned to take pride and pleasure in what I had at any given time instead of just looking to the future; I learned the joy of doing for and giving to others. I reminded her of how she distracted us in the hot June and July sun in the cotton field by teaching us Christmas carols, how she entertained us with ghost stories while we washed hundreds of mason jars for her to can on-the-halves for landowners. Although it frightened her, I believe she ultimately was pleased that I broadened my vision to encompass the world outside her life.

I am very fortunate to have known strong women as well as weak ones. I have learned from both. The more knowledgeable I become, the more aware I am of things I haven't done and the greater my desire for my life to make a difference. I support the underdog, campaign for women and children's rights, and stand against social injustices. My stubbornness hasn't abated with the years and I have experienced much beyond the straight, unpaved, hazy red road that beckoned me to explore life. I still look toward the horizon because I know there is more to be accomplished and discovered.

questioning

Janice H. Brazil

She starts with anger.
Toys with it, plays
with each letter as though
it were part of an elaborate puzzle.
She stands the A on its head
and swings it around the N
until so dizzy.
She falls on the G,
smothering the E—R.
Determinedly she connects the
letters again until she
feels their power.
But she needs to know
if their power is her power.
Or whether, it's a game.
A ritual.
Or the rites of passage
a woman bleeds through
in order to feel.

So she begins
again, first with the A.

Reprinted from *Outerbridge* (NY: The College of Staten Island) No. 25, 1994.

her place

Karen A. Waldron

Her bed a constant companion now,
eyes closed by time gone on too long.
Shaken alert, frail hand pushes angrily away.

A departed mother still with us,
she carried an umbrella on sunny days,
life's weighty fears in a fully stocked purse.

That purse lies empty now,
its contents scattered like ashes
across our universe of doubt.

Faithfully, she lived on and on,
no worry of chill in this hospital bed.
Heart still strong, conscience summoning Beyond.

Wasted frame forced fetally into trust,
she's in a different home these days.
Body a memory, soul a tantalizing promise.

They say she's alive, yet she's been gone awhile now.
Ivory wrinkles dissolved into rare softness
at odds with timeworn beads indenting her flesh.

Is there an end to this journey,
another beginning to sweep away the tiredness?
And if she finds nothing, where will she go?

no traveler

Ruth Kessler

The undiscovered country, from whose bourn
No traveler returns

—Hamlet

Upon our return from the islands of perpetual summer
   someone said you had left for the land of eternal darkness.
someone you and we barely knew.

We were dismayed at your self-inflicted exile,
               a destination more daring than any of ours,
and you so ordinary and timid.
We kept score:
how your winter buried our summer   snow-flake for sand-grain;
our palm trees shrouded in white like huge iciclic stalagmites,
   memorials to your willful defection.

We understood nothing:
the wounded angels that lured you to darkness,
   their wings' music audible to no one but you;
how you could not help but accept winter's unequivocal invitation,
   its long pointing finger of ice an eleventh commandment.

We never saw you tied to the mast, wax in your ears,
sailing past wrecked floes, life's infinite claims—
past the shadows and doubts attaching
   themselves like barnacles to your soul,
past all things that had ceased to matter:
parceled love,
a day-lily unfolding,
desperate telephone calls

of those who thought they knew who you were—
the world a grotesque bubble where all laws stammer,
the rainbow no longer a covenant between you and *any* God.

We never noticed your vessel
receding,
    surrender tangled in your hair,
your cold cold hands
your cold nets gathering darkness.

Later, we pinned down your shadow with
handy labels we found in textbooks.
Because the other language—
    doubt-ridden, winter-bound,
    in which you sang your laments and dirges to us
                            so softly, so audibly,
    the one spoken in parts we never intended to visit—
we branded foreign and refused to learn.

Reprinted from *The Evansville Review*, vol. X (University of Evansville, 2000)

stone house

Naomi Shihab Nye

My grandmother is dead
but her green trunk
must still be sitting.
Sitting in the stone room
with an arch
and a single window.
Sitting in the cool light
that touches
the chipped lid.
And I wonder where the key has gone.
The key that lived
between her breasts
whether she slept or woke.
And wouldn't let anybody touch.
I wonder if they have
emptied the trunk
or left her squares of velvet
carefully folded,
her chips of plates,
the scraps and rubble she saved
and wouldn't let us see.
Wouldn't let us see
because every life
needs a hidden place.
And I pray they
have not emptied it.

We brought her rosy soap
for the hidden place.
Heavy wedge of chocolate
twisted in foil.

She tried to eat the foil.
We brought her nothing big enough
but she saved it all.
The uncle made fun of her.
She lived too long.
The Queen of Palestine.
She would turn her face away
when he said that.
He died first.

And we never stayed.
No we never stayed.
The trunk stayed.
The grapes shriveled in the village
and didn't come again.
This was a sadness beyond telling.
Maybe if they didn't mention it
the grapes would return.
The clay they used for jugs
also went away.
The young men
went away.
It was a hard place to be
if you were staying.

Why do I think of that key
still planted firmly in the crack
over her heart?
She used to say the stone
was smarter than people
because it never went away.

Reprinted from 19 *Varieties of Gazelle: Poems of the Middle East* (Greenwillow, 2002).

elegy for an angel

Ruth Kessler

... and [Abraham] lifted up his eyes ... and , lo, three men stood over against him;
and he ran to meet them from the tent door, and bowed down to the earth and said:
... pass not away, I pray thee ... And I will fetch a morsel of bread ...

—Genesis

Look—
how again we
have turned away
from our door
the angel of Love
disguised as
mere mortal;
how she weeps
before God
of our failure
once more
to offer her bread
she would anyway
not have taken,
but picking it
up with her
suddenly visible
wings
would transform it
before our eyes
into the Heart
we have tried
to recover
to shield our
desperate nakedness
from the curse
of that
Primal Expulsion.

next year in jerusalem

Karen A. Waldron

I have never been so hated and terrified in all my life. As I walked alone into the Baghdad conference center, six enraged women approached me, one with her fist raised, others with voices shouting unfamiliar languages. A striking, dark-skinned woman grabbed my sleeve and yanked me close to her face.

"Our country is poor, our people starve, and you look away," she hissed. Another pushed her aside. "Your Hollywood is more important than our children's lives!" A third, "You are not welcome here. Why did you come?" Obviously, she and I had the same thought.

It was August 1989, the year before the first Persian Gulf War and American bombing of Baghdad. All visions of a fascinating, exotic trip to Iraq banished, I would have given anything to be in class with my students, home drinking tea, or even having a root canal.

Thoughts of escape vanished as I was abruptly shoved by a North Vietnamese reporter. "Murderer! Butcher! You have nothing to say that we want to hear!" Hiba, the Iraqi woman assigned as my "interpreter" pushed the reporter aside, and firmly holding my arm, moved me down the aisle of the modern, cavernous auditorium to a front row of tables. She seated me behind a card with my name and "United States" written in Arabic and English.

As much to escape the tirade of loud voices following me as fascinated by the simultaneous instructions in seven languages, I put on the headphones and studied the speakers' tables. Wiser than I, another American arrived through a side door and slid in next to me with a weak smile and wave at the annoyed-looking interpreter.

Hand outstretched, "Susan Bolton, Columbia University. I'm filling in for a colleague in Arab Studies who couldn't come at the last minute. But I'm not a speaker and will try to leave sooner if it gets too unsafe. Are you as petrified as I am?"

"Absolutely! I'm Karen Waldron, Trinity University, San Antonio. I'll be speaking the last day of the conference. Hopefully, things will settle down by then."

She observed, "There are two more American women attending, one who'll be presenting, and another, working in Paris for the State Department, who'll be here in a few days just to keep an eye on things." I already knew what that meant.

"Have you noticed that our 'interpreter' doesn't speak much English but never lets us out of sight?" I asked. "She's in several pictures with Saddam in the lobby. You know the Americans are the only ones staying at the Al Rasheed hotel?"

"Right," she exhaled. "Who invited you to speak?"

Ironically, I was a guest of the Iraqi government. The phone call had come suddenly at home, during the chaos and pizza of my son's fourteenth birthday party.

"Dr. Waldron?"

"Yes."

"I am calling from the Iraqi Embassy. The Council on U.S.-Arab Relations here in Washington gave us your name as a potential speaker at the Conference of the General Federation of Iraqi Women next month. We would like you to speak on issues around providing quality care for children world-wide."

As I motioned for my son to finish serving his friends, flashes of my visit earlier that year to Saudi Arabia and Bahrain immediately piqued my interest in this new adventure. The Council had sponsored a fascinating tour for a dozen college professors to further our understanding of the Arab world. Yet, as we travelled from Jedda to Riyadh to Dhahran, I was sure that I had disappointed their expectations by openly questioning the Saudi leadership about their harsh treatment of women. So I was very surprised when the Council recommended me for another foray into the Middle East.

He continued, "The conference will include approximately 1000 women from around the world. While most will be from Arab countries, predominantly Iraq and Egypt, others will come from North Vietnam, Lebanon, and as far away as Brazil and Finland. You will be one of two American speakers during the week. At the end of the conference, you will be our guest for tours of Basra and other areas along the Arab River."

As he waited, my mind moved quickly. It had not been a typical day. That morning, I had received a call from former neighbors in New York that my mother had suffered a small stroke. I would have to visit her immediately and arrange for her care. Always an independent woman, she would certainly resist, initiating a new and heartbreaking chapter in our lives.

I related to Susan other events of that day. At my older son's encouragement, during the party I visited for the first time with two brilliant Taiwanese brothers who desperately needed an American sponsor. They would otherwise return home to military duty and lost opportunities for future education. As I told my story in that Iraqi auditorium, I couldn't realize that just months later, these teenagers would become a permanent part of our family, kindred brothers to my sons, and eventually, American citizens and PHD engineers, one with an additional degree in law. Nor could I have known that I would come to love them as my own, welcoming thoughtful daughters-in-law and becoming *Ama* ("Grandma") to their beautiful children.

Also, single parents don't make quick decisions on the telephone. I would be gone almost two weeks and would have to arrange care for my sons and organize the start of their school year. But that hot Texas afternoon, I was startled when the Iraqi caller interrupted my thoughts. "We need to know *today* so we can begin to process your visa."

Later that day, with arrangements made and sons supportive of my venture, I heard myself say, "I'll be honored to speak," followed by a deep personal sigh acknowledging my craziness.

And now I was in Baghdad, again questioning my safety and sanity amidst the fury of women who just wanted my blood. *Why?* What had I done, what had the U.S. done, to provoke such anger? I learned over the next days, that often their rage was over what we *hadn't* done. The Brazilian woman who confronted me at the door announced heatedly that the U.S. could save her country's economy from bankruptcy, but we didn't care. The Palestinian delegate had lost a child who could have survived with treatments of basic antibiotics. She reminded me at every turn, "We are a homeless people. Why do you support rich Zionists and ignore our poverty?"

Hearing that I was from Texas, more anger was directed at me than at the other Americans. I appreciated their response, having recently seen re-runs of translations of the TV show *Dallas*, even in censored Saudi Arabia. The wealth and degradation of the Ewing family had become the benchmark for gauging Americans. I felt like Sue-Ellen in their eyes.

That day, I understood easily that a native Texan who was also U.S. President would be one of the most despised men in this region of the world. But I'm not sure what my emotions would have been had I also known that years later my own son would become an Army officer and risk his life on Iraqi soil. In the midst of such pervasive hatred, it was far better that only time brings such after-knowledge.

After the morning's ironically entitled "Welcoming Session," Susan and I headed for lunch with the interpreter in tow. Seated by ourselves, we were delighted when two Bangladeshi women dressed in brightly colored *saris* asked if they could join us. The conversation that followed opened my eyes to my own naïveté about life in other countries.

In excellent English, one woman commented softly, "We look forward to your talk on care for children. At times, our situation at home seems hopeless. Our parents love their children as much as you love yours. Yet, many are starving and uneducated and it seems better to sell their children for a meager amount to help the family. Other times, children are simply kidnapped as they walk to the market or school, never to see their families again."

"Why?" I asked in disbelief.

"Primarily for their body parts. There is a huge market for organ-donors, too great to be supplied by normal death rates and availability. So our children are bought for a pittance or stolen to be killed. Their hearts or kidneys sell for a fortune to wealthy families or medical foundations that are ignorant of the source. We hear that the biggest market is the United States."

I was horrified. And I slowly had a sinking realization that the paper I planned to present was all wrong. Listening to these women dedicated to saving children's lives dwarfed my proposed priorities of lengthening daycare hours and providing more training for workers. Back home, these needs would be applauded. Here, these issues would seem trivial, even laughable, when so many lacked a home, a parent, even a daily meal or hospital bed.

Afternoon sessions over, Susan and I walked back to the hotel, passing 20-foot pictures of Saddam on almost every corner. Saddam, the soldier in uniform, sternly holding a rifle. Saddam, the kindly father, smiling as he gently held a child on his lap. Saddam, the religious leader, looking blissfully toward heaven. Street vendors plied us with watches with Saddam faces. The interpreter hung close behind, never speaking.

But she couldn't be in two places, and when she left to meet the American arriving from Paris, Susan and I decided to see Baghdad for ourselves. Earlier, while on an official tour, as we stared upward in amazement at the Hands of Victory Monument, huge arches of crossed swords made from Iraqi and Iranian guns and helmets, a cabbie had approached us quietly. He promised that he would give us a personal tour of the bazaars and watch over our safety. But only if he were paid in American dollars, clearly a black-market item. While Hiba was preoccupied, we spent a morning with him in several loud, crushed marketplaces bargaining for crafts. He was our Arabic voice, interpreting prices by a shake of his head and walking away, returning with us later to bargain some more, with vendors shouting that our low offers were an outrage and he yelling back that their prices were exorbitant. When we ultimately reached agreement, smiles and quiet friendliness returned to their demeanor.

While clearly we were recognizable as Americans and unlikely visitors, I didn't need to wear my hijab from Saudi Arabia. Baghdad was far more liberal, with many women un-scarved, sporting casual but modest clothes as they laughed, visited, and shopped. Those in traditional Muslim dress wore colorful silk head-scarves along with bright pant-legs or long skirts peeking out from under abayas. Somehow these glimpses of flair added to the women's sensual allure. While never seen evenings in outdoor cafes, daylight and the marketplace openly belonged to the women.

There was an understandable curiosity, as vendors brought crates for our seats and poured us steaming coffee. Looking around nervously, the cabbie translated their questions about America.

Furious ones: "Do the Zionists run America? Is that why the U.S. lets Palestinians die?" "Why did your husbands let you come here without them?"

Yet, more were interested in clarifying their impressions: "Is Michael Jordan really that good?" "Do U.S. women have sex with everyone?" "Are all Americans rich?" And, most often, "Why are you in Baghdad?"

We knew that we were taking a chance by travelling with the cabbie and that he could be imprisoned for taking American money. Yet, over subsequent years, that remarkable 110-degree morning, made even hotter by the Turkish coffee, returned poignantly in stunned moments as I watched bombs erupt in Baghdad. The marketplace is gone, but the sounds and pictures of the people remain recorded in my memory.

Waiting vigilantly that early afternoon, Hiba saw the cabbie leave us a few blocks from the hotel with our goods and friendly farewells. Shouting furiously and following us, she threatened in very broken English to have him found and us sent home. Since it was typically difficult for us to understand her, we feigned ignorance and rushed off to the afternoon's solemn meetings.

Almost all the speakers elaborated the pitiful neglect of children. We saw slides of baby amputees in Lebanon and ten-year-old prostitutes in Bombay. A visceral sense of dread spread over us at grotesque pictures of circumcisions on young Northern African girls. Describing the child-kidnapping market for U.S. adoptions, the speaker stopped abruptly, stared at our table, and plaintively asked, "How can you steal our families from us?" My stomach turned.

As sessions ended that day, we met "Kay," the newly arrived American from the embassy in Paris. While giving us sparse information, she informed us that she was attending the conference "to keep an eye on things." Consistently and rudely, Hiba interrupted our attempts at conversations. She heralded Kay back to an isolated hotel away from all of us. Amused at her quiet acknowledgment as a spy by everyone, Kay managed to sustain Hiba's attention often enough for us to meet more of the conference women.

By now, anti-American sentiment had poured over into a tidal wave. Fueled by days of speakers' animosity and perceptions of U.S. negligence and materialism, Susan and I felt the risk of our very presence increase. With Kay's isolation, we were unsure of our alternatives. And the other U.S. conference speaker stirred the pot with a broad spoon.

As the party chair for a southern congressman, her heartfelt bitterness erupted in this supportive environment. In her speech, she described an America full of racial hatred and dismissive of the disadvantaged. She told countless stories of personal persecution as an African American woman. Adding that U.S. freedom and equality are mere propaganda, she described a country carried by the rich on the backs of the poor.

Listening in horror to details of dates and locations, I realized that these terrible experiences had indeed happened to her. She condemned the United States as powerful, threatening, and imperiously directing foreign policy to occupy and corrupt other nations. She ended by saying that she was ashamed to call herself an American. The audience cheered and applauded loudly, awarding her a standing ovation as she left the stage to scores of hugs and handshakes.

Leaving the auditorium worriedly, Susan and I discussed the speech. In her talk, the delegate had generalized her own experiences to those of all American women, minorities, and disadvantaged. Despite my childhood in a working-class family and Susan's ardent feminism, we hadn't shared these experiences. But we also knew that the racism she had endured was real and, clearly, that others have suffered poverty and gender discrimination for generations. Since few in the audience would have travelled to the U.S., she supported their worst fears and stereotypes. Irrespective of Susan's and my liberal personal and political beliefs at that moment, the speaker had indeed fueled an increasingly dangerous fire.

A tour of the Baghdad Museum and dinner at the Convention Center followed that day's sessions. Despite some glares, we quietly joined a small group of women conversing in English. When the Lebanese delegate, Samira, asked me my reaction to the conference, I told her honestly that I was horrified by what I had seen and heard.

I added, "I develop programs for children with disabilities, and I was particularly upset to see the number of child amputees in Lebanon after the war. Where are they being cared for?"

"Mostly at home or in orphanages, since there's no room in the hospitals.

But they won't be able to go back to school without assistance. Others who suffered burns or mental trauma will be cared for by any living family members. Sadly, we have nothing for the disabled."

She studied me carefully. "I can't imagine you would be willing to go there and help after we re-build?"

"Of course. Keep in touch and let me know when the time is right. Then we'll work out the arrangements." I gave her my business card.

"Then perhaps you would also do a smaller favor? My son lives in New York. We have lost mail and telephone service in Lebanon because of the war. I want to let him know that I'm alive and that I miss him. Can I give you a box of cigars to send him when you're back in America?"

Susan laughed. "I live in New York. I'll call him, tell him you're fine, and give him the cigars personally."

"Thank you!" as she wiped away tears streaming down her cheeks. She invited us to sit with her and a Brazilian woman for the dinner.

Despite her angry comments about the U.S. on my initial day at the conference, Celia turned out to be delightful, with an outrageously bawdy sense of humor. A stately and stunning woman from a wealthy family enmeshed in Brazil's conflicted government, she sacrilegiously joked about every political and social institution possible.

"Our men, they like women Rio-style. They wouldn't last here an afternoon!" We roared, finally remembering how to just laugh and enjoy the company of other women.

Even in the evening's more relaxed atmosphere, I worried about my speech. I had spent late nights writing revisions, but the message didn't have any heart. Since I was shunned by most women at the sessions, finding an Arab speaker to help personalize it was difficult.

But I remembered Rana, a friendly young Iraqi conference assistant who had greeted me with her story of fond memories of a childhood with her family in California. Slipping away from the table, I caught up with her as she left the hall.

Her open smile disappeared when I made my request. Inhaling, "Yes, I'll work with you on it, but only if no one's around. If you give it to me early tomorrow with your questions, I'll hand it back to you later. But don't tell anyone. It is a risk."

As I thanked her and returned to the table, my thoughts reflected on her world here in Baghdad. I have always felt that the air feels different in non-human-rights countries. From the moment we step off the plane, to subsequent observations of people coming and going between work and home, and even between those engaged in friendly conversations, there's a watchfulness, a sense of looking around to see who may be listening. But I was learning that even in such threatening environments where we exhale fear and anxiety, the commonalities among all of us are far stronger than that air we breathe and can certainly enrich our relationships.

Yet, it became obvious to me that the lack of open and honest personal and cultural exposure among the many nations represented at the conference had corrupted any sense of commonality. The only woman I could turn to for help had lived in California for years and had come to love Americans.

I realized that the conference delegates' hatred toward us was evident not only because of strong political and religious differences, but from their perception of America and its women. Not only the Iraqis, but the majority of delegates from around the world knew only MTV stereotypes and the conspicuous materialism they saw on filtered news reports. A universal trait that women share is their nurturing love for family. Yet, along with a divorce rate of almost fifty percent, images of many U.S. women dressed very sexually and of others as over-worked professionals appeared to be convincing evidence that we promote the breakdown of the family.

Or even if we did care about our own children, it ended there. So we supported kidnapping for body parts or adoptions and looked away when Palestinian teens died from violence and third-world children suffered poverty and disease. With profound personal loss and tragedies in so many families, anger and hatred had moved onto a need for revenge.

Samira's invitation to work with child amputees had been genuine, but also a test. Yet, her longing to contact her adult son and send him a present was universal. When Susan and I responded, she sensed that we cared. How could I reach the remainder of this huge audience? I pondered this after midnight as I completed my speech.

The following day sped by. Early, Susan and I waited on a line extending outside the building as we tried to change our Iraqi Air flights to leave the next day, immediately after conference closing ceremonies. Fearing that the ugly sentiments in the lecture hall might only worsen outside, we had decided to skip the tours of Basra and Babylon. We waited two hours behind women checking on their own flights home, apparently all too familiar with frequent changes and cancellations. But with one weary, irritable woman scheduling flights on a single computer, our chances were non-existent.

"Flights to Frankfurt are full. No other flights in Europe for two or three days. Next?!!"

To further engage her in our plight, I made a foolish attempt at humor as I placed a lollipop on the counter in front of her.

"*Baksheesh?*" I asked with a smile.

Not amused, she threw it fiercely in front of me and watched it smash on the floor.

"Next?" never making eye contact. We moved on.

I found Rana as we entered the conference hall and quietly handed her my next-day's speech.

"Here it is. I've re-written it completely. Just one request. Can you translate the sentences I've underlined into Arabic, giving me their phonetic pronunciation in English so I'll say the words properly?"

Surprised, "Are you expecting the simultaneous translators for the sessions to translate this new speech for the first time as you read it tomorrow?"

As I nodded, she gave an apprehensive headshake.

"They will be furious with you. They request speeches days in advance to cross-translate. Then they just read them at the sessions, maybe even tape them."

"Is there a chance that they'll read my former speech instead?"

"Not if we intervene. I'll contact the conference coordinator right now and ask her to let them know. But don't expect a present this holiday!" Rana smiled uneasily and moved on.

Finally, the day of my session arrived. I was certain that my paranoia had grown out of proportion and that things would go just fine.

"Perhaps no one will even show up," I mused hopefully as I made my way into the auditorium, noting scores of beautiful children waiting noisily in the lobby. They were all between five and ten years old, busily chatting with their mothers, many of whom were conference delegates. It appeared that the children would be part of this afternoon's closing session.

I was wrong about both the attendance and the children. For the first time that week, the auditorium overflowed to encompass more than a thousand women. The first morning speaker artfully elaborated potential social and health proposals in less-developed regions to increase mothers' survival in childbirth and reduce infant mortality. Her programs sounded wonderful, well-considered, and, as the audience was too well-aware, unlikely to ever happen because of lack of funding.

As she finished, with a deep breath, I gathered my notes and rose reluctantly to walk to the stage. Susan grabbed my arm.

"Wait!" she warned.

The doors opened and several delegates marshalled the large group of children into the auditorium and onto the stage. Only now each child carried a brightly written sign, written in Arabic and English:

"AMERICAN PIGS!" "ZIONIST-LOVERS!" "CHILD-MURDERERS!"

My heart pounding loudly, I watched in disbelief as the women led the children in wide circles on the stage screaming and shouting anti-American slogans. To the audience's delight, the simultaneous translators found no problem immediately informing us of these words of hatred.

At first, I was confused. The only previous demonstration I had witnessed personally had been earlier that year in downtown Riyadh. Saudi officials had good-naturedly rounded up workers out of their offices, handed them signs, and coached them to shout anti-Western slogans, louder and louder for the news cameras. Glad for the break from work, the demonstrators had participated with gusto, some raising fists in mock or real anger. With the cameras turned off, they joked and laughed immediately, making their way back to their offices.

But this was different. During the eternity of the fifteen-minute protest, I comprehended in horror that this demonstration had been carefully orchestrated to occur just before my speech. And there were no jokes or laughter this time. The organizers were using children purposefully to provoke revengeful anger through reaching the hearts of an all-female audience. It worked.

Most women stood, shouted along with the children, stomping their feet and clapping hands in cadence with the chants as the resounding decibel level increasingly filled the conference hall. Looking toward Celia and Samira, who sat with heads lowered, I realized that I had few supporters.

The demonstration ended in a fever pitch with a continuous standing ovation as the children marched out of the auditorium with their signs. Then the stomping continued impatiently. It was my turn to speak.

Moving almost robotically, I climbed the stage steps and approached the lectern. My eyes searched the wide audience vigilantly for any sign of violence. Along with hisses and apparently name-calling shouts, I noted that many of the women sat down, but removed their head-sets. Considering what might have occurred, I felt a sudden relief, smiling internally at this mild gesture of contempt.

At that moment, in order to re-engage their attention, I decided to open the speech with the words from Rana's Arabic translation. While my accent would be terrible, hopefully my intent would carry and even the more hostile delegates would decide to listen to the remainder of the speech. As I waited for the quiet to spread, I also saw others who sat and nodded at me, head-sets intact and interested. With their encouragement and Celia's broad grin, I began in Arabic:

أشكر احترامكم لكوني ضيفتكم و المتحدثة في هذا المؤتمر. و على الرّغم من حفيتها و ثقافتنا المختلفة اختلافا عظيما، فنحن كنساء نشارك التحدي النقدي في تربية أطفالا ذو صحة جسمانية و عقلية على الرغم من العالم المضطرب. دعوت هنا اليوم للكشف سويا عن ما أعرفه عن تطوير رعاية الأطفال ،و لكن جدت أني لأعرف شئ هذا الأسبوع على الإطلاق.

(I thank you for the honor of being your guest and speaker at this conference. While our backgrounds and cultures may differ greatly, as women we share the critical challenge of raising physically and mentally healthy children despite a troubled world. I was invited here today to explore with you what I know about improving children's care. But I've found this week that I really don't know very much at all.) At this comment, there were both laughter and hisses from the audience.

To great audience surprise, my opening words in Arabic were broadcast across the auditorium. I waited as loud murmurs responded along with some light applause. As I continued in English, a number of women picked up their discarded head-sets and quietly held one earpiece in place to follow the speech.

So I'll share what I've learned:

I've learned that governments hurt all women and children when they don't support them. We women bear and nurture our young. In turn, our children lead nations and become the future. But a mutilated or prostituted woman cannot bear or raise a healthy child. And a child who is malnourished or lacks an available medication dies or is under-prepared to become a leader. Each day of her life, a mother feels the trauma of losing her child or of seeing amputated limbs. Her anger and grief lessen her ability to nurture and guide her remaining children. She and her family turn to survival instead of hope. Without hope in the future, our resilience to withstand the present is lost.

I've learned that blame and lack of understanding breed hatred. If we women don't have each other and congresses such as this to share our ideas and negate stereotypes, we have nothing. While our cultures and religions differ, our love and concern for our families do not. Until more women are leaders of nations, we and our children will rarely be a priority over greed and politics. But as long as hatred prevails and divides us from the very commonality we share in raising and nurturing our families, we move backward and more children starve or play with land mines.

I've learned that revenge doesn't work. It can't bring back a lost husband or son, or give us food for our families. Revenge is bitter-sweet and momentary. But when it passes, our original pain returns even stronger. The only thing that remains after revenge is the

message to our children to expect to live their lives in anger and suffering and to hurt some-
one else first. The children of revenge become poisoned adults at a young age and view their
sole purpose as injuring or killing others. We as mothers can do better than this for our
families and our nations.

And I've learned from you, who sadly know it best, that war hurts everyone. There is
no real victor, no country that comes away unscathed, none without wounds inflicted on
its families forever. Who is the child that benefits from his father's death, his mother's rape?
War is not the answer.

While negative emotions were still powerfully present in the room, I could
feel audience attention and even agreement with my comments. Over the next
minutes, in the body of the speech, I explored specific physiological, emo-
tional, and educational needs of young children, enabling a solid foundation
for a healthy adulthood. Back on my "daily turf" here, I was able to relax more
and focus on elaborating the content.

Yet, as I concluded, I was very uncertain what the audience response
would be when I left the stage. Unsure that I could safely return to my seat, I
decided to end with the prayer Rana had translated and then leave the audito-
rium immediately.

Let us conclude with a prayer. The audience stood, heads bowed.

جنسية الطفل و عنصره لايهم، عندما طفل يموت و أم تبكي.أم تبكي لأم أم أخرى، و التي يوم ما سوف يكون
ألها. دعونا نوحد قلوبنا اليوم هنا لنقسم على إنها، أذى و موت الأطفال، و لنتشارك كل المصادر المتاحة ذات
المعاني السلمية.

(When a child dies, a mother cries. The child's nationality and race don't matter. One
mother cries for another mother's pain, which may someday be her own. Let us join our
hearts together here today to vow to end the harm and death of children and to share all
resources through peaceful means.)

As I looked out on this sea of strong women who wanted only a better life
for their children, I added the words that had been filling my heart that
remarkable afternoon:

Despite our different beliefs, may religions and governments come together to feed the
mutual roots that will support our children as they grow. For today's friends and foes
alike, Insha'Allah we will meet again in peace—Next year in Jerusalem.

To the echo of "*Insha'Allah*" across the vast room, I left the stage quickly and slid out the side door. As I heard some applause and progressively louder conversations, I realized in dismay that when ascending the stage, I had left the purse containing my passport on the speaker's table.

Another thing I had learned this trip was that without a passport, a person was country-less and in deep trouble. I saw Susan rush past delegates pouring out of the auditorium.

"Here, I thought you might need this!" I hugged her in gratitude as she solidly handed me the purse.

Before we could move outside to discuss the audience response, the North Vietnamese reporter grabbed my arm.

"Can I interview you?"

"Why?" I asked in surprise, afraid that my comments would be used as propaganda.

"Most of my readers will be surprised. Your words and ideas were respectful and important."

"OK," I agreed hesitatingly. "But no political questions. The article can be only about women and children."

Abashed, she nodded and moved me to a quieter corner. But individually and in pairs, a number of women followed us. As I stopped to visit with them, they thanked me for my comments, several having their words translated into English by others:

"We are ashamed that they used children in the protest."

"You're right! We have to focus our attention on what we can achieve in our families."

And mostly, "Thank you for being here and agreeing to speak."

I was taken aback most strongly as a Palestinian woman in a solemn black *abaya* waited for others to leave and then commented, "My English is not good, but I want to tell you that my son died in the *antifada* last year. My family mourn him each day and my younger sons plan their revenge. But we must not let this happen. I cannot lose any more children. Thank you for your words." Stoically, she walked away.

So the sentiment changed in a small way. Did most women there still feel anger and even hatred toward Americans? Of course. I knew that even if I were the cleverest of speakers, I couldn't change that. But I felt that the tide was moving again, that the earlier waves of sentiment had been buttressed for awhile. Despite their rage, they had invited me and allowed me to speak. And putting their emotions aside, they had listened.

But it was I who learned and changed the most. In the following days, as we boarded planes and vans to tour Basra, I sat with different women and heard stories of their families, of death and disappointment. As we observed the Iraqi and Iranian troops standing with weapons steadily pointed at each other across the Arab River, they spoke of fathers, brothers, and husbands still missing after seven years of war. We drove past men stripped to the waist in 119-degree desert heat, pushing boulders without equipment as they re-built roads and villages. At the ruins of Babylon, we stood together and marvelled over the brilliance of its architects and scientists, yet recognizing that a civilization had been lost.

There were light moments as well. We all watched two totally cloaked women dutifully follow their husbands as they walked down the street in conversation. Yet, each was holding out the front of her dark veil so as not to burn a cigarette hole.

On a tour, Celia and I were each grabbed by the arm and pulled roughly from a mosque by an angry man who felt it was blasphemy to allow us to enter. Shouting, he snatched off our *abayas* and yelled seemingly horrible things at us in Arabic. Seeing this, several Iraqi women from our group came to our assistance and chased him away. How we laughed afterwards when he stood in the receiving line in the reception hall. He was one of the hosts! Yet, as we passed through, all the women in our group moved by him quickly, none even acknowledging him or returning his now-friendly greeting.

It was time to go home. The conference and tour over, we were boarding the bus for the airport. Samira pressed a box of cigars into Susan's hands.

"I wrote my son a long letter too, with his address on the envelope. You'll see he gets these?"

"I can't wait to meet him," Susan responded, "and let him know about his wonderful mother."

Hugging me tightly, Samira whispered, "*Insha'Allah*, next year in Jerusalem."

"*Insha'Allah*," I prayed.

on the pulse of morning

Maya Angelou

Delivered at the Inauguration of President William Jefferson Clinton, 1993

A Rock, A River, A Tree
Hosts to species long since departed,
Marked the mastodon,
The dinosaur, who left dried tokens
Of their sojourn here
On our planet floor,
Any broad alarm of their hastening doom
Is lost in the gloom of dust and ages.

But today, the Rock cries out to us, clearly, forcefully,
Come, you may stand upon my
Back and face your distant destiny,
But seek no haven in my shadow,
I will give you no hiding place down here.

You, created only a little lower than
The angels, have crouched too long in
The bruising darkness
Have lain too long
Facedown in ignorance,
Your mouths spilling words
Armed for slaughter.

The Rock cries out to us today,
You may stand upon me,
But do not hide your face.

Across the wall of the world,
A River sings a beautiful song. It says,
Come, rest here by my side.

Each of you, a bordered country,
Delicate and strangely made proud,
Yet thrusting perpetually under siege.
Your armed struggles for profit
Have left collars of waste upon
My shore, currents of debris upon my breast.
Yet today I call you to my riverside,
If you will study war no more.

Come, clad in peace,
And I will sing the songs
The Creator gave to me when I and the
Tree and the Rock were one.
Before cynicism was a bloody sear across your brow
And when you yet knew you still knew nothing.
The River sang and sings on.

There is a true yearning to respond to
The singing River and the wise Rock.
So say the Asian, the Hispanic, the Jew,
The African, the Native American, the Sioux,
The Catholic, the Muslim, the French, the Greek,
The Irish, the Rabbi, the Priest, the Sheik,
The Gay, the Straight, the Preacher,
The privileged, the homeless, the Teacher.
They hear. They all hear
The speaking of the Tree.

They hear the first and last of every Tree
Speak to humankind today.
Come to me,
Here beside the River.
Plant yourself beside the River.

Each of you, descendant of some passed-
On traveler, has been paid for.
You, who gave me my first name, you,
Pawnee, Apache, Seneca, you,
Cherokee Nation, who rested with me, then
Forced on a bloody feet,
Left me to the employment of
Other seekers—desperate for gain,
Starving for gold.

You, the Turk, the Arab, the Swede,
The German, the Eskimo, the Scot,
The Italian, the Hungarian, the Pole,
You the Ashanti, the Yoruba, the Kru, bought,
Sold, stolen, arriving on a nightmare,
Praying for a dream.

Here, root yourselves beside me.
I am that Tree planted by the River,
Which will not be moved.
I, the Rock, I, the River, I, the Tree,
I am yours—your passages have been paid.
Lift up your faces, you have a piercing need
For this bright morning dawning for you.
History, despite its wrenching pain,
Cannot be unlived, but if faced
With courage, need not be lived again.

Lift up your eyes
Upon this day breaking for you.
Give birth again
To the dream.

Women, children, men,
Take it into the palms of your hands,
Mold it into the shape of your most
Private need. Sculpt it into
The image of your most public self.
Lift up your hearts.

Each new hour holds new chances
For a new beginning.
Do not be wedded forever
To fear, yoked eternally
To brutishness.

The horizon leans forward,
Offering you space
To place new steps of change.
Here, on the pulse of this fine day,
You may have the courage
To look up and out and upon me,
The Rock, the River, the Tree, your country.
No less to Midas than the mendicant.
No less to you now than the mastodon then.

Here, on the pulse of this new day,
You may have the grace to look up and out
And into your sister's eyes,
And into your brother's face,
Your country,
And say simply
Very simply
With hope—
Good morning.

Reprinted from *The Complete Collected Poems of Maya Angelou* (Random House, 1994).

contributors' biographies

WENDY BARKER

Wendy Barker's *Poems' Progress* (Absey & Co., 2002) is a selection of poems accompanied by autobiographical essays meditating on the process of writing. Her translations (with Saranindranath Tagore) from the Bengali of India's Nobel Prize-winning poet, *Rabindranath Tagore: Final Poems* (George Braziller, 2001), received the Sourette Diehl Fraser Award for Translation from the Texas Institute of Letters. Of her three collections of poetry, *Way of Whiteness* (Wings Press, 2000), received the Violet Crown Book Award, and *Let the Ice Speak* (Greenfield Review Press, 1991), won the Ithaca House Poetry Prize. Her poems and translations have appeared in magazines including *Poetry*, *The American Scholar*, *The Kenyon Review*, *Stand*, *Partisan Review*, and *Antioch*. As a scholar, she is author of *Lunacy of Light: Emily Dickinson and the Experience of Metaphor* (1987) as well as co-editor (with Sandra M. Gilbert) of *The House is Made of Poetry: The Art of Ruth Stone* (1996). Recipient of NEA and Rockefeller fellowships as well as other poetry awards, including the Mary Elinore Smith Poetry Prize from *The American Scholar*, and Gemini Ink's Award for Literary Excellence, her work has been translated into Hindi, Japanese, and Bulgarian. A Fulbright lecturer in Bulgaria in 2000, she is a professor of English and poet-in-residence at the University of Texas at San Antonio.

KIM BARNES

I am the daughter of a logger and was raised in the remote logging camps of northern Idaho. I am the author of two memoirs: *In the Wilderness: Coming of Age in Unknown Country* (Doubleday/Anchor), and *Hungry for the World* (Villard/Anchor). My first novel, *Finding Caruso*, was published by Marian Wood Books/Putnam in 2003. I am co-editor, with Mary Clearman Blew, of *Circle of Women*, an anthology of contemporary western women writers (University of Oklahoma Press). *Kiss Tomorrow Hello: Notes from the Midlife Underground by Twenty-Five Women Over Forty*, co-edited with Claire Davis, was published by Doubleday in 2006. I received my BA in English from Lewis-Clark State College in 1983, my MA in English from Washington State University in 1985, and my MFA in Creative Writing from the University of Montana in 1995. My work has appeared widely in anthologies and journals, including *The Georgia Review*, the 2002 Pushcart Prize anthology, and *Shenandoah*. I am the recipient of two grants (1991, 2001) from the Idaho Commission on the Arts. In 1997, I was honored with a Pacific Northwest Booksellers Association Award for *In the Wilderness*, which was also a finalist for the PEN/Martha Albrand Award, Quality Paperback Book Club's New Visions Award, and the Pulitzer

Prize. I teach creative writing and literature at the University of Idaho and live with my husband and children on Moscow Mountain.

Isaura Barrera

The daughter of Manuel Barrera and Rafaela T. Barrera, my perspective on courage and risk-taking is nested in the courage and risk taking that my parents modeled for me. Not only did they enter a cultural context other than the one they were born into, they also witnessed immense technological change: radios, cars, phones, planes, to name a few. The lessons they modeled for me, both implicitly and explicitly, are interwoven through both my personal and professional life. Personally, I am a Mexican American female with a passionate interest in reading, spirituality, teaching, and the dialectics of communication and paradox. Professionally, I have worked over 25 years in early childhood special education programs in San Antonio, TX and Western New York as well as in New Mexico. Currently I am an associate professor in the Special Education Graduate Program at the University of New Mexico in Albuquerque. I continue to work as a consultant nationally and have recently co-authored a book entitled *Skilled Dialogue: Strategies for Responding to Cultural Diversity in Early Childhood* (2003, Paul H. Brookes Publishing).

Janice Hosking Brazil

I grew up the middle child of a career army soldier and lived in Germany for seven years. There I developed a taste for travel and a sense of adventure. I hold a degree in European history from San Jose State University and my masters from San Jose State. I was in my thirties with two children when I discovered a love for creative writing and began to write poetry as well as essays. Much of my poetry deals with people and places in my life, while my essays revolve around my travels. I have had several pieces published in journals including *Outerbridge*, *Lucidity*, and *Springhouse*. Over the years I have been actively involved in Girl Scouts, Amnesty International, the Peoria YMCA Board, and the San Antonio Friends in Hospice program.

Valerie Bridgeman Davis

I am a poet. I learned in the past twenty years that there is a difference in being a poet and writing poetry. One is about being—the other about doing. I be a poet. I be writing poetry. I love to read it and to write it. I write to save my life. The women poets who fed me early on as I was learning to write and read poetry were Alice Walker, June Jordan, Lucille Clifton, Nikki Giovanni, and Audre Lorde. Growing up in the United States' Deep South and feeling very much like a creature from another world, I learned to question and savor and cry. And I love to people watch, which is where much of my poetry comes from. I've traveled throughout the United States, and to several other countries and I find that mothers want the same thing for their children—health, food, happiness. That's why people intrigue me. We can be so alike and so different at the same time. I teach at a seminary where I also direct the arts and theology institute, so I get the rare opportunity to combine my love of the arts and my concerns for theology. I have been fortunate to perform on the same stage with Naomi Shihab Nye, Susan Bright, Talaam Acey, DaShade, and the like. I have poetry in *My Soul is a Witness* (Beacon Press), wedged between Nikki and Lucille. I performed for "An Evening with Bill Moyer" at the KRLU Public Broadcasting Station for Austin, Texas. I was one of the main poets for the station's "Poetry Out Loud" series in 1995. I've had several individual poems published, in the anthologies *Kente Cloth* (University of North Texas Press), *Coming Full Circle,* and *Everywhere is Someplace Else* (Plain View Press), and *Red Boots and Attitudes: The Spirit of Texas Women Writers* (Eakin Press).

ROSEMARY CATACALOS

Growing up hearing and speaking three languages (Spanish, Greek, and English) caused me to have (1) one of the oddest ears around, (2) a painful sensitivity to misunderstanding, and (3) a healthy sense of compassion. These qualities can be useful to a poet, though the jury is still out as to whether or not I've made the most of them. I have received National Endowment for the Arts, Stanford University/Stegner, and Dobie-Paisano writing fellowships, and from 1997–2003 was an Affiliated Scholar at Stanford's Institute for Research on Women and Gender. My poems appear widely in trade anthologies and textbooks and have twice appeared in *Best American Poetry.* I am a former executive director of The Poetry Center and American Poetry Archives in San Francisco, and have consulted extensively on arts funding and policy in various states, as well as nationally and internationally. Currently, I am executive director of Gemini Ink, San Antonio's center for literary arts and ideas.

ROSETTA MARANTZ COHEN

Born in New Jersey and educated at Yale and Columbia, I began my professional career as a high school teacher in New York City. For the past 15 years, I have been a professor in the Department of Education and Child Study at Smith College, where I teach courses in the history and philosophy of education and in American Studies. I'm the author of five books, four on education-related subjects (school reform, the history of the teaching profession, etc.), and one poetry collection which, unsurprisingly, is no longer in print. Several of my books were written in collaboration with my husband, Samuel Scheer, a high school English teacher. Sam's many years of work in the public schools—and daily stories about teaching—help me maintain street credibility as a professor of education. Sam and I are currently collaborating on an ethnography of his school, a large comprehensive high school outside Hartford, Connecticut, where the best and worst aspects of public education are on view each day. We are assisted in our writing efforts by our daughter Elizabeth, who, at 16, has a keen critical eye as well as an obvious personal investment in the topic.

PAULA M. COOEY

Paula Cooey holds the Margaret W. Harmon Chair in Religion at Macalester College in St. Paul, Minnesota. After receiving her PHD in Religion from Harvard University

(1981), she taught for eighteen years at Trinity University, San Antonio, Texas, before going to Macalester in 1999. She teaches courses in history of Christianity, Christianity and culture, and theory and method in the study of religion. In addition to numerous articles in scholarly journals, she has published several books, among them, *Religious Imagination and the Body: A Feminist Perspective* (Oxford University Press, 1994) and *Family, Freedom, & Faith: Building Community Today* (Westminster John Knox Press, 1996). Her most recent book is *Willing the Good: Jesus, Dissent, and Desire* (Ausburg Fortress Press, 2006). She is married to Philip C. Nichols, Jr., the mother of Benjamin Charles Cooey Nichols, and the mother-in-law of Rebecca Rosser.

Nan Cuba

My beliefs about the value of literature were confirmed while I studied with Richard Russo, Robert Boswell, and Chuck Wachtel in the Warren Wilson MFA Program for Writers. Along with my degree came a responsibility to investigate the human condition through the crafting of fiction. My stories spotlight existential situations, raising questions for readers to consider. Besides offering entertainment and solace, art should inform and provoke, ultimately challenging the status quo. I, at least, aspire to that. Besides having poems, reviews, and stories published in journals such as *Quarterly West*, *Harvard Review*, and *Columbia: A Magazine of Poetry and Prose* and in anthologies such as *New Texas '92* and *Inheritance of Light*, I have recently completed a novel, *Body and Bread*, and am now editing an anthology of work by San Antonio writers. I am the proud founder and Executive Director Emeritus of Gemini Ink (www.geminiink.org), but now teach literature and writing as an assistant professor of English at Our Lady of the Lake University.

Constance Curry

Constance Curry is a writer, activist, and a fellow at the Institute for Women's Studies, Emory University, Atlanta. She has a Juris Doctor degree from Woodrow Wilson College. Curry did graduate work in political science at Columbia University and was a Fulbright Scholar at the University of Bordeaux in France. She earned her BA degree in History, graduating Phi Beta Kappa and *summa cum laude* from Agnes Scott College in Decatur, Georgia. During the early 1960s, she was the first white woman on the executive committee of the Student Nonviolent Coordinating Committee, and from 1964 to 1975, Curry was Southern Field representative for the American Friends Service Committee (AFCC). From 1975 to 1990, she was the City of Atlanta Human Services Director, a Mayor's appointee. Curry is the author of several works, including her award-winning book, *Silver Rights* (Algonquin Books of Chapel Hill, 1995), which won the Lillian Smith Book Award for nonfiction in 1996. Curry is the producer of a documentary film, *The Intolerable Burden*, based on *Silver Rights*, but showing today's resegregation in public schools and the fast track to prison for youth of color. She has written, edited, or partnered in writing four other books about people who worked in the freedom movement. Connie Curry has helped illuminate the struggle for justice.

JEAN FLYNN

When you are a poor farmer's child in Northwest Texas, you do not grow up dreaming of becoming a writer, or a teacher, or a librarian with a Master's Degree. You dream of owning your own farm or ranch with a two-storyed house and a white picket fence. Or you fantasize about beating the pants off the boys pulling bolls or chopping cotton with you. I did both. I dreamed and I fantasized but I never expected to achieve the things I have in my lifetime. I have experienced immeasurable joy and unmitigated tragedy and have come out a stronger woman because of the experiences. My story is not unique among women my age. We all grew up in turbulent times, but unfortunately, some women never get beyond the pain or are too complacent to try anything new. I did take risks and profited by it. After nine years, a marriage, and two children, I finished my BA at Baylor University and taught English for thirteen years. It was as an elementary school librarian that I began to write biographies for young readers. My first book was *Jim Bowie: A Texas Legend* and my most recent and tenth book is the biography, *Henry B. Gonzalez: A Rebel with a Cause*. I am currently working on a book about Texas ranchwomen.

GAYNELL GAVIN

After practicing law in the Boulder-Denver area for several years while raising my son, I decided to go to graduate school in English, thereby making myself a living study in economic downward mobility. I practiced law primarily in the areas of juvenile and family law, particularly the latter; most of my juvenile practice was in the area of abuse and neglect, although I handled occasional delinquency cases also. *What I Did Not Say: Reflections of an Attorney-at-Large*, my book about that experience, was a finalist in the AWP Award Series in Creative Nonfiction. "Choosing" is one of the chapters from *What I Did Not Say*, which deals with social justice issues of race (including racialized levels of care sometimes provided to children in the abuse and neglect system), gender, and class. I am also the author of *Intersections* (Charlotte: Main Street Rag, 2005). I have prose and poetry published or forthcoming in such publications as *The Chronicle of Higher Education*, *The Comstock Review*, *Fourth Genre*, *Natural Bridge*, *North Dakota Quarterly*, *Prairie Schooner*, *Quercus Review*, *Texas Journal of Women and the Law*, *Viet Nam War Generation Journal*, *Best New Poets 2006* (Charlottesville: Samovar Press, 2006), and *Times of Sorrow, Times of Grace* (Omaha: Backwaters Press, 2002). I am a past recipient of the Academy of American Poets Wilbur Gaffney Award (University of Nebraska-Lincoln) and the Audre Lorde Creative Writing Award (The Poetry Center at San Francisco State University). My poetry chapbook, *Intersections*, was published by Main Street Rag Publishing in late 2005.

GAIL HOSKING GILBERG

I live in Rochester, New York, and divide my time among teaching, writing, and literature at Rochester Institute of Technology and writing my own work. My memoir, *Snake's Daughter: The Roads in and out of War*, was published by the University of Iowa Press in

1997, the same year I received an MFA from the Bennington Writing Seminars at Bennington College in Vermont. Since then my essays and poems have appeared in such places as *The Threepenny Review, Florida Review, The South Dakota Review, Tar Hill Poetry, The Fourth Genre, The New Jersey Ledger, The Chattahoochee Review, Nimrod,* and *The Cream City Review.* My poem "Poetry's Beginnings" was published in *Visiting Frost,* an anthology of poems about Robert Frost, published by the University of Iowa Press. I am nearly finished with a second memoir—this one about my mother and the effects of the military culture and war on families. Its working title is "Oh Glorious."

BÁRBARA RENAUD GONZÁLEZ

I was a monthly columnist for the *San Antonio Express-News* from 1992 until the post-9/11 purges. My columns/essays have appeared in the *Dallas Morning News, Los Angeles Times, La Opinión, Houston Chronicle, Fort Worth Star-Telegram, The Nation, The Progressive, Ms. Magazine,* and others. I have been a finalist for six Katys (the five-state journalism awards). My work is in diverse anthologies, including *Cornbread Nation* (University of North Carolina Press, 2004); *Aztlan and Vietnam* (University of California Press, 1999); and McGraw-Hill's anthology for middle school students, *The Reader's Choice,* 2000. *Glimmer Train* recently chose an excerpt from my unpublished novel, *Golondrina: A Texas Story,* for their top 25 in their fall 2006 fiction contest. I am most proud of having led the establishment of the Latino Cultural Center in Dallas, Texas, as the only Chicana on the city's Commission for Cultural Affairs.

DIANE GRAVES

I was born in Pittsburgh, Pennsylvania, and grew up in Hudson, Ohio, a small town between Cleveland and Akron. (*New Yorker* fans may recognize it as the home of Ian Frazier.) I attended Emory University, worked for the publications office there for a year, and then went back for my master's in Librarianship. Serving first as director, then dean, of Library and Information Services at Hollins University in Roanoke, Virginia, I have also been a library administrator at the University of Mississippi and at Loyola University, Chicago. I am now university librarian at Trinity University, San Antonio, where I focus on information literacy and marketing services to students and faculty, as well as promoting positive change from the traditional academic library to a more dynamic service and access environment. I am active in the higher education and technology organization, EDUCAUSE, and in the Oberlin Group of Library Directors.

TERRI BRONOCCO JONES

I grew up knowing that I was blessed and that something special was in store for me. My earliest memories are of the constant encouragement my parents gave me at whatever endeavor I was undertaking. I believed that with hard work, integrity, and a generous heart that I could accomplish anything. And I did! I even conquered breast cancer, an experience that transformed my life forever. With blessings come responsibility, however. I no longer reach up trying to grab the brass ring. Instead, I reach down to lift up women less fortunate than I. By forming WINGS (Women Involved in Nurturing, Giving, and Sharing) to pay for breast cancer treatment for uninsured women, I am able to touch hundreds of lives—each lived with such grace and dignity—of women who face financial, health, and emotional devastation when they hear the words, "It's cancer." My husband David and I hope to leave a legacy of kindness to the next generation, to make the world just a little bit better because we passed through and stopped to help.

CATHERINE KASPER

Currently, I am an associate professor at the University of Texas in San Antonio. My books include *Field Stone* (winner of the 2004 Winnow Press first book contest), *A Gradual Disappearance of Insects* (Pecan Grove Press 2005), and *Optical Projections* (Obscure Publications). A collaborative novel with authors Rikki Ducornet and Amy England is forthcoming from Leaping Dog Press. I am interested in interdisciplinary approaches to the humanities, in particular the intersections of visual arts, architecture, science, and literature. In addition to teaching creative writing, I teach a wide range of courses on twentieth century literature including courses on hybrid-genres, long poem sequences, and Modernism. Before returning to school in my thirties, I was a babysitter, a bookstore clerk, a pastry chef, an assembly line worker on the night shift, a caterer, a secretary, and a marketing director (among other things). A great deal of my life has been spent helping take care of sick and ageing parents. Both these realities enter my poetry and fiction, but also contribute to an overwhelming awareness of the brevity of life.

RUTH KESSLER

Ruth Kessler was born in Poland, grew up in Israel, and currently lives in Rochester, New York. Her poetry, translations, and short fiction appear in such publications as *Seneca Review, Southern Poetry Review, Hawai'i Pacific Review, Puerto Del Sol, Nimrod, Evansville Review, The MacGuffin, Adirondack Review, Texas Observer, Gihon River Review, Switched-on Gutenberg,* and the *Anthology of Magazine Verse & Yearbook of American Poetry.* She is the recipient of grants and fellowships from the New York State Council on the Arts, Yaddo, MacDowell, VCCA, and VSC. She has completed two poetry collections, a short fiction collection, and a children's book.

LAURA MARTIN LABATT

I earned my BA and MA in Speech and Language Pathology at our Lady of the Lake University, San Antonio. Teaching provided me with an opportunity to travel. After teaching one year for the Department of Defense in Misawa, Japan, I returned to San Antonio and worked in a psychiatric center with children with emotional problems. Subsequently, with several psychologists, I began an educational clinic for children with learning differences. After my own two children reached school age, I opened a private practice. Education has been my focus even in my community service, including women's issues, literacy, career development, Hospice, and care for the elderly. As President of Bexar Country Women's Center and as an instructor teaching women career development at San Antonio's Ecumenical Center and Junior League, I enjoyed helping other women discover their potential to become independent and successful. Currently my attention is focused on raising awareness and funds for San Antonio Hospice. It is a rewarding opportunity to appreciate the precious value and dignity of life.

AMY FREEMAN LEE

Raised in Seguin, Texas, by her grandmother, Amy Freeman Lee was a poet and a painter. In 1949, she was a founder of the Texas Watercolor Society, and more than 1,250 exhibitions of her own work were sponsored locally and nationally. She received an Honorary Doctorate and was president of the Board of Trustees at the University of the Incarnate Word. Always witty and irreverent, she was an arts critic for newspapers and a radio hostess, and received the Maury Maverick Award from the ACLU, with special recognition given to her courage and outspokenness during the days of communist-hunting by Sen. Joseph McCarthy. Entirely in longhand, she wrote four books, volumes of poetry for her personal collection, and was an author for hundreds of publications. Her prodigious writings are collected at Texas Tech University. In 1985, she was the subject of a CBS documentary on her life and accomplishments. While her art and writings were recognized hundreds of times, one of her most precious honors was the Joseph Wood Krutch Medal from the Humane Society of the U.S. Their highest award underscored her love for animals and profound reverence for life. While still writing and painting, Dr. Lee died in 2004, at 89. She had reflected that she didn't know if she would make it to heaven, but "If I get up there and my dogs aren't there, I'm asking God for my money back."

BARBARA LOVENHEIM

Barbara Pitlick Lovenheim has a BA from Ohio University, an MA from Tufts University, and a PHD from the University of Rochester. She is presently a Professor in the English Department at Monroe Community College, Rochester, where she teaches critical and creative writing in addition to Honors courses in Critical Theory and Witchcraft. She is the editor of *The Flower City Review* at Monroe Community College. Her critical publications are "Lydia Coonley-Ward," *Women Building Chicago, 1790-1990: A Biographical Dictionary*; "Joanne Goldenberg Greenberg," *Jewish American Women Writers: A Bio-Bibliographical and Critical Sourcebook*; "Picturing Webs of Significance: Adult Truths and Knowledge in Picture Books," *Community College Humanities Review*; and "Anne Sexton's 'Cinderella': Teaching Poetry in the Developmental Classroom," *Perspectives on Practice in Developmental Education*. She has had the poem "Lies That Were Told" published in *Hazmat* and additional critical work in *The Encyclopedia of Chicago Women* and *New York College English Association Journal*.

Joan Loveridge-Sanbonmatsu

Joan Loveridge-Sanbonmatsu, poet, writer, and professor emerita in Communications Studies, Women's Studies, and Intensive English at SUNY Oswego, has recently published her third book, *Imperial Valley Nisei Women: Transcending Poston*(2006), now in its second printing. Her first collection of poetry and stories is entitled, *Winged Odyssey: Poems and Stories*. Dr. Loveridge-Sanbonmatsu co-authored *Feminism and Woman's Life* with Nancy Seale Osborne, Kiyoe Sugimoto, and Teruko Nakata. In addition, her articles, poems, stories, and non-fiction have been printed in such publications as *The Howard Journal of Communications*; *Phoebe, A Feminist Journal*; *Women Public Speakers, 1925–1993*; *Life in a Fishbowl: A Call to Serve*; *Starfish*; *The Oversea'r*; and others. She has read from *Winged Odyssey* at the National Women's Studies Conference Writers Series in Las Vegas, San Juan, Colorado Springs, Vermont, Massachusetts, New York, Florida, Pennsylvania, and from her latest book. She shares her life with Akira Loveridge-Sanbonmatsu, her sons Jamie and Kevin, and her two cats, in Oswego, New York.

Bonnie Lyons

A professor of English at the University of Texas at San Antonio, Bonnie Lyons received her BA from Newcomb College and her MA and PHD from Tulane University. She has taught at Newcomb College, Boston University, as a Fulbright Visiting Professor at the Institute for American Studies in Rome, the University of Florence, the University of Haifa, the University of Athens, and the University of Tel Aviv, and as a Fulbright Senior Lecturer at Aristotelian University (Thessaloniki, Greece) and Central and Autonoma Universities in Barcelona. Her first book, *Henry Roth: The Man and His Work*, was published by Cooper Square Publishers in 1977. She has published more than fifty articles on Margaret Atwood, Kate Chopin, Tillie Olsen, Grace Paley, Cynthia Ozick, Henry Roth, Philip Roth, Delmore Schwartz, and Bernard Malamud, among others. Her second book, *Passion and Craft* (co-authored with Bill Oliver) was published by the University of Illinois Press (1998), and another book of literary interviews is in progress. Her first chapbook of poems, *Hineni*, was published in 2003, and a full-length book of poems, *In Other Words* (from which poems in this volume were selected) was published in 2004. A second chapbook, *Meanwhile*, appeared in 2005. She calls *In Other Words* "my favorite project. It combines two of my deepest interests—feminism and Judaism. Reading the scriptures and trying to imagine the characters as real women rather than symbols or allegorical figures made the stories come alive in new, fascinating ways. Imagining myself into Jezebel and Lilith was a delicious, freeing process. My current book manuscript, *Bedrock*, is a spiritual autobiography in poems. I intend to spend the rest of my writing life fashioning the strongest poems I can."

Pat Mora

Reflecting on her sixth poetry collection, *Adobe Odes* (University of Arizona Press, 2006), Pat notes, "I was, of course, inspired by Pablo Neruda's odes and wrote praise songs to much that I love from apples to words." Her poems, characterized as "proudly bilingual" by *The New York Times*, include the collections *Aunt Carmen's Book of Practical Saints, Communion, Borders,* and *Chants. Agua Santa: Holy Water* is being re-issued by University of Arizona Press. The *Washington Post* described her memoir *House of Houses* as "a textual feast ... a regenerative act ... and an eloquent bearer of the old truth that it is through the senses that we apprehend love." *Nepantla: Essays from the Land in the Middle* will soon be re-issued. An award-winning author of poetry, nonfiction, and more than twenty-five children's books, Pat is completing *Dear Teacher: Seven Practices for Creative Educators.* She is the recipient of an Honorary Doctorate in Letters from Buffalo State College (SUNY). Among her other awards are the 2006 National Hispanic Cultural Center Literary Award, The University of Texas at El Paso's Distinguished Alumna for 2004, and a Civitella Ranieri Fellowship to write in Umbria, Italy. Pat was also a Visiting Carruthers Chair at the University of New Mexico, a recipient and judge of the Poetry Fellowships from the National Endowment for the Arts, and a recipient and advisor of the Kellogg National Leadership Fellowships.

NAOMI SHIHAB NYE

Naomi Shihab Nye grew up in St. Louis, in Jerusalem, and in San Antonio, her current home. Her books include *You & Yours; Going Going; A Maze Me; 19 Varieties of Gazelle; Baby Radar; Poems of the Middle East* (a National Book Award finalist in 2002); *Come with Me: Poems for a Journey; Words Under the Words: Selected Poems; Never in a Hurry; Fuel; Mint Snowball; Red Suitcase;* and *Habibi,* a novel for teens which won six Best Book awards. Her books for young readers include *Come with Me: Poems for a Journey; Sitti's Secrets; Benito's Dream Bottle; Lullaby Raft.* Editor of poetry anthologies: *This Same Sky, The Tree Is Older Than You Are, I Feel a Little Jumpy Around You* (co-edited with Paul Janeczko); *The Space Between Our Footsteps: Poems & Paintings from the Middle East; What Have You Lost? Salting the Ocean: 100 Poems by Young Poets,* and *Is This Forever or What? Poems and Paintings from Texas.* Nye's award-winning work has been featured on PBS poetry specials including NOW with Bill Moyers, "The Language of Life with Bill Moyers," and "The United States of Poetry." Her work has been presented on National Public Radio (*Prairie Home Companion* and *Writer's Almanac,* among other shows), and she is poetry editor for *The Texas Observer* and a regular columnist for *Organica.* In 2001, she received a presidential appointment to the National Council of the National Endowment for the Humanities, one of many honors.

GINGER PURDY

A long-time advertising and public relations professional, Ginger Purdy holds degrees from Texas Woman's University and sits on the University's Foundation Board. She served on the local, district, and national boards of the Association of Women in Communications for many years and received their Headliner Award for outstanding service. She has been a member of the state steering committee for Women's Legislative Days, a trustee for the Women's and Children's Hospital, and active in the task force for development of the University of Texas at San Antonio inner-city campus. She was a founding member of the first University Women's Center. A member of the

International Women's Forum, she received their "Women Who Make a Difference Award" in 1992 and was one of the first inductees in her city's Women's Hall of Fame. Honored with a lifetime achievement award from the YWCA and named State Woman of the year by BPW/Texas, in 2004 the Women's Studies Institute of the University of Texas at San Antonio made her their first annual "Women's Advocate of the Year" for her service to the community through her dedication to helping women. She is the author of *Come On In, There's Room for Us All!*, a motivational book for women. Speaking engagements have taken her throughout the country, as well as to Mexico, Germany, and China. She is the proud mother of five daughters, including two step-daughters.

HILDA RAZ

I'm the Glenna Luschei Endowed Editor of the literary quarterly *Prairie Schooner*, now entering its 81st year of continuous publication and also the founding editor of the *Prairie Schooner* Book Prize Series in Poetry and Short Fiction. Professor of English and Women's and Gender Studies at the University of Nebraska and a past president of AWP, I serve as a member of the Board of Directors for the Goucher College MFA in creative nonfiction. My new book of essays, written with my son Aaron Raz Link, is called *What Becomes You*, and is an account of our experience of Aaron's transsexual transformation. Previous books of my poems, most recently *Divine Honors* and *Trans*, were published in the Wesleyan University Press Poetry Series, and *Living on the Margins: Women Writers on Breast Cancer*, was published by Persea Books. As a journals editor, I'm proud of publishing widely in other journals, *Creative Nonfiction, Fourth Genre, GenderQueer, Pleiades, Puerto del Sol, Paterson Literary Review*, and elsewhere, and proud to report that recent essays were listed in the 100 Best in Best American Essays.

DORIS SAGE

I grew up in rural Oregon and married at age 17, two weeks after graduating from high school. My husband, age 19, had just returned from the Navy to enter the University of Oregon on the GI Bill. Because some members of our family were convinced our marriage would not last, I took business courses to ensure employment and homemaking courses so we could survive otherwise, while my husband was completing his degrees. During this time our two sons, Michael and Douglas, were born, and I continued to enjoy part-time study. When my husband began teaching at Syracuse University, my scattered course work up until then qualified me to become a teacher and I was assigned to an inner city school. This was during the late 60's, and in Syracuse, a time of racial conflict. It was an experimental program of change, attempting to make integration work; it was an exciting time and where I knew I wanted to be. After 21 years of teaching in the Syracuse Public Schools, I retired to become a full time storyteller and to travel extensively. My husband and I developed an interest in how our government intervenes in the affairs of Latin American countries. What we witnessed there and the stories we heard led to advocacy and civil disobedience that resulted in our arrest and six-month imprisonment in 1998. We were recognized, in absentia, with the Kharas Award by the ACLU and the Adin Ballou Social Justice Award at the Unitarian Universalist General Assembly in Rochester, New York. We now have three beautiful grandchildren, continue to be active in peace work, and in June 2007 celebrated our 60th wedding anniversary.

JOAN E. SHALIKASHVILI

Born in Portland, Oregon, Joan Shalikashvili received both her Bachelor and Master of Arts degrees in Education from Oregon State University. Through her extensive travels with her husband, the Chairman of the Joint Chiefs of Staff of the United States Armed Forces, and son, Brant, she had the opportunity to work closely with youth activities and military families in the United States, Europe, and the Pacific. Joan has always had a special concern for military members and their families stationed far from home. Awards she has received throughout the years are the Red Cross Clara Barton, Field Artillery Molly Pitcher, VII Corps Helping Hand, Heidelberg Star, USAREUR Soaring Eagle, three civilian public service medals, and Distinguished Public Service awards from the Secretary of the Army and the Secretary of Defense. One of the highlights in her life was being selected as the sponsor of a Navy Aegis-class guided missile destroyer, DECATUR (DDG73), which was christened in November of 1996 and commissioned in August of 1998 in her hometown. She is currently on the USO-Puget Sound Area board of directors, is the treasurer of her PEO chapter, has served as the vice-president and membership chairman for the Steilacoom Historical Museum Association, and helps with fundraising for the local community theater, the Lakewood Playhouse. She continues to maintain her membership on the Board of Advisors of the National Military Family Association.

ESTELLE M. SHANLEY

Estelle Shanley was an award-winning journalist in Boston and Chicago and has extensive U.S. and international journalistic experience. She is also a public relations expert who has worked in academia, business, government, and the not-for-profit sector. She is a frequent contributor to *Desert Magazine* and lives in Palm Springs with her husband, Dr. John B. Duff, retired President of Columbia College, Chicago. Shanley's work has been published in literary journals, magazines, and newspapers, as well as the *Dictionary of American Biography*. She is a native of the Republic of Ireland and is currently writing a series of short stories focusing on growing up in Ireland. In 1979, she had the distinction of being the first female journalist in the locker room of the Boston Red Sox, days following the Supreme Court action lifting the ban on women reporters entering the locker room.

BERT KRUGER SMITH

From 1952 until 1999, Bert Kruger Smith served as Special Consultant to the Hogg Foundation for Mental Health at the University of Texas, Austin. Throughout her years of service, she wrote and edited over 120 publications, and taught courses in mental health information, special education, and gerontology. She developed a partnership between Austin Groups for the Elderly (of which she was a founding member) and the Gerontology Institute at the University of Texas, and was honored with the creation of the Bert Kruger Smith Centennial Professorship in the School of Social Work. For more than 40 years, she was an advisor to community, state, and volunteer organizations, and served as a role model to young women involved in mental health, community, and communication. She won numerous awards, including Texas Woman of the Year and Austin's Most Worthy Citizen and was inducted into the Texas Women's Hall of Fame. Her alma mater, the University of Missouri, awarded her an honorary Doctor of Humane Letters degree. Her books include a novel, A Teaspoon of Honey, and non-fiction, Looking Forward, The Pursuit of Dignity, His World Upside Down, and No Language But Cry, among others. Her books have been selected by Women in Communications to be honored on three occasions. The organization named her their National Headliner in 1966. In an interview some years ago, she is also quoted as saying, "The thing that makes me the happiest is the feeling that I have touched other lives in meaningful ways. I can't think of a better way to live than to know you've made a difference." Bert Kruger Smith died on July 26, 2004. Indeed, she did make a difference.

Susan J. Tweit

I'm a field ecologist who studied grizzly bears, sagebrush, and wildfires before turning to writing when I realized that I loved the stories in the data more than I loved collecting the data itself. To me, nature's plots and intrigues are as compelling as any in fiction: who sleeps with whom, who eats whom, who cooperates and who competes and who cannot survive without whom. My writing celebrates the connections between individuals and species that animate the landscapes where we live. I'm the author of ten books that explore the relationship between "human" and "nature," including Barren, Wild, and Worthless: Living in the Chihuahuan Desert, hailed by Southwest Book Views as "one of the greatest titles ever for the Southwest." I've written hundreds of essays, newspaper columns, articles, and commentaries for audiences as diverse as Audubon Magazine, the Los Angeles Times, Popular Mechanics, and listeners to the Martha Stewart Living Radio Network. You can hear my weekly commentaries on "The Nature of Life" on my website: http://susanj.tweit.com.

Karen A. Waldron

I am a Professor of Education Emerita and former Director of Special Education at Trinity University, San Antonio, Texas, my position for 28 years. As a lecturer and consultant in Eastern and Western Europe, the Middle East, Australia, New Zealand, and Hong Kong, my focus has been on healthy child and family development, as well as the design of programs in general and special education so that we can meet the needs of all of our children. Currently, I consult with school districts and families of at-risk youth, as well as children and adolescents with disabilities. In support of teachers and families, I have published four previous books, numerous research articles, three professional handbooks, and a website with international colleagues. I serve as a Trustee for the George W. Brackenridge Foundation, dedicated to awarding scholarships and educational resources to students from underserved, minority backgrounds. In 2005, I was honored to receive the Professional Achievement Award from the Association for Women in Communications for my publications, media appearances, and consultations with parents and professionals. My PHD in Special Education Administration and my MS in Reading Education are from Syracuse University. My BA in Education is from the State University of New York, with a major in English and concentration in writing. I have taught students ranging from early childhood to graduate school. Throughout my research, professional, and personal experiences, I have found that the role of women as role models and risk-takers is critical to the family and community. Consequently, I decided to explore why some women are motivated to take more risks than others and the impact of their journeys on themselves and society. This book, containing prose and poetry by these brave women, is the result of this exploration.

DEMETRICE ANNTÍA WORLEY

Born and raised on Chicago's westside, I came of age in Peoria, Illinois. This combination of urban and small city living provided me with a foundation constructed of (in Nikki Giovanni's words) "Black love is Black wealth" (a shout-out to Chi's K-town), Black feminism (via my family, bell hooks, and Nikki Giovanni), and Black humor (praises to Peoria for nurturing Richard Pryor who taught the world about Black pain and joy through laughter). This foundation served me well while earning the following degrees: BA, *cum laude*, English, Bradley University; MA, English, University of Illinois, Urbana; DA, English, Illinois State University. I am a Cave Canem Poetry Fellow Workshop alumna. My poetry has appeared in literary journals such as *Permafrost*, *The Spoon River Poetry Review* (where I was a finalist for the 2002 Editor's Prize), *Clackamas Literary Review*, and *Rambunctious Review*. In addition, my poetry appears in several anthologies including *Temba Tupu! (Walking Naked) Africana Women's Poetic Self-Portrait* (Africa World Press/The Red Sea Press 2006), *Spirit & Flame: Contemporary African American Poets* (Syracuse University Press, 1997), and *Reflections on a Gift of Watermelon Pickle and Other Verse*, 2nd edition (ScottForesman, 1994). My scholarly publications include co-editing *Language and Image in the Reading-Writing Classroom: Teaching Vision* (LEA, 2002), *African American Literature: An Anthology* (McGraw-Hill, 1998), and *Reflections on a Gift of Watermelon Pickle ... And Other Verse* (ScottForesman, 1994). Currently, I am an associate professor of English at Bradley University, where I teach courses in creative writing, African American literature, composition, business writing, technical writing, and writing theory. In every spare moment, I visualize peace.

MITSUYE YAMADA

In 1942, along with my mother and three brothers, I was sent to a concentration camp in Minidoka, Idaho, a few months after the outbreak of World War II. Ten camps were built in the desert areas of western United States to house 120,000 Japanese nationals and Japanese Americans. I was permitted to leave camp after a year and a half to attend college in Ohio. I describe my impressions of being exiled in the desert in my first book of poetry, *Camp Notes and Other Poems* (Shameless Hussy Press, 1976). My collection of short stories and poems, *Camp Notes and Other Writings* (Rutgers University Press, 1988), is a combined edition of my first two books. My poems, essays, and short stories have been published in numerous anthologies, including: *This Bridge Called My Back: Writings by Radical Women of Color* (Cherrie Moraga and Gloria Anzaldua, Eds.); *Women Poets of the World* (Joanna Bankier and Deirdre Lashgari, Eds., Macmillan Pub,1983); *Introduction to Literature* (Sylvan Barnet, Morton Berman, William Burto, Eds., Harper Collins, 1993); *Bold Words: A Century of Asian American Writing* (Rajini Srikanth and Esther Y. Iwanaga, Eds., Rutgers University Press, 2001); *New Worlds of Literature: Writings from America's Many Cultures* (Jerome Beaty and J. Paul Hunter, Eds. WW Norton & Co.); *No More Masks! A Flowering of Asian American Arts* (Florence Howe, Ed. HarperCollins, 1993); and *Yellow Light: The Flowering of Asian American Arts* (Amy Ling, ed. Temple University Press, 1999). I served on the Board of Directors of Amnesty International USA from 1987 to 1993, and am an active member of the Committee on International Development of AIUSA which funds and promotes development of human rights work in Third World countries. I am a member of Interfaith Prisoners of Conscience (IPOC), an organization that works to free political prisoners in the United States, and Director of Multicultural Women Writers. Now, as Professor Emerita and grandma to six grandchildren, I continue to teach, write, and learn.

NANETTE HELENA YAVEL

Nanette (Nina) Yavel was born in Brighton Beach, Brooklyn and graduated Phi Beta Kappa from Brooklyn College in Chemistry and Psychology in 1971. Nina lives in Greenport, NY with her loving felines, Ruby and Billie; and shares a home in Southhampton with her life partner, Jesse. She reflects, "I had wanted to be a doctor, but soon after graduation I became severely depressed and spent 2 years in and out of hospitals. Over the next 20 years, I found my way back to health and self-sufficiency." She has written poetry since age 14, published in journals and magazines, and won prizes in local competitions. She has published poems in *Civic News; Bitterroot International Poetry Quarterly; The Mac Street Journal* (Haiku); and has won numerous awards for her poetry from organizations and art guilds. At 50, Nina received her MSW and began to practice as a therapist. She now works with autistic children and developmentally disabled adults. In her private practice, she counsels caregivers. Her dream is to become a novelist in her retirement years and to continue to write poetry.